D0510574

PLANNING APPLICATIONS

THE RMJM GUIDE

THIRD EDITION

Henry Brown, RIBA, MRTPl, DipArch, Cert AA (UD)
Consultant architect planner
Adrian Salt, DipArch, DipTP, FRSA, FRTPI
Consultant, RMJM Ltd

LLYFRGELL COLEG MENAI LIBRARY

064076

b

**Blackwell
Science**

© RMJM Ltd 1987, 1991, 1998

Blackwell Science Ltd
Editorial Offices:
Osney Mead, Oxford OX2 0EL
25 John Street, London WC1N 2BL
23 Ainslie Place, Edinburgh EH3 6AJ
350 Main Street, Malden
 MA 02148 5018, USA
54 University Street, Carlton
 Victoria 3053, Australia
10, rue Casimir Delavigne
 75006 Paris, France

Other Editorial Offices:

Blackwell Wissenschafts-Verlag GmbH
Kurfürstendamm 57
10707 Berlin, Germany

Blackwell Science KK
MG Kodenmacho Building
7–10 Kodenmacho Nihombashi
Chuo-ku, Tokyo 104, Japan

All rights reserved. No part of this publication may be
reproduced, stored in a retrieval system, or transmitted,
in any form or by any means, electronic, mechanical,
photocopying, recording or otherwise, except as
permitted by the UK Copyright, Designs and Patents Act
1988, without the prior permission of the publisher.

First Edition published 1987
Reprinted 1988
Second Edition published 1991
Third Edition published 1998

Set in 11/13pt Palatino
by DP Photosetting, Aylesbury, Bucks
Printed and bound in Great Britain by
MPG Books Ltd, Bodmin, Cornwall

The Blackwell Science logo is a trade mark of
Blackwell Science Ltd, registered at the United Kingdom
Trade Marks Registry

DISTRIBUTORS

Marston Book Services Ltd
PO Box 269
Abingdon
Oxon OX14 4YN
(*Orders:* Tel: 01235 465500
 Fax: 01235 465555)

USA
 Blackwell Science, Inc.
 Commerce Place
 350 Main Street
 Malden, MA 02148 5018
 (*Orders:* Tel: 800 759 6102
  781 388 8250
  Fax: 781 388 8255)

Canada
 Login Brothers Book Company
 324 Saulteaux Crescent
 Winnipeg, Manitoba R3J 3T2
 (*Orders:* Tel: 204 224-4068)

Australia
 Blackwell Science Pty Ltd
 54 University Street
 Carlton, Victoria 3053
 (*Orders:* Tel: 03 9347 0300
  Fax: 03 9347 5001)

A catalogue record for this title
is available from the British Library

ISBN 0-632-04117-X

Library of Congress
Cataloging-in-Publication Data
is available

While every care has been taken to ensure the accuracy of
the information at the time of compilation, the authors
would be grateful to be informed of any errors detected,
and also for suggestions for additions and improvements.
Neither they, nor the publisher can accept responsibility
for loss or damage resulting from inaccuracies.

The material reproduced in Appendix H is Crown Copyright.

LLYFRGELL COLEG MENAI LIBRARY
SAFLE FFRIDDOEDD SITE
BANGOR GWYNEDD LL57 2TP

CONTENTS

Scope

The guide covers the process of applying for planning permission but does not include other possible subsequent issues such as appeals, compensation claims, enforcement, building regulations, etc. The Flowchart and Procedures apply in all cases including applications and notifications by or on behalf of a local authority, government department or the Crown.

Scotland

The guide applies to development in England and Wales, where the main controlling legislation is the Town and Country Planning Act 1990. In Scotland the procedures are the same to all intents and purposes but derive from the Town and Country Planning Act (Scotland) 1997. Although the contents of the 1990 and 1997 Acts are almost identical, the section numbers are not; a section 65 Notice in England and Wales is a section 35 Notice in Scotland. All references in this guide are to the 1990 Act, for which we ask the indulgence of the Scots and hope they will be content with the equivalence table of critical sections under 'References'. The local government system in Scotland is different to that in England and Wales: applications are made to district councils except in certain cases where the regional council has responsibility. The list in Appendix J makes clear to which districts this applies.

Northern Ireland

In Northern Ireland the planning system differs from the remainder of the UK in that the district councils have no planning powers. The six divisional offices of the DETR for Northern Ireland are responsible for all statutory planning functions but district councils are consulted on all planning applications. The list of the divisional offices appears in Appendix J.

Abbreviations used in the text:

AONB	Area of Outstanding Natural Beauty
Art.	Article
BPN	Building Preservation Notice
CA	Conservation area
CCTV	Closed circuit television
Circ.	Circular (Department of Environment)
CLEUD	Certificate of Lawful Existing Use or Development
CLOPUD	Certificate of Lawfulness of Proposed Use or Development
DCMS	Department for Culture, Media and Sport
DETR	Department of Environment, Transport and the Regions
EA	Environmental assessment
ES	Environmental statement
EZ	Enterprise zone
GDPO	Planning (General Development Procedure) Order 1995
GPDO	Planning (General Permitted Development) Order 1995
HSA	Planning (Hazardous Substances) Act 1990
HSA	Hazardous Substances Authority
LA	Local Authority
LBCA	Planning (Listed Buildings and Conservation Areas) Act 1990
LPA	Local Planning Authority
MPA	Mineral Planning Authority
MPG	Mineral Planning Guidance Notes
PCA	Planning and Compensation Act 1991
PPG	Planning Policy Guidance Notes
RCHME	The Royal Commission on the Historic Monuments of England
SI	Statutory Instrument

s.	Section (of Act)
Sch	Schedule (of Act or Statutory Instrument)
SDO	Special Development Order
S of S	Secretary of State
SPG	Supplementary planning guidance
SPZ	Simplified planning zone
SSSI	Site of Special Scientific Interest
TCPGR	Town and Country Planning General Regulations 1992
TPO	Tree preservation order
UDC	Urban Development Corporation

INTRODUCTION

Planning control

This is the third edition of the Planning Guide and the second time it has been revised to take account of legislative changes. The third edition takes account of many new Acts, Circulars and Statutory Instruments, the most significant of which are the Planning and Compensation Act 1991, the General Development Procedures Order 1995 and the General Permitted Development Order 1995.

Development is a complicated business and the planning system in the UK reflects this completely. It is an accumulation of checks and balances which seeks to regulate the development and use of land in the public interest.

This guide does not attempt to duplicate the many excellent descriptions of the background or structure of planning in this country, but it is important to be aware of the nature of planning control. Control of development in its present form started with the Town and Country Planning Act 1947 and now derives mainly from three Acts of Parliament: the Town and Country Planning Act 1990 (referred to throughout the guide as the 1990 Act); the Planning (Listed Buildings and Conservation Areas) Act 1990 (LBCA); and the Planning (Hazardous Substances) Act 1990 (HSA). This legislation was amended significantly by the Planning and Compensation Act 1991 (PCA).

The planning control process consists of both the making of development plans and the day-to-day control of development. The powers to do both come from Parliament through the Secretary of State for the Environment, but in this guide we go no further than the appropriate Local Planning Authority (LPA). It is the LPAs that administer the system on behalf of the Secretary of State; that draw up the development plans; and that grant or refuse planning permission in their areas.

What are the LPAs? In England and Wales they include county councils and district councils (which overlap in a two-tier system), London boroughs and metropolitan districts (which are Unitary Authorities). The Local Government Act 1992 created more Unitary Authorities, some of which have yet to come into being. They also include UDCs, National Parks Authorities and, when such things existed (or if they are recreated), New Town Development Corporations.

What are development plans? Section 54A of the 1990 Act (inserted by the PCA) is the statutory power behind what is officially described as a plan-led system. This requires that planning applications shall be determined in accordance with the development plan unless material considerations indicate otherwise. The development plan or plans for an area are, generally speaking, the adopted structure plan (produced by counties) together with the local plan (produced by districts) or the unitary development plan (produced by London boroughs and metropolitan districts). But because the process of adopting a development plan involves several stages of consultation and review, at any one time there may be old plans gradually diminishing in importance against new ones that are emerging towards adoption. In addition, statutory development plans are often supplemented by LPA guidelines on such issues as conservation areas, design standards, minerals etc. These are called supplementary planning guidance (SPG). The policies contained in all these documents are the legal yardstick for deciding on any planning application. It is always as well to check the current position in a particular area.

Who determines planning policy? Policy-making mirrors the hierarchy of the planning system as a whole. Government sets the tone of planning policy by means of three types of Policy Guidance Notes (Planning, Regional and Mineral) known as PPGs, RPGs and MPGs. Government also has a decisive role in approving development plans. Within these constraints, LPAs then draw up and adopt their local planning policies in the various development plans. It is worth noting, however, that the policy framework as a whole is often ambiguous in relation to particular development proposals: policies in favour of conservation and restraint need to be weighed against policies promoting the growth of jobs or housing. This means that planning officers are constantly called upon to make judgements and to interpret their policies, and that a potential developer is well advised to achieve a broad understanding of the policy context before submitting a planning application.

Who controls development? In some circumstances it could be a county, or some other body such as a UDC, but in general all applications go to the district council, London borough or metropolitan district. Appendix J contains a list of them for easy reference.

How is development controlled? In general any proposal classified as 'development' as defined by the 1990 Act, and several other activities, need approval. If such development is carried out without permission, the LPA can invoke a variety of enforcement procedures and penalties.

The normal way to obtain approval is to make formal applications to the LPA. An LPA can approve but can also prevent or modify development by refusing an application or imposing conditions. This opens up a variety of processes including planning appeals, inquiries and compensation which we have chosen not to describe in this guide.

After the application

After an application has been submitted, the LPA carries out a series of checks, consultations and analyses before making its decision. An applicant is entitled by law to have a decision within eight weeks (16 weeks if an environmental assessment is involved) and it is usually wise to assume that it will take at least that length of time even for simple applications. The following is a simplified flowchart of the LPA's actions during this time. At any stage in the process the LPA may ask the applicant for more information. It is advisable for an applicant to check up on the progress of the application: they sometimes get delayed in favour of more urgent business and sometimes get refused for lack of some minor design change or piece of information that could have been volunteered.

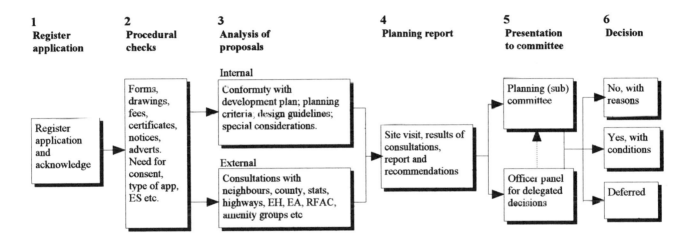

The Guide

With such complexity of statute and authority, it is hardly surprising that anyone trying to promote development may get lost in a maze of apparently uncoordinated and arbitrary procedures. This guide is an attempt to map the maze. It has evolved out of practical experience of trying to work and understand the system and is aimed at anyone with similar practical interests. We have designed it as a reference book for anyone who gets involved in the development process. Its primary aim is to save time, money, wasted effort and frustration. We do not claim that the guide is comprehensive on all issues which might impinge on planning applications, but we do claim that it covers most of the field in sufficient detail to avoid recourse to other reference books. It is as well to remember, however, that some aspects of development control are notoriously open to interpretation: interpretations can differ between authorities and even between officers in the same authority. Case law frequently throws up important new precedents, making government and local planning guidance something of a moving target.

Form of the Guide

There are three main sections of the guide. The first is the flowchart which helps the applicant determine if his particular development proposal needs planning permission, and, if so, what type or types of application is needed. The second section amplifies the flowchart, and clarifies some of the terminology peculiar to planning and planning legislation. The third section sets out step-by-step procedures to be followed for each of 22 different types of planning application.

We have consigned much of the detail to the appendices. These cover, amongst other things, official and useful definitions, fees, use classes, permitted development and environmental assessments.

January 1998

Adrian Salt
RMJM
83 Paul Street
London EC2A 4NQ

Henry Brown
7 Strand-on-the-Green
London
W4 3PQ

Introduction

The flowchart is designed to answer two fundamental questions in respect of any particular development proposal: is a planning application required? and, if so, which of the many planning application procedures should be followed? The flowchart is broken down into a series of component questions that have 'yes' or 'no' answers. These are arranged in a sequence that starts at the top left-hand corner of the flowchart. Along the route are two recurring symbols:

These are references to specific procedures for applying for planning consent which are set out in detail in Section 4.

These indicate that no planning application is required, so far as one particular line of enquiry is concerned. In some instances they are dead-ends and indicate that development can proceed.

Form of the flowchart

The questions are grouped in five vertical columns dealing with different aspects of development:

1   *The planning history of the site:* are any previous planning permissions or consents relevant? does the site have an established use?

2   *Is it development:* does the proposal constitute development within the meaning of the 1990 Act? (See Appendix A for the definition of development)

3   *Is it a special case:* does the site or the buildings on it constitute one of the many special cases which affect or add to the number of approvals to be sought?

4   *Is it permitted development:* is the proposal within one of the categories of 'permitted development' that does not require planning permission?

5   *Other issues:* the final column focuses on standard planning applications and the issues that relate to them.

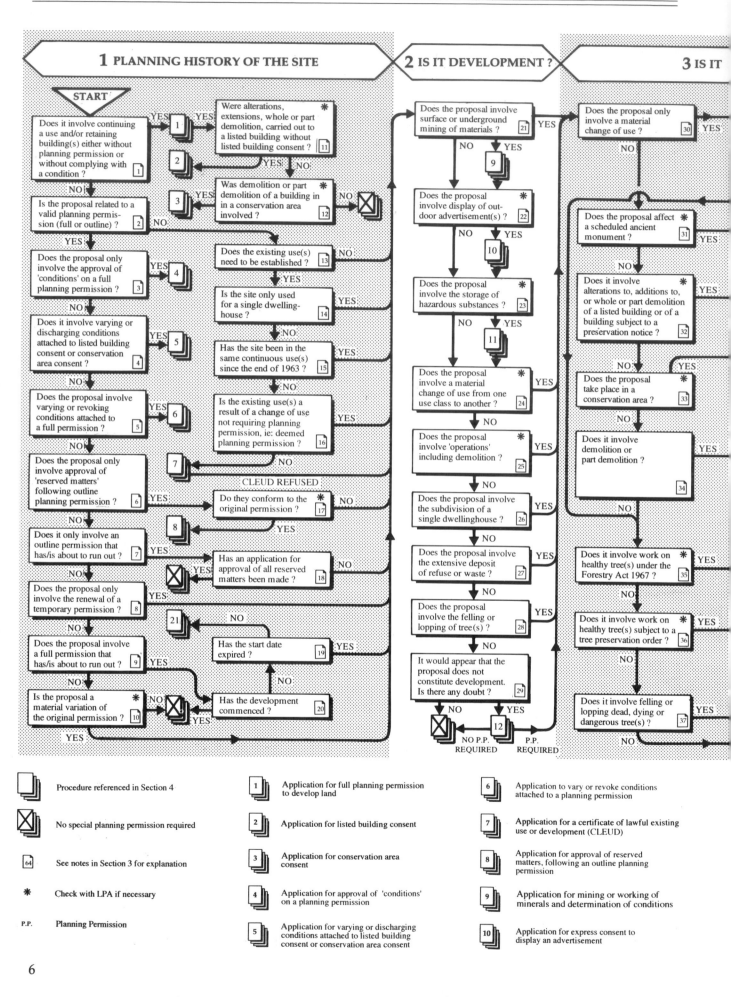

1 PLANNING HISTORY OF THE SITE

2 IS IT DEVELOPMENT ?

3 IS IT

START

Does it involve continuing a use and/or retaining building(s) either without planning permission or without complying with a condition ? [1]

Were alterations, extensions, whole or part demolition, carried out to a listed building without listed building consent ? * [11]

Was demolition or part demolition of a building in in a conservation area involved ? [12]

Is the proposal related to a valid planning permission (full or outline) ? [2]

Does the existing use(s) need to be established ? [13]

Does the proposal only involve the approval of 'conditions' on a full planning permission ? [3]

Is the site only used for a single dwelling-house ? [14]

Does it involve varying or discharging conditions attached to listed building consent or conservation area consent ? [4]

Has the site been in the same continuous use(s) since the end of 1963 ? [15]

Does the proposal involve varying or revoking conditions attached to a full permission ? [5]

Is the existing use(s) a result of a change of use not requiring planning permission, ie: deemed planning permission ? [16]

CLEUD REFUSED

Does the proposal only involve approval of 'reserved matters' following outline planning permission ? [6]

Do they conform to the original permission ? * [17]

Does it only involve an outline permission that has/is about to run out ? [7]

Has an application for approval of all reserved matters been made ? [18]

Does the proposal only involve the renewal of a temporary permission ? [8]

Has the start date expired ? [19]

Does the proposal involve a full permission that has/is about to run out ? [9]

Is the proposal a material variation of the original permission ? * [10]

Has the development commenced ? [20]

Does the proposal involve surface or underground mining of materials ? [21]

Does the proposal involve display of outdoor advertisement(s) ? * [22]

Does the proposal involve the storage of hazardous substances ? * [23]

Does the proposal involve a material change of use from one use class to another ? * [24]

Does the proposal involve 'operations' including demolition ? * [25]

Does the proposal involve the subdivision of a single dwellinghouse ? [26]

Does the proposal involve the extensive deposit of refuse or waste ? [27]

Does the proposal involve the felling or lopping of tree(s) ? [28]

It would appear that the proposal does not constitute development. Is there any doubt ? [29]

NO P.P. REQUIRED

P.P. REQUIRED

Does the proposal only involve a material change of use ? [30]

Does the proposal affect a scheduled ancient monument ? * [31]

Does it involve alterations to, additions to, or whole or part demolition of a listed building or of a building subject to a preservation notice ? * [32]

Does the proposal take place in a conservation area ? [33]

Does it involve demolition or part demolition ? [34]

Does it involve work on healthy tree(s) under the Forestry Act 1967 ? * [35]

Does it involve work on healthy tree(s) subject to a tree preservation order ? * [36]

Does it involve felling or lopping dead, dying or dangerous tree(s) ? [37]

Procedure referenced in Section 4

No special planning permission required

[64] See notes in Section 3 for explanation

* Check with LPA if necessary

P.P. Planning Permission

1 Application for full planning permission to develop land

2 Application for listed building consent

3 Application for conservation area consent

4 Application for approval of 'conditions' on a planning permission

5 Application for varying or discharging conditions attached to listed building consent or conservation area consent

6 Application to vary or revoke conditions attached to a planning permission

7 Application for a certificate of lawful existing use or development (CLEUD)

8 Application for approval of reserved matters, following an outline planning permission

9 Application for mining or working of minerals and determination of conditions

10 Application for express consent to display an advertisement

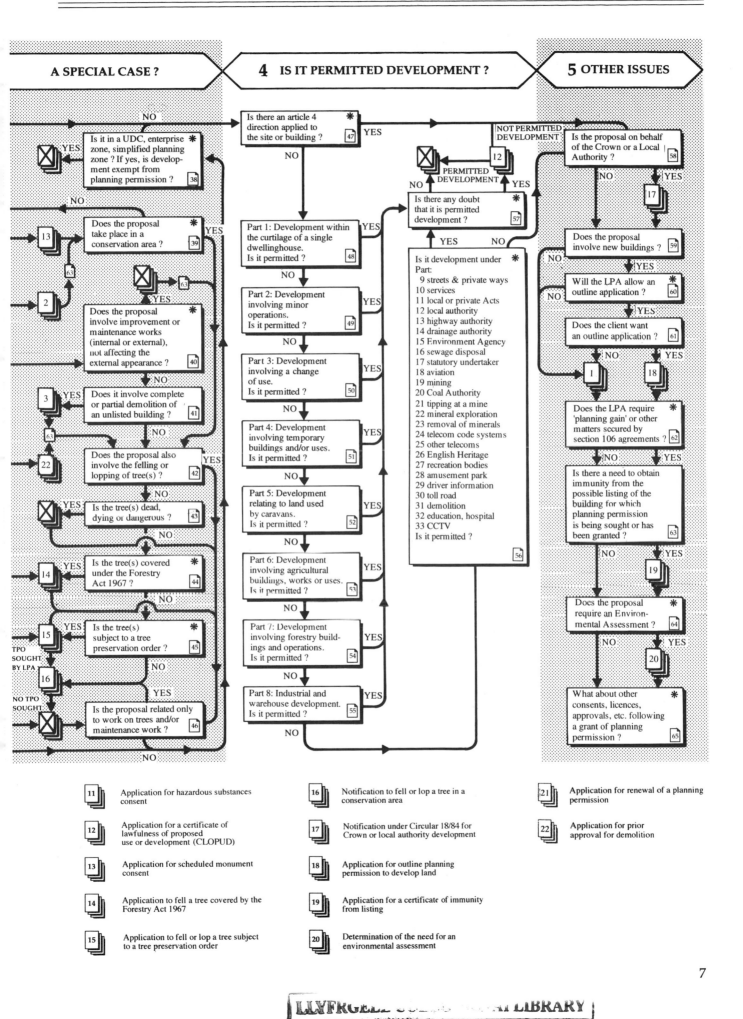

A SPECIAL CASE ?

4 IS IT PERMITTED DEVELOPMENT ?

5 OTHER ISSUES

Is it in a UDC, enterprise ✳ zone, simplified planning zone ? If yes, is development exempt from planning permission ? |38|

Does the proposal take place in a ✳ conservation area ? |39|

Does the proposal involve improvement or ✳ maintenance works (internal or external), not affecting the external appearance ? |40|

Does it involve complete or partial demolition of an unlisted building ? |41|

Does the proposal also involve the felling or lopping of tree(s) ? |42|

Is the tree(s) dead, dying or dangerous ? |43|

Is the tree(s) covered ✳ under the Forestry Act 1967 ? |44|

Is the tree(s) ✳ subject to a tree preservation order ? |45|

TPO SOUGHT BY LPA

NO TPO SOUGHT

Is the proposal related only to work on trees and/or maintenance work ? |46|

Is there an article 4 ✳ direction applied to the site or building ? |47| YES

Part 1: Development within the curtilage of a single dwellinghouse. Is it permitted ? |48| YES

Part 2: Development involving minor operations. Is it permitted ? |49| YES

Part 3: Development involving a change of use. Is it permitted ? |50| YES

Part 4: Development involving temporary buildings and/or uses. Is it permitted ? |51| YES

Part 5: Development relating to land used by caravans. Is it permitted ? |52| YES

Part 6: Development involving agricultural buildings, works or uses. Is it permitted ? |53| YES

Part 7: Development involving forestry buildings and operations. Is it permitted ? |54| YES

Part 8: Industrial and warehouse development. Is it permitted ? |55| YES

NOT PERMITTED DEVELOPMENT

PERMITTED DEVELOPMENT |12|

Is there any doubt ✳ that it is permitted development ? |57|

Is it development under Part:
9 streets & private ways
10 services
11 local or private Acts
12 local authority
13 highway authority
14 drainage authority
15 Environment Agency
16 sewage disposal
17 statutory undertaker
18 aviation
19 mining
20 Coal Authority
21 tipping at a mine
22 mineral exploration
23 removal of minerals
24 telecom code systems
25 other telecoms
26 English Heritage
27 recreation bodies
28 amusement park
29 driver information
30 toll road
31 demolition
32 education, hospital
33 CCTV
Is it permitted ? |56|

Is the proposal on behalf of the Crown or a Local Authority ? |58| |17|

Does the proposal involve new buildings ? |59|

Will the LPA allow an ✳ outline application ? |60|

Does the client want an outline application ? |61|

|1| |18|

Does the LPA require ✳ 'planning gain' or other matters secured by section 106 agreements ? |62|

Is there a need to obtain immunity from the possible listing of the building for which planning permission is being sought or has been granted ? |63| |19|

Does the proposal ✳ require an Environmental Assessment ? |64| |20|

What about other ✳ consents, licences, approvals, etc. following a grant of planning permission ? |65|

|11| Application for hazardous substances consent

|12| Application for a certificate of lawfulness of proposed use or development (CLOPUD)

|13| Application for scheduled monument consent

|14| Application to fell a tree covered by the Forestry Act 1967

|15| Application to fell or lop a tree subject to a tree preservation order

|16| Notification to fell or lop a tree in a conservation area

|17| Notification under Circular 18/84 for Crown or local authority development

|18| Application for outline planning permission to develop land

|19| Application for a certificate of immunity from listing

|20| Determination of the need for an environmental assessment

|21| Application for renewal of a planning permission

|22| Application for prior approval for demolition

7

LLYFRGELL .... LIBRARY

Short-cut through the flowchart

Most development proposals entail only one procedure and the first four headings can be treated as a short cut through the flowchart leading, in most cases, to Procedure 1 (application for full planning permission).

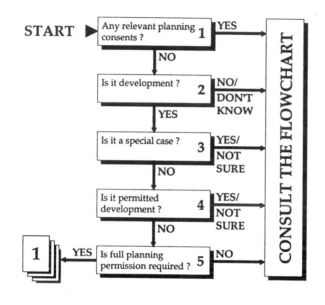

Many proposals will, however, involve other issues such as listed buildings, conservation areas, or tree preservation orders. These occur in box 3 (*left*) and are a frequent cause of technical errors in planning applications. The flowchart should be treated in the first instance as a checklist: go through it quickly to see if any issues are raised that give rise to separate procedures. The flowchart can thus help to identify relevant questions about both the proposal and the site.

The flowchart is designed in such a way that it is important to follow the sequence carefully, otherwise critical procedures may be missed. It may be best to divide a multi-use proposal into its components and take each through the flowchart separately.

The notes

 Each of the boxes contains a number that serves as a cross-reference and as an index to the notes (Section 3). It is always advisable to check the notes: the questions in the boxes have been distilled to the least number of words for obvious reasons, as a result of which some critical nuance may be overlooked.

 Many of the boxes contain an asterisk. These are questions that are often best referred to the LPA for advice or confirmation.

Introduction

The following notes refer to the numbered boxes in the flowchart. They are necessarily succinct: many of the topics could be, and some are, the subject of entire books rather than a humble paragraph, and some are affected by esoteric case law and often variable practice by LPAs.

Consultation

In the case of the boxes containing an asterisk, we suggest discussion with the LPA. If the application is not dealt with entirely by a planning officer under delegated powers, then at the end of the day it is presented to a lay planning committee (or its equivalent) usually (but not always) by a planning officer, on the basis of a report often written by another planning officer, after consultations with other technical officers (highways and services, engineers, statutory authorities, conservation and listed building specialists, architects, solicitors, etc.). Outside bodies are often consulted as well (resident groups, amenity groups, chambers of commerce, English Heritage, Royal Fine Arts Commission, etc.). Planning officers are always overworked and need all the help they can get. They also want to make a contribution, and many have a knowledge of political and aesthetic sensitivities that it would be foolish to ignore. We have already stressed the importance of the local development plan in determining an application. So make contact with the planning officers; find out how the local system works; explain your proposals; listen; understand the local policies, expectations and political pressures; make sure the planning officer has everything necessary for an accurate and positive report. A discussion with the right officer at the right time can save days and months of wasted effort.

Explanatory Statement

A concise explanatory statement with the planning application, describing the proposals and addressing the issues that the case officer will have to cover in his report to committee, can be a great help to both planning officer and applicant. Appendix B outlines the key topics.

Notes to the flowchart

1

Does it involve **continuing a use and/or retaining building(s)** *either without planning permission or without complying with a condition?*

Where a change of use and/or a development has taken place without the necessary planning permission, or without complying with a condition attached to a permission (see note 3), the owner and occupier of the land may be in breach of planning control and could be liable to enforcement action under Part IV of the 1990 Act, as amended by the PCA.

In the case of a material change of use (see note 24) without planning permission, the change must have occurred within ten years for there to be a breach of planning control or within the last four years if it is a change of use to a single dwellinghouse.

For building, mining, engineering or other 'operations' (note 25), or breach of any condition or limitation (see note 3) attached to a planning permission for operations, the enforcement notice can only be issued by the LPA within four years of the breach.

The LPA has discretion as to whether to use its powers of enforcement. The Secretary of State may also issue a notice after consulting the LPA. Enforcement action is generally reserved for situations where the amenity of an area is seriously harmed or where it prejudices future planning schemes.

An enforcement notice will give details of the alleged breach, reasons for the enforcement, the steps to be taken (within a given period) to remedy the breach, and the date the notice takes effect. Failure to comply with the notice is an offence, leading on conviction to a fine of up to £20 000 in the Magistrate's Court, unlimited in the Crown Court.

In the case of advertisements (see note 22) the LPA, under section 220 of the 1990 Act, can require the person responsible for its display to make an application for its retention (see Appendix F).

Section 73A of the 1990 Act (as amended by the PCA), allows for retrospective planning applications for buildings, works, or change of use. The procedure is usually the same as for a full planning application.

2 — *Is the proposal related to a* **valid planning permission** *(full or outline)?*

When planning permission is granted it is valid only for the site specified and for the works and/or change of use stated in the notification letter. Additionally, the permission, which becomes 'active' on receipt by the applicant/agent of the notification, only remains valid for a limited period (stated in the notification letter as a 'condition'). For full permission this period is generally five years. For an outline permission it is three years to submission of all necessary applications for approval of reserved matters (see note 6), and development must begin within five years of the date on which the outline permission was granted, or within two years of the last approval of reserved matters, whichever is the later. If the permission is not acted on during this period it becomes void. Any number of permissions can be valid at the same time on the same site.

3 — *Does the proposal only involve the approval of* **'conditions'** *on a planning permission?*

Sections 72 and 73 of the 1990 Act give LPAs wide powers to impose conditions on all types of planning permission. Conditions can include a range of issues, e.g. approval of facing materials or details of landscaping, time limits for commencing operations, etc. Circular

11/95 recommends that good practice should involve informal discussions with the LPA, and the use of standard conditions with reasons and notes or 'informatives' to give guidance on the other statutory approvals which must be obtained. The Circular recommends that LPAs should always impose conditions rather than require section 106 agreements (see note 62) because the latter deprive the developer of the right to appeal to the Secretary of State. (Many LPAs ignore the recommendation and tie up all major conditions with section 106 agreements precisely for that reason.)

The Circular sets out six tests for conditions: they should be necessary (i.e. the permission would be refused if the condition were not imposed); relevant to planning; relevant to the development permitted; enforceable; precise; and reasonable. The second test, 'relevant to planning', is sometimes overlooked by LPAs who seek, for instance, to ensure that housing is occupied by people on the housing list, or that open spaces or leisure facilities are open to the public.

The Circular sets out guidelines on many types of conditions, including outline permission, time limits, completion of development, phasing, highway conditions, contaminated sites, archaeological sites, maintenance and planning obligations. It gives examples of unacceptable conditions and models for acceptable conditions.

*Does it involve **varying or discharging conditions** attached to listed building consent or conservation area consent?*

In the case of listed building consent and conservation area consent, conditions may be attached which a person with an 'interest' in the building may wish to change or discharge altogether by application to the LPA under section 19 of the LBCA. The relevant Regulation covering this type of application is the Town and Country Planning (Listed Buildings and Buildings in Conservation Areas) Regulations 1990 (No. 1519).

*Does the proposal involve **varying or revoking conditions** attached to a permission?*

Section 73(2)(a) of the 1990 Act allows application to be made to the LPA for varying or revoking conditions (see note 3) attached to a planning permission.

*Does the proposal only involve approval of **'reserved matters'** following outline planning permission?*

These are matters which relate to design details not submitted with an outline planning application (see note 60) but which would be necessary for a full planning application. They can include one or more of siting, design, external appearance, means of access and landscaping.

*Does it only involve an **outline permission** that has, or is about to, run out of time?*

Outline planning permission can only be granted on proposals that do, or will, involve new buildings. It does not apply to changes of use, listed buildings, or usually, in conservation areas. Outline permission can be viewed as a first stage of a full application, with the approval of the 'reserved matters' (see note 6) forming the second stage, but it is important to remember that the outline permission establishes the principle of development. An application for approval of reserved matters should usually be made within three years, and the development must begin within five years of the date on which the outline permission was granted, or within two years of the approval of 'reserved matters', whichever is the later. On the expiry of its time limit an outline planning application cannot be renewed except by making a new application.

8 *Does the proposal only involve the renewal of a* **temporary permission**?

In certain instances planning permission can be granted on a temporary basis, i.e., after a specified length of time the use ceases, any buildings or structures are removed, and the site is restored to its original state or as agreed with the LPA. A temporary permission can be renewed for a further limited period by applying within the lifetime of a valid permission.

9 *Does the proposal involve a* **full planning permission** *that has, or is about to, run out of time?*

The 'time' condition on the start of works following the grant of a planning permission can be varied but if the time limit expires a new application is required. A planning application can also be renewed (see Procedure 21) before the end of its time limit.

10 *Is the proposal a* **material variation** *of the original permission?*

Once planning permission has been granted the development can only be implemented according to the approved details. The degree of variation allowed before a fresh application is necessary is determined by the LPA, judging each case on its merits. There is no rule of thumb on what is 'material' and only negotiation with the LPA will resolve it.

11 *Were* **alterations, extensions**, *whole or part* **demolition, carried out** *to a listed building* **without listed building consent**?

It is an offence to demolish, part demolish (see note 12), alter or extend a listed building (see note 32) without first obtaining listed building consent. Section 8 (3) of the LBCA allows an application to be made which can give retrospective listed building consent.

12 *Was* **demolition or part demolition** *of a building in a conservation area involved?*

In the context of conservation areas, the legal definition of demolition is now limited to total demolition: that which creates a new development site. Anything less is 'alteration' and the alteration must significantly affect the building's character before it requires a separate consent. See notes 32, 34 and 41.

13 *Does the existing* **use(s)** *need* **to be established**?

Without a planning permission for a specific use, there may be doubt as to the lawful use of a building or piece of land. This could lead to a situation where the LPA believes there may be a breach of planning control (see note 1). Section 191 of the 1990 Act (as amended) allows for an application to the LPA for a certificate of lawful existing use or development (CLEUD). A CLEUD is the equivalent of a planning permission. It establishes that an existing use or operation, or one such in breach of a condition, is lawful. The applicant must prove that:

- the use was begun more than ten years before the application and has continued without a break;
- the use, if changed or begun less than ten years before the application, would not have required planning permission;

- the use of a single dwellinghouse began more than four years before the application;
- other reasons for the use being lawful.

14 *Is the site only used for a* **single dwellinghouse?**

This refers to a single dwelling unit such as a detached, semi-detached or terraced house, but not including a building containing one or more flats, or a flat contained in a building having some other use (i.e. flat over a shop, or a caretaker's flat in an office block).

15 *Has the site been in the same* **continuous use(s)** *for ten years?*

Ten years continuous use for most purposes, or use as a single dwellinghouse for more than four years is sufficient to establish the lawful use of a building. A continuous use in this context does not only have the obvious connotation but also means a use that has not been abandoned by the landowner, with no view of resumption.

16 *Is the existing use(s) a result of a change of use not requiring planning permission, i.e.* **deemed planning permission?**

Not all changes of use require planning permission: for some there is automatic or 'deemed' planning permission as a result of their being 'permitted development' (see note 57).

17 *Do they* **conform to the original permission?**

'Reserved matters' (see note 6) must relate to the original permission, i.e. the site must be exactly the same or, if smaller, must relate to an area which can form part of a whole, e.g. a single house plot. The proposal must be within the parameters of the outline permission.

18 *Has an application for* **approval of reserved matters** *been made?*

An outline planning permission cannot be acted upon until the critical reserved matters (see note 6) have been approved by the LPA and a written notification is issued to that effect. Check with the LPA what the critical matters consist of. Approval of landscape details can often be obtained after development has started and on complex developments this can also apply to building details and materials. Consented reserved matters can have conditions attached to them that may require approval (see note 3).

19 *Has the* **start date** *expired?*

The notification of full planning permission usually contains a condition which states the period for which the permission is valid. Where no such time period is given, it is deemed to be five years. Only within this period is a start on site permitted.

20 *Has* **development commenced?**

Development will be deemed to have commenced when a start is made on any of the following 'specified operations':

- any work of construction in the course of the erection of a building;

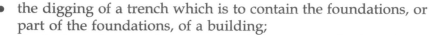

- the digging of a trench which is to contain the foundations, or part of the foundations, of a building;
- the laying of any underground main or pipe to the foundations of a building or to any such trench as mentioned above;
- any operation in the course of laying out or constructing a road or part of a road;
- any change in the use of any land, where that change could be considered 'material' (see note 24).

The start on site must be bona fide and not purely to keep permission alive and it must not be in breach of any conditions. Tree planting, not being development, is not a 'specified operation'.

21 *Does the proposal involve surface or underground* **mining of minerals***?*

The phrase relates to the winning and working of minerals and includes underground mining, opencast mining and drilling for hydrocarbons as well as the removal of material of any description from disused mineral workings and railway embankments.

22 *Does the proposal involve the display of outdoor* **advertisement(s)***?*

The definition of advertisement includes any word, letter, model, sign, placard, board, notice, awning, blind, device or representation, whether illuminated or not, in the nature of and employed wholly or partly for the purposes of, advertisement, announcement or direction. It includes any hoarding or similar structure used or adapted for use for the display of advertisements, including tethered balloons. There are three types of advertisement:

- those that do not need consent to be displayed (exempted classes);
- those that have deemed consent but are subject to a discontinuance order if the LPA consider it expedient (deemed consent classes);
- those for which express consent must be obtained before being displayed (express consent classes).

The various types are described in Appendix E. The relevant Regulations are contained in SI 1992 No. 666.

> Special note: A flag, other than a national flag, is deemed an advertisement and may require express consent for its display. Erecting the flagpole, on the other hand, involves 'building' (see note 25) and may require planning permission and possibly even listed building consent.

23 *Does the proposal involve the* **storage of hazardous substances***?*

Certain substances, when stored in sufficient quantity, are potentially hazardous and require planning consent before they can be stored on, over or under land. Excluding the situation where the material is being transported, the term storage in this context has the dictionary definition. Note that if during transportation the material is unloaded, it becomes 'storage'. Procedure 11 has a list of the substances and the quantities regarded as being hazardous, derived from the Notifications of Installations Handling Hazardous Substances Regulations 1982 (SI 1982, No. 1357).

24 *Does the proposal involve a* **material change of use** *from one use class to another?*

Some changes of use are declared by statute to be 'material' (the subdivision of a dwelling into flats; the use of dwellings in London as temporary sleeping accommodation or a time share; the enlargement of a refuse dump by further deposits) but otherwise there is no definition. Changes of use within the use classes (e.g. B1a to B1c) are not regarded as development. Certain changes of use between use classes as defined in the GPDO (Appendix E part 3) do not require permission. All other changes from one use class to another require planning permission. The question of whether a change is 'material' often arises in relation to mixed use developments or where the intensity of a use is increased.

25 *Does the proposal involve* **'operations'**, *including demolition?*

The concept of 'operations' is central to the definition of development in the 1990 Act: 'the carrying out of building, engineering, mining or other operations...'

Building operations include the demolition of buildings, rebuilding, structural alterations or additions to buildings, and other operations 'normally undertaken by a person carrying on business as a builder'.

'Building' means any structure or erection or part of a building, but excludes:

- plant or machinery in a building
- caravans (see Appendix A)
- repair and maintenance works (e.g. scaffolding)
- gates, fences, walls or other means of enclosure, within certain criteria (see Appendix E).

'Engineering or operations' include:

- the formation or laying out of a means of access to a highway
- the building and maintenance of roads
- laying of sewers, water mains, etc.
- the formation or removal of earth embankments

but excludes:

- maintenance or improvement of a road by the LA
- inspection, repair and renewal of sewers, mains, cables, etc. by the LA or statutory undertaker.

Other 'operations' include mining (see note 21), the removal of materials from mineral working deposits, from a deposit of pulverised fuel ash, from a deposit of iron, steel or other metallic slags, or the extraction of minerals from a disused railway embankment.

Other operations also include the assembly of a tank in inland waters for fish farming, and the display of an advertisement on the external part of a building. Planting trees does not constitute an 'operation'.

Does the proposal involve the subdivision of a single dwellinghouse?

'Single dwellinghouse' is defined in note 14. Dividing a single dwellinghouse into two or more self-contained dwelling units is development and requires planning permission. Reducing the number of dwelling units in a building, however, does not of itself necessarily constitute development.

Does the proposal involve the extensive deposit of refuse or waste?

The deposit of refuse or waste only constitutes development if a new tip is proposed or, on an existing tip, the superficial area is extended or the height is increased above natural ground level.

Does it involve the felling or lopping of a tree(s)?

There is no statutory definition of a tree and this has given rise to much confusion. There is no doubt in the case of trees or groups of trees that are specifically mentioned in preservation orders, or, in the terms of one judgment, that a tree with a trunk of over seven or eight inches diameter (measured 1.5 m from the base) is indeed a tree. The question arises in relation to saplings which clearly need to be preserved in the interests of the regeneration of woodland. A more recent judgment has held that anything that would ordinarily be called a tree, a term that is deemed to include saplings, can be protected under a tree preservation order. In the case of coppices, the stools from which the saplings grow, being neither a tree nor a sapling, would need special protection.

Dead, dying or dangerous trees are not protected by blanket preservation orders or by the law concerning conservation areas. Other exceptions include trees affected by the needs of statutory undertakers, those affecting airfields or defence establishments, and works on fruit trees so long as they are cultivated for fruit production.

It would appear that the proposal does not constitute development. Is there any doubt?

Whether a particular proposal involves development within the meaning of the 1990 Act (and therefore whether planning permission is needed), or whether it qualifies under one of the many exemptions is not always self-evident. Under section 192 of the 1990 Act (as amended) an application can be made to the LPA for a Certificate of Lawfulness of Proposed Use or Development (CLOPUD). This provides a definitive statement as to the need for planning consent. A CLOPUD is the legal equivalent of a planning permission. Circular 17/92 provides background and detailed information. The definition of development is given in Appendix A.

Does the proposal only involve a material change of use?

In this context, for the proposal to consist only of a material change of use (as defined in note 24), it should not involve any 'operations' (as defined in note 25) or the felling or lopping of trees (see note 42).

26

27

28

29

30

31 *Does the proposal affect a* **scheduled ancient monument***?*

This term includes all monuments which are in the schedule of monuments described in section 1 of the Ancient Monuments and Archaeological Areas Act 1979. Although the majority of scheduled monuments are archaeological sites, ruins or structures for which there is no present day use, there are some buildings that are both scheduled and listed (see note 32 for a definition of 'listed'). However, section 61 of the LBCA provides that the legislative controls relating to listed buildings are subordinate to ancient monument legislation.

32 *Does the proposal involve alterations to, additions to, or whole or part demolition of a* **listed building** *or of a* **building** *subject to a* **preservation notice***?*

(a) Listed buildings:
The Secretary of State for the Environment is required under section 1 of the Planning (Listed Buildings and Conservation Areas) Act 1990 (referred to here as the LBCA) to compile lists of buildings of special architectural or historic interest. There are currently about half a million list entries which are classified in grades to show their relative importance, i.e. Grade I, Grade II* ('Grade II star') and Grade II. Each list entry may represent more than one building. The term 'building' can include any object or structure fixed to a building or within its curtilage (covered by 'Building' in section 1(5) of the LBCA). The LPA keeps a register of all the listed buildings in its jurisdiction and this is available to the public for inspection. The Royal Commission on the Historic Monuments of England (RCHME), English Heritage, and the Department for Culture, Media and Sport (DCMS) have produced a computer-based national index of listed buildings with 24 hour access by phone or fax. Details of buildings can be obtained free of charge from the London branch of RCHME. The comprehensive archive is kept at RCHME's headquarters at Swindon.

RCHME
55 Blandford Street
London W1H 3AF
tel: 0171 208 8221
fax: 0171 224 5333
Email: london@rchme.gov.uk

National Monuments Record Centre
Kemble Drive
Swindon SN2 2GZ
tel: 01793 414628
fax: 01793 420728
Email: info@rchme.gov.uk

The owner of any listed building to be altered should notify the Emergency Recording unit of RCHME at the above London address, telephone number 0171 208 8220.

PPG15 contains a full statement of the criteria used to identify and grade listed buildings and what type of works require listed building consent. The control is comprehensive. Once a building is listed in any category, it and any object or structure fixed to it or within its curtilage which has been there since 1948, becomes protected. Both the exterior and interior of a listed building are protected regardless of whether any internal features are mentioned in the listing description. Any works or repair which would affect the building's 'special interest' require permission: even, in some cases, internal repainting. This, as PPG15 says, is a matter of degree which must be determined in each case.

The legal position over demolition and part demolition of listed buildings and buildings in conservation areas has been altered by a recent ruling by the House of Lords (*Shimizu (UK)* v. *Westminster City Council*, 1997). The judgment defines demolition as that which creates a site for redevelopment – in other words, the virtual removal of the building. Anything less is defined as alteration and, as long as it does not affect the building's character, it does not require listed building or conservation consent. This applies particularly to internal alterations but also has significance for extensions and other later additions in the curtilage of listed buildings. Circ. 14/97 has been produced to clarify the situation and should be referred to in any listed building application involving partial demolition.

(b) Building Preservation Notice (BPN):
An LPA can issue a BPN under section 3 of the LBCA if it believes an individual building is under threat of alteration or demolition and is potentially 'listable'. A BPN has the effect of protecting the building as fully as if it were listed for a period of six months. During this period an assessment is made and if the building qualifies against the approved selection criteria it is added formally to the statutory list. A BPN may not be served in respect of an ecclesiastical building which is still in ecclesiastical use. Section 29 provides for compensation to be paid by the LPA for any loss or damage resulting from the service of a BPN which is not upheld by the DETR.

> Special note: Although there is no formal right of appeal against the decision to list a building, an owner may at any time put to the Secretary of State evidence that his building does not have the architectural or historic interest identified. If it is accepted that the original assessment was not justified, the Secretary of State will de-list the building.

33 *Does the proposal take place in a conservation area?*

A conservation area is an area identified and designated by the LPA under section 69 of the LBCA as being 'an area of special architectural or historic interest, the character or appearance of which it is desirable to preserve or enhance'. A register of conservation areas is kept by the LPA and is available for public inspection. Planning controls are much more strict in conservation areas and some permitted development rights may be removed. Refer also to PPG 15 for a statement and discussion of policy, and to Circ. 14/97 for detailed guidance.

34 *Does it only involve* **demolition**, *or part demolition?*

Demolition or part demolition of a dwelling or any building adjoining a dwelling requires the prior approval of the LPA for the method of demolition and the proposed restoration of the site (Procedure 22). All demolition was brought within the definition of development by the PCA, but all buildings other than dwellings were then exempted from the definition by Part 31 of the GPDO as 'permitted development'. Circ. 10/95 describes the various controls over demolition. Any building which is listed, in a conservation area, or a scheduled monument, requires the relevant consents (see notes 31, 32 and 33). Where demolition of a dwelling is urgently required for reasons of health and safety, the developer must give the LPA a written justification as soon as possible after demolition. Demolition is not permitted under Part 31 if the owner's actions or negligence have rendered the building unsafe, or if it is practicable to repair the building or to provide temporary support.

Planning permission is not required to demolish a building of less than $50\,m^3$ or if the demolition is part of a development with planning permission. The demolition of gates, fences, walls and other means of enclosure do not require planning permission. See also Appendix E (part 31).

Under section 80 of the Building Act 1984 it is necessary to give six weeks written notice to the local authority, adjoining occupiers, gas and electricity suppliers, before the demolition of any building (see note 65).

35 *Does it involve work on healthy tree(s) under the* **Forestry Act 1967**?

Many areas of forest and woodland are on land coming under a 'forestry dedication covenant' entered into with the Forestry Commission under the Forestry Act 1967. In such an area a licence must be obtained to fell any healthy tree above a given size with exceptions specified in section 9 of the Act, e.g. those in orchards, gardens or public open spaces. Lopping a tree covered by the Forestry Act, however, does not require a licence.

36 *Does it involve work on healthy tree(s) subject to a* **tree preservation order**?

The LPA may, in the interests of amenity, designate under section 198 of the 1990 Act a TPO on a single tree, a group of trees or a woodland. The effect of a TPO is to prohibit the cutting down, topping, lopping or wilful destruction of trees except with the consent (which may be given subject to conditions) of the LPA.

37 *Does it involve felling or lopping* **dead, dying or dangerous tree(s)**?

To be subject to the prohibitions listed in note 36 above, trees subject to a TPO and trees covered by the Forestry Act 1967 must be healthy and growing. A tree that is dead, dying or dangerous can, therefore, be felled without consent or licence. Despite this, it is prudent to inform the LPA (in the case of a TPO tree), or the Forestry Commission's local Conservator of Forests (in the case of a tree covered by the Forestry Act) of the intention to fell the tree(s). Trying to prove after the event that the tree was dead, dying or dangerous is very difficult.

| 38 | *Is it in a* **UDC, enterprise zone or simplified planning zone**? *If yes, is the development exempt from planning permission?* |

These types of area are intended to encourage industrial and commercial activity. An aspect common to them is the relaxation of planning controls for development proposals that conform with the approved scheme. Planning permission under such a scheme may be unconditional or subject to conditions, limitations or exceptions. If a proposal does not conform, or there is no approved scheme, then normal planning controls apply.

(a) Urban Development Corporations (UDC):
UDCs are designated under Part 16 of the Local Government, Planning and Land Act 1980 and section 7 of the 1990 Act. Under section 59, an SDO may be made which grants automatic planning permission for developments which accord with the approved plan. Check with the LPA whether such an SDO exists.

(b) Enterprise zones (EZ):
Section 179 and Schedule 32 of the Local Government, Planning and Land Act 1980 and section 6 of the 1990 Act make provision for EZs. In addition to fiscal benefits, developments that conform with the published scheme for the EZ do not require planning permission or incur fees. Development proposals in EZs should be checked with the EZ Authority and if they do not conform, then the appropriate planning application must be made in the normal way to the LPA (section 88 of the 1990 Act).

(c) Simplified planning zones (SPZ):
Sections 82 to 87 of the 1990 Act cover SPZs. They are similar to EZs, but without the fiscal advantages, and are designated by the LPA, whether or not they own the land. Adoption or approval of the SPZ scheme has the effect of granting planning permission for specified development or class of development. These exclude any proposals dealing with hazardous substances, mineral or waste disposal proposals (see note 27), or those for which an environmental assessment is required. No planning application or fee is required for approved developments. Nothing in an SPZ scheme affects the right of anyone to carry out development for which planning permission is not required or for which permission has already been granted. SPZ schemes cease after ten years.

| 39 | *Does the proposal take place in a* **conservation area**? |

See note 33 above.

| 40 | *Does the proposal involve* **improvement or maintenance works** *(internal or external), not affecting the external appearance?* |

If the works to an unlisted building in a conservation area are restricted to improvement or maintenance works that do not affect the external appearance of the building, and do not involve demolition, conservation area consent need not be applied for (see note 41).

41 *Does it involve* **complete or partial demolition** *of an unlisted building?*

A proposal to demolish all of an unlisted building in a conservation area is treated in the same way as if it were a listed building, i.e., listed building consent must be obtained or, as it is termed, 'conservation area consent'. A recent House of Lords decision (see note 32) has held that 'partial demolition' is an oxymoron: demolition means the clearing of the site; anything less is 'alteration'. Conservation area consent is only required if the 'alteration' significantly affects the building's character.

42 *Does the proposal also involve the* **felling or lopping** *of a tree(s)?*

'Felling or lopping' has come to be interpreted as meaning any action resulting in a physical change to a tree (tree has been discussed in note 28). This action can range from simple pruning of branches to the complete destruction and removal of the tree. To be accurate, 'topping', 'root pruning', 'uprooting' and 'wilful destruction' should be added to 'felling and lopping' as they are all actions that might, or do, prejudice the healthy growth of the tree. The relevant sections in the 1990 Act relating to trees are specifically devised to protect healthy trees that provide amenity value to an area. The procedures relating to proposed work on trees in conservation areas apply to all trees, the only exception being if the tree is dead, dying or dangerous; if it is a productive fruit tree, or if it is in the way of some statutory undertaking, airfield or defence establishment (notes 28 and 37). If there is any doubt about whether work to a particular tree requires permission, it is prudent to consult with the LPA.

43 *Is the* **tree(s) dead, dying or dangerous?**

See note 37 above.

44 *Is the tree(s) under the* **Forestry Act 1967?**

See note 35 above.

45 *Is the tree(s) subject to a* **tree preservation order?**

See note 36 above.

46 *Is* **the proposal** *related only to work on trees and/or maintenance work?*

The proposal in question may involve a whole variety of components of which work to trees and/or maintenance work may only be a part.

47 *Is there an* **Article 4 direction** *applied to the site or building?*

Article 4 of the GPDO provides that the Secretary of State or LPA can direct that all or any 'permitted development' (note 57) under the GPDO shall not be carried out in a particular area or to a particular building without specific permission. If permission is refused, or permission is conditional, the applicant is entitled to compensation.

Part 1: **Development within the curtilage** *of a single dwellinghouse. Is it permitted?*

There is no definition in the 1990 Act of 'curtilage', but it is generally accepted as being ground which is used for the enjoyment of a house and that in some necessary or reasonably useful way serves the purpose of the house.

'Development in the curtilage of a dwellinghouse' comes under Part I of Schedule 2 of the GPDO. Part I only applies to single dwelling-houses and not to flats or a single flat above, for example, a shop, or office (see note 14). Development is permitted in eight classes:

Class A enlargement, improvement or other alteration, within certain limits
Class B enlargement or alteration by addition to its roof, within certain limits
Class C any other alteration to the roof within certain limits
Class D erection or construction of a porch, within certain limits
Class E erection or construction of a building or enclosure required for a purpose incidental to the enjoyment of the dwellinghouse (shed, etc.) within certain limits
Class F construction of a hard surface
Class G installation of a tank for the storage of domestic heating oil, up to a certain size and within certain limits
Class H erection of a satellite dish aerial, within certain limits.

Details of these are contained in Appendix E.

Part 2: Development involving **minor operations.** *Is it permitted?*

Minor operations include the erection, maintenance, improvement or alteration of gates, fences, walls or other means of enclosure, and the painting of the exterior of a building. They also include the construction of an access to a highway (see Appendix E for details).

Part 3: Development involving a **change of use.** *Is it permitted?*

For a change of use to be development, it must be material (see note 24). 'Changes of Use' come under Part 3 of Schedule 2 of the GPDO (see Appendix E for details). There have been a number of planning appeal decisions in which the residents of dwellings who own adjoining agricultural land, have extended their gardens into their unused fields. This is not permitted development as the agricultural character of the land, whether it is in current agricultural use or not, is thereby changed to a domestic character. Planning permission for the change of use must be applied for.

Part 4: Development involving **temporary buildings and/or uses.** *Is it permitted?*

Temporary buildings and works include buildings, works, plant or machinery needed temporarily in connection with building or construction work, and some other types of moveable structures. 'Temporary Buildings and Uses' come under Part 4 of Schedule 2 of the GPDO (see Appendix E for details).

Part 5: Use of land for **caravan sites.** *Is it permitted?*

The GPDO refers to the Caravan Sites and Control of Development Act 1960, the first schedule (paragraphs 2 to 10) of which lists the main types of exempted use:

- use by persons travelling with a caravan for one or two nights
- use of holdings of two hectares or more, for not more than five caravans
- sites occupied and supervised by exempted organisations
- sites approved by exempted organisations for not more than five caravans
- meetings organised by exempted organisations for not more than five days
- use by occasional agricultural or forestry works
- use for building or engineering operations
- use by travelling showmen between October and March
- use by the licensing authority for the area.

53 *Part 6: Development involving* **agricultural buildings, works or uses**. *Is it permitted?*

As defined in section 336(1) of the 1990 Act, the term 'agricultural uses' includes the following:

> horticulture, fruit growing, seed growing, dairy farming, the breeding and keeping of livestock (including any creature kept for the production of food, wool, skins or fur or for the purpose of its use in the farming of land), the use of land as grazing land, meadow land, osier land, market gardens and nursery grounds, and the use of land for woodlands where that use is ancillary to the farming of land for other agricultural purposes.

A notable exception is land/buildings used for the breeding and training of horses. However land used for grazing horses is deemed to be in agricultural use.

'Agricultural buildings, works and uses' comes under Part 6 of Schedule 2 of the GPDO. Development is permitted for buildings connected with agricultural use, within certain size limitations. To qualify the agricultural land area must be greater than 0.4 ha (see Appendix E for a summary).

54 *Part 7: Development involving buildings or works on* **forestry land**. *Is it permitted?*

Forestry land is land coming under a 'forestry dedication covenant', entered into with the Forestry Commissioners under the Forestry Act 1967. 'Forestry buildings and works' come under Part 7 of Schedule 2 of the GPDO. Permission is given for building and other operations required for forestry and for the formation, alteration and maintenance of private ways (see Appendix E for a summary).

55 *Part 8:* **Industrial and warehouse development**. *Is it permitted?*

'Industrial' involves any process for, or incidental to, any of the following purposes, namely:

- the making of any article or part of any article (including a ship or vessel, or a film, video or sound recording) or
- the altering, repairing, ornamenting, finishing, cleaning, washing, packing or canning, or adapting for sale, or breaking up, or demolition, of any article, or
- the getting, dressing or treatment of minerals,

in the course of trade or business other than agriculture, or a use carried out in or adjacent to a mine or quarry.

The definition of 'warehouse' appears in Appendix A.

'Industrial and warehouse development' comes under Part 8 of Schedule 2 of the GPDO and includes the extension or alteration of industrial buildings within certain limits and the installation or replacement of plant or machinery (see Appendix E for a summary).

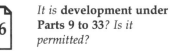

56 *It is* **development under Parts 9 to 33**? *Is it permitted?*

As can be gathered from the flowchart, Parts 9 to 33 of Schedule 2 of the GPDO include a miscellaneous collection of different types of development. Appendix E gives a summary of the permitted development for each class, but the GPDO must be referred to for details.

57 *Is there any doubt that it is* **permitted development**?

Certain types of 'classes' of development provided for by section 59 of the 1990 Act and specified in the GPDO do not require planning permission. There are currently 33 GPDO classes. As with 'development' (see note 29) it is not always clear whether a particular proposal is permitted development or not, and precedents have been set over the years. Where there is doubt, an application for a Certificate of Lawfulness of Proposed Use or Development (CLOPUD) Act (Procedure 12) puts the onus on the LPA to resolve the issue.

58 *Is the proposal on behalf of* **the Crown or a local authority**?

The Crown is shorthand for the Crown Estate, government departments (including Health Authorities and the like) and the Duchies of Lancaster and Cornwall. Development by the Crown does not require planning permission but a routine of consultation has evolved, and is enshrined in Circ. 18/84, which amounts to much the same thing. The Crown gives Notice of Proposed Development and invites the views of the LPA. The LPA deals with the Notice as if it were any other planning application. If the LPA objects, the DETR acts as referee between it and the developing department.

The Circ. 18/84 procedures are used if the Crown intends to develop for its own use. If the Crown wants to sell the land with the permission on the open market, an ordinary planning permission should be secured rather than go through the Notice procedures.

Development under the notification procedures is subject to the same rules as other development as regards such things as section 65 notices and permitted development.

Development by an LPA, either alone on its own land or jointly with a developer, is governed by section 316 of the 1990 Act as modified by section 20 of the PCA. The general principle is that an LPA must make applications in the same way as any other developer, and the detailed procedures are set out in the Town and Country Planning General Regulations 1992, SI 1992, 1492 (TCPGR) and explained in Circ. 19/92. In general terms the provisions are as follows:

- If an LPA is seeking to develop its own land either by itself or jointly with a developer, and if the LPA's interest in the development is significant, Regulation 3 of the TCPGR applies. As for other developers, the application must be registered and go through the same publication and consultation procedures; the same fees are payable and the requirements for an environmental assessment are the same but any listed building application must be made direct to the Secretary of State.
- The Regulations separate the LPA's landowning functions from its planning functions: the planning decision cannot be made by the same committee that is responsible for the land or building to which the application relates. If the landowning committee disagrees with the planning committee there is no right of appeal. If permission is granted under Regulation 3 it is personal to the LPA or to the other interested parties: it does not go with the land and cannot pass to third parties.
- Regulation 4 enables an LPA to grant consent which does run with the land and therefore enables it to dispose of land with the benefit of planning permission.

59   *Does the proposal involve* **new buildings?**

Where a proposal requiring planning permission involves the development of a new building or buildings, as distinct from an extension to, or the alteration of, an existing building, it may be possible to submit an outline application (see note 60).

60   *Will the LPA allow an* **outline application?**

An application for outline planning permission enables an applicant to test or establish the principle of a particular proposal without the trouble and expense of preparing full details. If successful the applicant receives a planning permission but with various 'reserved matters' (see note 6) which must be submitted and agreed before any works can start. The applicant can, to some extent, choose what aspects are to be reserved but he must obtain the agreement of the LPA on how much detail is submitted.

An outline application can only be used for the development of buildings: it cannot be used for alterations, extensions or changes of use. Outline applications are rarely accepted in conservation areas.

An applicant can choose to submit an outline application but the LPA must be satisfied that there is enough detail on which to make a formal decision. The LPA can, within a month of the application, ask for more detail on any or all reserved matters (under Article 4 of the GPDO) but cannot direct an applicant to supply further information. The LPA can also ask for details which need not form part of the official application but which are nevertheless taken into consideration as 'illustrative material'. If the applicant declines to supply further details, the LPA may reject the application, upon which the applicant may appeal to the Secretary of State. This would only be advantageous in exceptional circumstances. Reserved matters can be one or more of five aspects: siting, design, external appearance, means of access and landscaping.

61 *Does the **client** want an outline application?*

Submitting an outline application (see note 60) has advantages for an applicant in some circumstances: a formal indication is gained as to the LPA's attitude towards the proposals without involving detailed design work. On the other hand, the process of an outline application followed by the approval of details may be longer than applying for full planning permission in the first place.

62 *Does the LPA require **planning obligations** or other matters secured by **section 106 agreements**?*

(a) Planning obligations:
The securing of planning obligations through section 106 agreements is now well established in law. Their intended purpose is to enhance the quality of development and to enable proposals to go ahead which might otherwise be refused. They are a means of reconciling the interests of developers with those of the local community and environment. Circ. 1/97 sets out Government guidelines on planning obligations.

The Circular sets out five tests for such obligations: they should be necessary; relevant to planning; directly related to the proposed development; fairly and reasonably related in scale and kind to the proposed development; and reasonable in all other respects. They should not duplicate or replace planning conditions.

The Circular states that acceptable development should not be refused because an applicant is unwilling to offer benefits, and unacceptable developments should not be permitted because of unnecessary or unrelated benefits offered by the applicant. It stresses that obligations are not a way of paying for planning permission or taxing development.

Obligations may be unconditional or subject to conditions; they may be indefinite in time or limited to a specific period; and they may consist of specific works or payment of money to the LPA for specific things such as infrastructure, schools or affordable housing.

The obligations run with the land and are a 'local land charge', which means, amongst other things, that the agreements are public documents. The Crown (see note 58) may enter into planning obligations under section 299A of the 1990 Act as amended by section 12 of the PCA.

(b) Section 106 agreements

Section 106 of the 1990 Act has been extensively modified by section 12.1 of the PCA. It enables LPAs to enter into agreements to restrict or regulate the development or use of land. They can be positive or negative covenants and are enforceable by the LPA against successors in title. There is no immediate recourse of appeal to the Secretary of State as there is in the case of planning conditions. They can only be discharged or modified by mutual consent of the applicant (or his successor) and the LPA, or by appeal after the 'prescribed period' originally agreed, or after five years from the date of the agreement.

In discussion with the applicant and his advisers, the LPA determines the scope and content of section 106 agreements before a planning application is determined. The formal drawing-up of the agreement is a legal matter and is usually concluded by the LPA's solicitor and the applicant's solicitor. It can be a lengthy business and often takes place after the planning committee has approved the application subject to the agreement; the LPA's solicitor is usually only briefed by the planning officers after the committee has had its say. The planning permission is only granted after the section 106 agreement has been completed.

In cases of an appeal, or any other circumstance in which the LPA fails to agree on planning obligations, a developer can make a 'unilateral undertaking': a voluntary offer of planning obligations which should be in accordance with the guidelines of the Circular.

63 *Is there a need to obtain* **immunity from the possible listing** *of the building for which planning permission is being sought or has been granted?*

A building judged to be worthy of listing can be 'spot-listed'. This could prove economically disastrous for a developer who was otherwise preparing to proceed on the basis of a full planning permission. The outcome of an application for immunity from listing will give greater certainty to the developer as he will know he must seek listed building consent, or that he has five years to carry out his development without the possibility of spot-listing disrupting the programme.

64 *Does the proposal require an* **environmental assessment***?*

Certain types of development proposals require a formal environmental assessment (EA) before they can be determined by the LPA. Appendix G contains a summary of the legislative background, the categories and criteria for projects requiring EA, and the procedures for deciding whether you need one, and for carrying them out. Procedure 20 gives more detail on the steps to be taken. Only a small proportion of projects require a formal EA, but developers are well advised to produce voluntary environmental statements (ES) to support any application that raises environmental concerns in the widest sense, which helps the planning officer, the public and the applicant.

What about **other** **consents, licences, approvals, etc.,** *following a grant of planning permission?*

This is a cautionary note that obtaining all the correct planning permissions, or being exempt from them, does not necessarily mean that work can start on site or a change of use be implemented immediately. Other consents or licences may be necessary, related, for example, to the structural integrity, safety and public health aspects of buildings under the Building Regulations. In particular, attention should be drawn to the procedures it is necessary to follow before demolition can be carried out.

(a) Demolition:
Regardless of the need for other permissions, under section 80 of the Building Act 1984, no demolition of any building can begin until:

- the local authority has been notified and either a period of six weeks has elapsed or the local authority have issued a section 81 notice
- notice has been given to all occupiers of any adjacent buildings
- gas and electricity suppliers have been notified.

Exceptions to this are when the demolition involves either:

- internal works only
- a volume less than $50\,\text{m}^3$
- subsidiary buildings (e.g. greenhouse, conservatory, shed or prefab. garage)
- agricultural buildings
- a demolition order.

(b) Demolition of listed buildings:
If the building to be demolished is listed or subject to a BPN (see note 32), then, in addition to the Building Act requirements above, the Royal Commission on Historic Monuments must be given an opportunity to make a record of the building. Either before or immediately after gaining consent to demolish a listed building, contact the LPA which will issue a form for the purpose of informing the Royal Commission. Having submitted the form, at least a month must elapse during which time reasonable access to the building must be given to the Royal Commission. (The Royal Commission should not be confused with the Historic Buildings and Monuments Commission for England).

If the Royal Commission completes its records or states that it does not wish to make a record, the building can be demolished. If, after the Royal Commission has been informed, no word is heard for a month, demolition can go ahead.

(c) Development on sites of potential archaeological importance:
Another consent required relates to development on sites of potential archaeological importance. Some areas are designated as being of archaeological importance under the Ancient Monuments and Archaeological Areas Act 1979. This designation does not

directly affect an application for planning permission but can have repercussions after it has been granted. The developer is obliged under section 35 of the above Act to serve an 'operational notice' on the district council (or London borough) giving six weeks notice of starting work on site and the archaeologists must be allowed up to four months to carry out investigations.

The format of the notice to be submitted to the LPA is contained in Part I of Schedule 1 to the Operations in Areas of Archaeological Importance (Forms of Notice etc.) Regulations 1984. An example of the certificate to accompany the notice is contained in Part II of Schedule 1.

LLYFRGELL COLEG MENAI LIBRARY

Introduction

Taking a particular development proposal through the flowchart will lead either to a 'no application required' symbol or to one or more 'application procedure' symbols. In this section each of the application procedures is set out as a self-contained sub-section. Most are divided into four parts:

Introduction:
> This contains explanations, conditions and/or exceptions to the procedure. It should be read carefully as you may find, on reading the small print, that your proposal might not need that type of application after all.

Steps for the applicant:
> Assuming that the introduction to the procedure has not invalidated the need for completing the procedure, this part is the complete list of steps that the applicant should follow in order to submit an application. (Because each procedure is written to be self-contained, there may be an element of repetition between one procedure and another.)

Relevant LPA action:
> These are just some of the actions taken by the LPA or relevant authority on receipt of the application, but are the actions which are of particular interest to the applicant. Note that the internal machinations of the determining authority and those of consultees are not discussed.

Forms:
> Where appropriate, forms relating to the application are set out in full at the end of each procedure. It should be noted, first, that some LPAs have their own versions of the application forms and that they should be used rather than those illustrated, and second, where a form is derived from the legislation, the wording should not be altered as this may render it invalid.

We stress the point that before submitting an application, particularly for complex, large or potentially contentious proposals, you should meet the LPA officer likely to be dealing with the application. It may be the case that several officers are involved on different aspects (conservation, local plan, development control etc.): meet as many as possible and get their advice on the number, form and content of all necessary applications.

Where a proposal results in a need for more than one type of application, treat each application separately but try to submit them simultaneously. Remember that the officer dealing with the application for listed building consent is not necessarily the same one that is dealing with the application for express consent to display an advertisement, etc.

Multiple applications

There are some circumstances in which it is desirable to submit more than one of the same type of application simultaneously for the same site. One instance is if an applicant wants to test formally which of several possible uses for a site would be permitted. A second is if an applicant wants a full permission for one part of a development (such as an access road) but wants only an outline permission on the rest. A third is where an applicant knows that only part of the proposal is contentious and therefore submits a separate application for this part, thus not putting 'all his eggs in one basket'. A fourth and common circumstance is if an applicant knows that the proposal is contentious and that the LPA is likely to refuse it, but that there is scope for negotiation: the applicant submits two identical applications, appeals to the Secretary of State on one (either on grounds of refusal or deemed refusal after eight weeks) and continues to negotiate and amend the other.

For complex proposals, the best combination of multiple applications can only be decided on a case by case basis. Once again, the LPA may be willing to advise.

An LPA may decline to determine an application which is made within two years of a similar application being dismissed at appeal.

Application for Full Planning Permission to Develop Land

This is the most common type of planning application and is required for any proposal:

- that constitutes development, i.e., building or engineering operations (see note 25), and/or a material change of use to which the land is put (see note 24), which is not 'permitted development' (see note 57), or
- involving the continuation of a use and/or retaining a building that has been constructed without the necessary planning permission, or without complying with a condition (see note 3) attached to a planning permission.

A planning application submitted for either of the above does not preclude the need for other types of permission to be obtained if relevant, e.g. listed building consent, express consent to display an advertisement, etc.

The procedures are set out in the Town and Country Planning (General Development Procedure) Order 1995 (GDPO). With two exceptions a planning application can be made by anyone – the applicant does not need to own or have an 'interest' in the site. The first exception is in the case of Crown land, where an applicant must have written permission from the relevant Crown department, or be a tenant. The second exception is in the case of trunk roads, where only the highway authority may make applications.

An application for the renewal of a temporary permission (i.e. a permission granted for only a limited time period) follows the procedure below, but without the need to submit copies of the original drawings – only a site plan need be submitted.

Outline planning applications follow the same procedures as full applications, but with the exceptions given in Procedure 18.

Steps for the Applicant:

1   Obtain the application forms from the LPA including examples of the notices and certificates required under section 65 of the 1990 Act. The application forms generally come from the LPA as a package containing:

Part 1   A form requesting general information on the application. (See Form 1A for an example.) Part 1 sometimes includes Certificate A (see step 5 below).

Part 2   Certificates of ownership (see step 5 below) and examples of notices (see step 4 below) under section 65.

Part 3   A form requesting additional information in respect of applications for industrial, office, warehousing, storage, shops or catering facilities (see Form 1B for an example).

Part 4   A form asking supplementary questions in connection with an application for permission to extract minerals.

Notes   Instructions for applicants and scale of fees.

2   Prepare the number of copies, as required (usually four), of the application form(s) and a plan (usually at 1:1250 scale) to identify the site, plus, if relevant, other plans as are necessary to describe the development. The site plan should have the site to which the application relates edged in red. Adjoining land owned by the applicant, but not part of the application, should be edged in blue.

3   Calculate the fee payable. See Appendix C for the scale of fees and method of calculation. Make the cheque or money order payable to the LPA.

Circ.31/92

Article 6 Notices

4   Section 65 of the 1990 Act as amended and Art. 6 of the GDPO deal with ownership of the site. If the applicant is not the sole owner, then notice must be served on all the owners using a form of notice shown in Form 1C, but use the LPA's own form if it has one.

Art.6, Sch.2, Part 1

If the land is part of an agricultural holding, then an Art. 6 Notice must be served on any person who was a tenant on the day 21 days before the application is made (Form 1C, as above).

If none or only some of the owners can be given notice, then an advertisement must be put in a local newspaper. The format of the advertisement is the same as for Form 1C, but use the LPA's own format if it has one.

Article 7 Certificates

5   Complete only one of either Certificate A, B, C or D, together with an Agricultural Holdings Certificate. This latter certificate is usually incorporated in the printed Certificates A, B, C and D obtained from the LPA.

Art.7

Certificate A
    a certificate stating that 21 days before the date of the application, no person other than the applicant was the owner of any of the land to which the application relates; see Form 1D

Sch.2, Part 2

Certificate B
a certificate stating that the applicant has given the requisite notice of the application to all persons who, 21 days before the date of the application, were owners of any of the land to which the application relates; see Form 1E

Certificate C
a certificate stating that the applicant is unable to issue either Certificate A or B, that he has given the requisite notice of the application to one or more owners, that he has taken such steps as are reasonably open to him to ascertain the names and addresses of the remainder of those persons and that he has been unable to do so; see Form 1F

Certificate D
a certificate stating that the applicant has taken such steps as are reasonably open to him to ascertain the names and addresses of the owners and that he has been unable to do so; see Form 1G.

If Certificate C or D is appropriate, then a copy of the actual newspaper advertisement must be attached.

Note: For the purposes of this procedure, 'owner' means a person having a freehold interest or a leasehold interest the unexpired term of which is not less than seven years.

6 Any application should be accompanied by an explanatory note of some kind, however brief. Appendix B contains a list of some of the issues that should be covered.

7 Applications for large scale or potentially environmentally disruptive developments may need to be accompanied by an 'environmental statement' (ES). It is mandatory for certain types of major projects to have an ES. See Appendix G and Procedure 20 for more details.

Summary of Activities to Submit a Full Planning Application

Before submission day:

Send an Art. 6 advertisement to the local newspaper, if necessary. Allow sufficient time for publication.

Submission day:

(a) Package to be sent to the LPA:

- application form Part 1, plus, if necessary, Part 3 or Part 4 (number of copies as indicated in 'notes to applicants')
- site plan and drawings as necessary (number of copies as indicated)
- list of drawings (number of copies as indicated)
- cheque or money order for the fee, made out to the LPA
- explanatory statement
- environmental statement, if necessary (number of copies as agreed with the LPA)
- appropriate Art. 7 Certificates
- copy of the Art. 6 newspaper advertisement, if required
- covering letter listing the contents of the submission package.

(b) Other actions:

- Art. 6 Notice sent to owners/occupiers, if necessary.

Note: The planning permission does not become active until formal notification, the Notice of Planning Consent, is received by the applicant.

Relevant LPA Action:

1 Acknowledge receipt of the application using the prescribed form.

2 The application must be registered and a copy of the application form(s) and a set of plans and drawings made available for public scrutiny. If the application is for a proposal in a Conservation Area, then it must be advertised in a local newspaper and a notice displayed on or near the site.

s.73/67 LBCA

3 The LPA can request, in writing, more information to verify any particulars.

4 Circulate copies of the application form(s) and plans and drawings to consultees (Appendix K).

5 Publicity is now primarily the responsibility of the LPA, including those developments which used to be known as 'bad neighbours'. The LPA must put up a site notice for all applications and leave it up for 21 days. In the case of proposals which are the subject of Environmental Statements, which do not accord with the development plan, or which are considered major developments, the LPA must, in addition, advertise in a local paper. In the case of both major and minor developments the LPA must also serve notice on any adjoining owner or occupier (GDPO Art. 8).

6 The decision should be made within eight weeks from the receipt of the application, or such extended periods as agreed with the applicant. For applications requiring an environmental assessment the period is extended to 16 weeks. The decision must not be made in less than 21 days if the land is not all owned by the applicant, or if others have an interest, or if agricultural tenants are involved.

7 The LPA may be directed to refer the application to the Secretary of State if it comes within a class specified in a direction issued under section 77.

s.77

Results

The outcome of the application can be:

- non-determination, i.e. deemed refusal
- refusal (reasons to be given)
- permission, subject to condition (reasons to be given)
- permission with no conditions.

The applicant can appeal to the Secretary of State against the decision, but only within six months of receipt of the decision notice or, in the case of non-determination, six months from the date the decision should have been made. If the applicant is aggrieved by one or more of the conditions, then he can apply to vary or revoke them (see Procedure 6) or appeal against their imposition.

s.78

FORM 1A   Typical application form (Part 1)

TOWN AND COUNTRY PLANNING ACT 1990

> For official use:
> fee paid:
> ref no.:
> date lodged:

GENERAL INSTRUCTIONS – PLEASE

1 Read the notes below before completing the application.
2 Complete Part A. Industrial, office, warehouse, retail, hotel, leisure or ancillary storage applications also complete Part B.
3 Enclose fee if applicable.
4 Certify ownership of the site under section 65 of the Act and serve notice on owners and tenants of the site other than yourself – see Certificates under section 65, below.
5 Send four copies of this completed form, and four copies of the plans and drawings to:

. . . . (a) . . . .

PART A

1 **The Applicant**

Name . . . .

Address . . . . postcode . . . .

Tel. No. . . . .

2 **Agent** (if any)

Name . . . .

Address . . . . postcode . . . .

Tel. No. . . . .

3 **Address or location of site:**

4 **Site area:**

5 This application is for (tick one box only)

    (a) **full planning permission** ☐
    (b) **outline planning permission** ☐

6 If you have **ticked box 5(b)**, tick any of the following matters which you have not included in this application but wish to reserve for subsequent approval:

    siting ☐
    external appearance ☐
    landscape ☐
    design ☐
    access ☐

7 **Present use** of buildings/land (if none, state last previous use):

4

FORM 1A continued

8 (a) Give brief **description** of proposed development, including works to be carried out, buildings to be demolished and the proposed use of the buildings/land:

   (b) Tick one or more boxes as appropriate:

   new build ☐
   alteration/extension ☐
   change of use ☐
   other ☐

9 If development is **residential**, state number and type of units:

10 Tick box if development involves:

   new access to highway ☐
   altered access to highway ☐

11 Tick box if development involves **felling tree(s)**
   (show positions on plan) ☐

12 Describe how **surface water** will be disposed of:

13 Describe how **water** will be supplied:

14 Tick box for method of **foul sewage disposal**:

   main sewer ☐
   other (specify and state whether involves existing system) ☐

15 List all **drawings, plans and other documents** forming part of this application:

Note: A site plan is needed showing the site and adjoining properties and roads. That plan should be at a scale of 1:1250 or larger and show the direction of north. The application site should be edged in red and any adjoining land the applicant owns or controls edged in blue. For a full application for building or other works you must also submit plans at a scale of 1:100 or larger. These plans must show the existing features of the site including any trees and the layout, elevations and sections of the development. If existing works are shown, they should be distinguished from new. Materials visible from outside the works must be described (including colour). The means of access to the site and type of enclosure (wall, fence, etc.) must also be shown.

16 **I/WE HEREBY APPLY** for planning permission to carry out the development described in this application and the accompanying documents, and in accordance with them.

   Signed: .... Date ....

   On behalf of* ....

* delete where applicable

(a) Name and address of local planning authority

FORM 1A
Typical application form
Source: RMJM and others

FORM 1B   **Typical application form (Part 3)**

TOWN AND COUNTRY PLANNING ACT 1990

PART B

Complete this part if your application involves industrial, office, warehouse, retail, hotel, leisure or ancillary storage development.

---

1   For industrial development, describe process and products and type of plant/machinery to be installed:

---

2   If the proposal forms part of a larger scheme for which permission is not yet asked, briefly describe ultimate development:

---

3   If the proposal is related to an existing use on or near the site, explain relationship:

---

4   How much new floorspace will be provided for each proposed use on the site:

    Total floorspace . . . .

---

5   How many staff will be employed on the site as a result of the proposed development:

    (a)   Full time . . . .

    (b)   Part time . . . .

---

6   Describe parking/loading/unloading provision (also show location on plan, unless you are reserving design for further approval):

---

7   State estimated traffic to the site during a normal working day:

    (a)   heavy goods vehicles . . . .

    (b)   other vehicles . . . .

---

8   State nature, volume and proposed means of disposal of any trade effluents or trade refuse:

---

9   Tick box if hazardous substances in the quantities listed in Schedule 1 of the Town and Country Planning (Hazardous Substances) Regulations 1992 will be kept on the land:

    ☐

FORM 1B
Typical application form
Source: RMJM and others

FORM 1C
Notice to owners and newspaper advertisement
Source:
GDPO 1995
Sch.2 Part 1

Town and Country Planning (General Development Procedure) Order 1995

NOTICE UNDER ARTICLE 6 OF APPLICATION FOR PLANNING PERMISSION

Proposed development at . . . . (a) . . . .

I give notice that . . . . (b) . . . .

is applying to the . . . . (c) . . . . Council

for planning permission to . . . . (d) . . . .

Any owner* of the land or tenant** who wishes to make representations about this application should write to the Council at

. . . . (e) . . . .

by . . . . (f) . . . .

* 'owner' means a person having a freehold interest or a leasehold interest the unexpired term of which is not less than seven years, or, in the case of a development consisting of the winning or working of minerals, a person entitled to an interest in a mineral in the land (other than oil, gas, coal, gold or silver).

** 'tenant' means a tenant of an agricultural holding any part of which is comprised in the land.

Signed . . . .

#On behalf of . . . .

Date . . . .

Statement of owners' rights

The grant of planning permission does not affect owners' rights to retain or dispose of their property, unless there is some provision to the contrary in an agreement or in a lease.

Statement of agricultural tenants' rights

The grant of planning permission for non-agricultural development may affect agricultural tenants' security of tenure.

delete where inappropriate

(a) address or location of the proposed development
(b) applicant's name
(c) name of Council
(d) description of the proposed development
(e) address of the Council
(f) date given a period of 21 days beginning with the date of service, or 14 days beginning with the date of publication, of the notice (as the case may be).

FORM 1D
Certificate A
Source
GDPO 1995
Sch.2 Part 2

* delete where inappropriate

(a) 'Owner' means a person having a freehold interest or a leasehold interest the unexpired term of which is not less than seven years, or, in the case of a development involving the winning or working of minerals, a person entitled to an interest in a mineral in the land (other than oil, gas, coal, gold or silver).

Town and Country Planning (General Development Procedure) Order 1995

CERTIFICATE UNDER ARTICLE 7

Certificate A

I certify that:

on the day 21 days before the date of the accompanying application nobody, except the applicant, was the owner(a) of any part of the land to which the application relates.

* None of the land to which the application relates is, or is part of, an agricultural holding.

or

* I have/The applicant has* given the requisite notice to every person other than my/him/her* self who, on the day 21 days before the date of the application was a tenant of an agricultural holding on all or part of the land to which the application relates, as follows:

Tenant's name	Address at which notice was served	Date on which notice was served
. . . .	. . . .	. . . .

Signed . . . .

*On behalf of . . . .

Date . . . .

4

FORM 1E
Certificate B

Source:
GDPO 1995
Sch.2, Part 2

* delete where inappropriate

(a) 'Owner' means a person having
a freehold interest or a
leasehold interest the unexpired
term of which is not less than
seven years, or, in the case of a
development involving the
winning or working of
minerals, a person entitled to an
interest in a mineral in the land
(other than oil, gas, coal, gold or
silver).

Town and Country Planning (General Development Procedure) Order 1995
CERTIFICATE UNDER ARTICLE 7

Certificate B

I certify that:

I have/The applicant has* given the requisite notice to everyone else who, on the day 21 days before the date of the accompanying application was the owner of any part of the land to which the application relates, as listed below:

Owner's name (a)	Address at which notice was served	Date on which notice was served
. . . .	. . . .	. . . .

*   None of the land to which the application relates is, or is part of, an agricultural holding.

or

*   I have/The applicant has* given the requisite notice to every person other than my/him/her* self who, on the day 21 days before the date of the application was a tenant of an agricultural holding on all or part of the land to which the application relates, as follows:

Tenant's name	Address at which notice was served	Date on which notice was served
. . . .	. . . .	. . . .

Signed . . . .

*On behalf of . . . .

Date . . . .

FORM 1F
Certificate C
Source:
GDPO 1995
Sch.2, Part 2

Town and Country Planning (General Development Procedure) Order 1995

CERTIFICATE UNDER ARTICLE 7

Certificate C

I certify that:

I/The applicant* cannot issue a Certificate A or B in respect of the accompanying application.

I have/The applicant has* given the requisite notice to the persons specified below, being persons who on the day 21 days before the date of the accompanying application were owners of any part of the land to which the application relates:

Owner's name (a)	Address at which notice was service	Date on which notice was served
. . . .	. . . .	. . . .

I have/the applicant has* taken all reasonable steps open to me/him/her* to find out the names and addresses of other owners of the land, or of a part of it, but have/has* been unable to do so. These steps are as follows:

(b) . . . .

Notice of the application, as attached to this Certificate, has been published in the

. . . . (c) . . . . on . . . . (d)

* None of the land to which the application relates is, or is part of, an agricultural holding.

or

* I have/The applicant has* given the requisite notice to every person other than my/him/her* self who, on the day 21 days before the date of the application was a tenant of an agricultural holding on all or part of the land to which the application relates, as follows:

Tenant's name	Address at which notice was served	Date on which notice was served
. . . .	. . . .	. . . .

Signed . . . .

*On behalf of . . . .

Date . . . .

---

* delete where inappropriate

(a) 'Owner' means a person having a freehold interest or a leasehold interest the unexpired term of which is not less than seven years, or, in the case of a development involving the winning or working of minerals, a person entitled to an interest in a mineral in the land (other than oil, gas, coal, gold or silver)

(b) description of steps taken

(c) name of newspaper circulating in the area where the land is situated

(d) date of publication (which must not be earlier than the day 21 days before the date of the application).

4

FORM 1G
Certificate D
Source:
GDPO 1995
Sch.2, Part 2

* delete where inappropriate

(a) 'Owner' means a person having
a freehold interest or a
leasehold interest the unexpired
term of which is not less than
seven years, or, in the case of a
development involving the
winning or working of
minerals, a person entitled to an
interest in a mineral in the land
(other than oil, gas, coal, gold or
silver)

(b) description of steps taken

(c) name of newspaper circulating
in the area where the land is
situated

(d) date of publication (which must
not be earlier than the day 21
days before the date of the
application).

Town and Country Planning (General Development Procedure) Order 1995

CERTIFICATE UNDER ARTICLE 7

Certificate D

I certify that:

I/The applicant* cannot issue a Certificate A in respect of the accompanying application.

I have/the applicant has* taken all reasonable steps open to me/him/her* to find out the names and addresses of other owners(a) of the land, or of a part of it, but have/has* been unable to do so. These steps are as follows:

. . . . (b)

Notice of the application, as attached to this Certificate, has been published in the

. . . . (c)

on . . . . (d)

* None of the land to which the application relates is, or is part of, an agricultural holding.

or

* I have/The applicant has* given the requisite notice to every person other than my/him/her* self who, on the day 21 days before the date of the application was a tenant of an agricultural holding on all or part of the land to which the application relates, as follows:

Tenant's name	Address at which notice was served	Date on which notice was served
. . . .	. . . .	. . . .

Signed . . . .

*On behalf of . . . .

Date . . . .

Application for Listed Building Consent

The legislation covering listed buildings is the Planning (Listed Buildings and Conservation Areas) Act 1990 (LBCA) (referred to in note 32). Any object or structure fixed to a listed building or, if there since before 1 July 1948, any object or structure within the curtilage of the building, is treated as part of the building and therefore subject to listed building control. PPG15 contains a full description of Government policy on listed buildings, and this guidance has been clarified, particularly with reference to partial demolition by Circ. 14/97.

The following types of work require listed building consent:

s.7/8 LBCA

- demolition or removal of whole or part of a listed building or a building or structure in the curtilage of a listed building. Part demolition is now considered to be alteration which only requires consent if the character of the building is affected (see note 32)
- alterations to the exterior and/or interior of a listed building which would affect its special character including painting the exterior a different colour or internal decoration in some buildings
- extensions of whatever size, to a listed building
- addition of advertisements to the exterior of a listed building
- works already carried out to a listed building and for which listed building consent was not obtained.

Exceptions to the above include any listed ecclesiastical building (being used for ecclesiastical purposes), and any listed building which is also a scheduled ancient monument, in which case scheduled monument consent is required and Procedure 13 should be followed.

s.60 LBCA

Although one effect of listing a building makes it an offence to carry out demolition, external alterations or extensions unless listed building consent is first obtained, permitted development rights granted under section 59 of the 1990 Act are not forfeited (unless of course an Article 4 direction has been issued). Thus, certain proposals will need listed building consent but not planning permission, while other proposals will need both. Listed building consent does not imply or confer planning permission.

Occasionally an alteration or extension to a listed building can be authorised by a planning permission provided it is a specific grant of permission and that the permission specifically refers to the works. However, it is much more common for the LPA to insist that an application for listed building consent is submitted simultaneously with the planning application.

Circ.8/87

Any proposal to display an advertisement (excluding statutory notices) on or inside a listed building requires listed building consent even if the advertisement complies with the advertisement regulations and does not need express consent (see Appendix F). Granting listed building consent for an advertisement does not imply or confer express consent to display the advertisement.

Circ.8/87, para 5

Normal listed building control applies in UDCs, enterprise zones and simplified planning zones (see note 38).

Recent legislation gives express authority for the imposition of conditions requiring the later approval of details. However, the application must show enough detail for the impact of the works on the building to be assessed, i.e. this change must not be assumed to be similar in function to an outline planning permission.

s.17(2) LBCA

Steps for the Applicant:

SI 1990 No. 1519

1 Obtain the listed building consent application forms from the LPA. (These vary from one authority to another and in some cases are combined with the application forms for permission to develop land.)

2 Complete and sign the consent application form and make the appropriate number of copies as requested.

3 If not the sole owner of the building, the applicant must notify all other owners. For the form of notice, see Form 2A. 'Owner' in this context means a person having a freehold or leasehold interest, the unexpired term of which is not less than seven years.

4 If the applicant is unable to notify any or all owners, then an advertisement is required in a local newspaper circulating in the area. For the form of advertisement, see Form 2B.

s.11 LBCA

5 Complete only one of either Certificate A, B, C or D:

Certificate A
a certificate stating that 21 days before the application date, no person other than the applicant was the owner of the building to which the application relates; see Form 2C

Certificate B
a certificate stating that the applicant has given the requisite notice of the application to all persons who, 21 days before the date of the application, were owners of the building to which the application relates; see Form 2D

Certificate C
a certificate stating that the applicant is unable to issue either Certificate A or B, that he has given the requisite notice of the

application to one or more owners, that he has taken all reasonable steps to ascertain the names and addresses of the remainder of the owners and that he has been unable to do so; see Form 2E

Certificate D
a certificate stating that the applicant has taken all reasonable steps to ascertain the names and addresses of the owners and that he has been unable to do so; see form 2F.

If Certificate C or D is appropriate, then a copy of the actual newspaper advertisement must be attached.

6 The application must be accompanied by a plan to show the site to which it refers in relation to surrounding properties. (The appropriate scale is usually 1:1250.) The plan should have the site edged in red.

7 If alterations and/or extensions are involved, drawings in sufficient detail are required to give a clear picture of the works proposed. The number of copies of the sets of drawings required by the LPA should be checked in the application notes.

Circ.8/87

8 Although not mandatory, it is helpful if applications are accompanied by photographs of all elevations if consent is sought for demolition, or for the part affected by alterations and extensions (including the interior).

Circ.8/87

Circ.31/92

9 No fee is payable.

Note: If a consent is granted for demolition, notice will be sent to the LPA to the Royal Commission on the Historical Monuments of England (or Wales and Monmouthshire, in the case of Wales) both known as the Royal Commission. The Royal Commission must be given at least one month before work is commenced in which to make a record of the building or, alternatively, must have indicated that it does not want to record the building. (The Royal Commission should not be confused with 'the Commission' which is the Historic Buildings and Monuments Commission for England, or English Heritage as it is known.)

s.8(2)(c) LBCA

Relevant LPA Action:

1 On receipt of the application, the applicant should be notified. The application is then registered and available for public inspection.

2 Notify the Secretary of State of application and wait 28 days before determining the application.

s.13 LBCA

3 With the exception of applications for consent to carry out works which affect only the interior of a Grade II (unstarred) building,

s.11 LBCA

s.73 LBCA

s.14 LBCA

applications must be advertised by the LPA in a local newspaper and a notice posted on or near the site for a period of not less than seven days. These state that the plans etc. can be inspected by the public for a period of 21 days thereafter.

4 In Greater London, the LPA must give notice of all applications for listed building consent to the Historic Buildings and Monuments Commission for England (the Commission). Outside London, only applications for Grade I or Grade II* (Grade II star) buildings in England need be referred to the Commission. In England, notice of applications (and the decisions) for demolition must be given to:

> The Ancient Monuments Society
> The Council for British Archaeology
> The Georgian Group
> The Society for the Protection of Ancient Buildings
> The Victorian Society
> The Royal Commission on the Historical Monuments of
>   England.

5 The decision should be made within eight weeks from the receipt of the application, or such extended periods as agreed with the applicant.

Results

The outcome of the application can be either:

- non-determination, i.e. deemed refusal
- refusal (reasons to be given)
- consent, with conditions (reasons to be given)
- consent, with conditions requiring the later approval of details
- consent.

The applicant can appeal to the Secretary of State against the decision within six months of receipt of the decision notice or, in the case of non-determination, six months from the date the decision should have been made. If the applicant is aggrieved by any of the conditions, he can apply to vary/discharge them (see Procedure 5).

s.20 LBCA

If a consent is granted for demolition, the LPA shall inform the Royal Commission.

FORM 2A
Notice to owners

Source:
SI 1990, No. 1519,
Schedule 2, Part 2

* Delete where inappropriate

(a) Name, address or location of building with sufficient precision to ensure identification of it
(b) Name of LPA
(c) Name of applicant
(d) Description of proposed works and name, address or location of building
(e) Date not less than 20 days later than the date on which the notice is served or published
(f) Address of LPA.

PLANNING (LISTED BUILDINGS AND CONSERVATION AREAS) ACT 1990

Notice for service on individuals

Proposal for *demolishing/altering/extending/varying or discharging conditions

. . . . (a) . . . .

TAKE NOTICE that application is being made to the

. . . . (b)   Council

by . . . .(c)

for listed building consent at . . . . (d)

If you wish to make representations about the application, make them in writing,

not later than . . . . (e)

to the Council at . . . . (f)

Signed . . . . *On behalf of (c) . . . .

Date . . . .

FORM 2B
Advertisement in newspaper

Source:
SI 1990, No. 1519,
Schedule 2, Part 2

* Delete where inappropriate

(a) Name, address or location of building with sufficient precision to ensure identification of it
(b) Name of LPA
(c) Name of applicant
(d) Description of proposed works and name, address or location of building
(e) Date not less than 20 days later than the date on which the notice is served or published
(f) Address of LPA.

PLANNING (LISTED BUILDINGS AND CONSERVATION AREAS) ACT 1990

Certificates C and D

NOTICE FOR PUBLICATION IN LOCAL NEWSPAPERS WHERE NOT ALL OWNERS ARE KNOWN, PURSUANT TO REGULATION 6(2) OF THE TOWN AND COUNTRY PLANNING (LISTED BUILDINGS AND CONSERVATION AREAS) REGULATIONS 1990

Proposal for *demolishing/altering/extending/varying or discharging conditions

. . . . (a) . . . .

Notice is hereby given that application is being made to the

. . . . (b)   Council

by . . . . (c)

for listed building consent at . . . . (d)

Any owner of the building (namely a freeholder, or a leaseholder entitled to an unexpired term of at least seven years) who wishes to make representations to the above-mentioned Council about the application should make them in writing

not later than . . . . (e)

to the Council at . . . . (f)

Signed . . . . *On behalf of (c) . . . .

Date . . . .

FORM 2C
Certificate A
Source:
SI 1990, No. 1519,
Schedule 2, Part 1

* Delete where inappropriate.

(a) Insert name of applicant.

PLANNING (LISTED BUILDINGS AND CONSERVATION AREAS) ACT 1990

Certificate A

I hereby certify that no person other than *myself/the applicant was an owner of the building to which the application relates at the beginning of the period of 20 days before the date of the accompanying application.

Signed . . . . *On behalf of (a) . . . .

Date . . . .

FORM 2D
Certificate B
Source:
SI 1990, No. 1519,
Schedule 2, Part 1

* Delete where inappropriate.

(a) Insert name of applicant.

PLANNING (LISTED BUILDINGS AND CONSERVATION AREAS) ACT 1990

Certificate B

I hereby certify that:

*I have/The applicant has given the requisite notice to all the persons other than *myself/the applicant who, 20 days before the date of the accompanying application, were owners of the building to which the application relates, viz:

Owner's name	Address	Date of service of notice
. . . .	. . . .	
	. . . .	. . . .

Signed . . . . *On behalf of (a) . . . .

Date . . . .

FORM 2E
Certificate C

Source:
SI 1990, No. 1519,
Schedule 2, Part 1

**PLANNING (LISTED BUILDINGS AND
CONSERVATION AREAS) ACT 1990**

Certificate C

I hereby certify that:

1. *I am/The applicant is unable to issue a certificate in accordance with either sub-paragraph *(a)* or sub-paragraph *(b)* of regulation 6(1) of the Planning (Listed Buildings and Conservation Areas) Act 1990 in respect of the accompanying

   application dated . . . . (a)

2. *I have/The applicant has given the requisite notice to the following persons other than *myself/the applicant who, 20 days before the date of the application, were owners of the building to which the application relates, viz:

Owner's name	Address	Date of service of notice
. . . .	. . . .	
	. . . .	. . . .

3. *I have/The applicant has taken the steps listed below, being steps reasonably open to *me/him, to ascertain the names and addresses of the other owners of the building and *have/has been unable to do so:

   . . . . (b)

4. Notice of the application as set out below has been published in the

   . . . . (c)

   on . . . . (d)

   Copy of notice is attached.

   Signed . . . . *On behalf of . . . . (e)

   Date . . . .

* Delete where inappropriate.

(a) date of application
(b) description of steps taken
(c) name of a local newspaper circulating in the locality in which the building is situated
(d) date of publication (which must not be earlier than 20 days before the application)
(e) name of applicant.

FORM 2F
Certificate D

Source:
SI 1990, No. 1519,
Schedule 2, Part 1

* Delete where inappropriate.

(a) date of application
(b) description of steps taken
(c) name of a local newspaper
circulating in the locality in
which the building is situated
(d) date of publication (which must
not be earlier than 20 days
before the application)
(e) name of applicant.

**PLANNING (LISTED BUILDINGS AND
CONSERVATION AREAS) ACT 1990**

Certificate D

I hereby certify that:

1. *I am/The applicant is unable to issue a certificate inaccordance with sub-paragraph *(a)* of regulation 6(1) of the Town and Country Planning (Listed Buildings and Buildings in Conservation Areas) Regulations 1987 in respect of

the accompanying application dated . . . . (a)

and *have/has taken the steps listed below, being steps reasonably open to *me/him, to ascertain the names and addresses of all the persons other than *myself/himself who, 20 days before the date of the application, were owners of the building to which the application relates and *have/has been unable to do so:

. . . . (b)

2. Notice of the application as set out below has been published in the

. . . . (c)

on . . . . (d)

Copy of notice is attached.

Signed . . . . *On behalf of . . . . (e)

Date . . . .

Application for Conservation Area Consent

Demolition of an unlisted building within a conservation area requires conservation area consent, which is consent required by section 74 of the Planning (Listed Buildings and Conservation Areas) Act 1990 (LBCA). Applications for conservation area consent are covered by the Town and Country Planning (Listed Buildings and Buildings in Conservation Areas) Regulations, 1990 (No. 1519). The procedure is similar to that for applying for listed building consent, again, PPG15 and Circ. 14/97 should be referred to for guidance, the latter particularly in the case of partial demolition.

Conservation area consent is not needed if:

Circ.8.87

- the building is protected under the ancient monument legislation (see Procedure 13 instead)
- the building is listed (see Procedure 2 instead)
- it involves only part demolition of an ecclesiastical building
- it involves demolition of a building with a **total** cubic content not exceeding 115 m³ or any part of such building (in this instance 'building' does not include part of a building)
- it involves demolition or part demolition of any gate, wall, fence or railing which is less than 1 m high where it abuts a highway (including a public footpath or bridleway) or public open space, or 2 m high in any other case
- it involves demolition or part demolition of any building erected since 1 January 1914 and used, or last used, for the purposes of agriculture or forestry
- it involves demolition of any part of a building used, or last used for an industrial process, if such part (taken with any other part which may have been demolished) is less than 10% of the cubic content of the original building (as ascertained by external measurement) or less than 500 m² of floor space, whichever is the greater
- the building is required to be demolished by virtue of a condition of planning permission granted under section 70 of the 1990 Act, or an agreement made under section 106 of the 1990 Act
- the building is required to be demolished by virtue of a discontinuance order made under section 102–104 of the 1990 Act, or is subject to an enforcement notice served under either sections 172 or 182 of the 1990 Act, or sections 38 or 46 of the LBCA, or is subject to a demolition order or compulsory purchase order made under Part IX of the Housing Act 1985
- a redundant building (within the meaning of the Pastoral Measure 1983) or part of such a building where demolition is in pursuance of a pastoral or redundancy scheme (within the meaning of that measure).

Conservation area consent is unlikely to be granted until there are acceptable and detailed plans for the redevelopment of the site.

LLYFRGELL COLEG MENAI LIBRARY

4

Steps for the Applicant:

1 Obtain the conservation area consent application forms from the LPA. (These vary from one LPA to another and in some cases are combined with the application forms for permission to develop land).

2 Complete and sign the consent application form and make the appropriate number of copies as requested (usually two plus original).

3 If not the sole owner, the applicant must notify all other owners. For the form of notice, see Form 2A (Procedure 2). 'Owner' in this context means a person having a freehold interest or a leasehold interest the unexpired term of which is not less than seven years.

4 If the applicant is unable to notify any or all owners, then an advertisement is required in a local newspaper circulating in the area. For the form of advertisement, see Form 2B.

5 Complete only one of either Certificate A, B, C or D:

Certificate A
a certificate stating that 21 days before the date of the application, no person other than the applicant was the owner of the building to which the application relates; see Form 2C

Certificate B
a certificate stating that the applicant has given the requisite notice of the application to all persons who, 21 days before the date of the application, were owners of the building to which the application relates; see Form 2D

Certificate C
a certificate stating that the applicant is unable to issue either Certificate A or B, that he has given the requisite notice of the application to one or more owners, that he has taken such steps as are reasonably open to him to ascertain the names and addresses of the remainder of the owners and that he has been unable to do so; see Form 2E

Certificate D
a certificate stating that the applicant has taken such steps as are reasonably open to him to ascertain the names and addresses of the owners and that he has been unable to do so; see Form 2F.

If Certificate C or D is appropriate, then a copy of the actual newspaper advertisement must be attached.

6 The application must be accompanied by a plan to show the site to which it refers in relation to surrounding properties. (The appropriate scale is usually 1:1250.) The site should be edged in red and the building proposed for demolition clearly marked. The number of copies of the sets of drawings required by the LPA should be checked in the application notes.

Circ.31/92

7 No fee is payable.

Relevant LPA Action:

1 On receipt of the application, the applicant should be notified using the prescribed form and the application registered and made available for public inspection.

2 If the application is accompanied by either Certificate B, C or D, the application should not be determined for 21 days from the date of the last notice issued to owners.

3 The Historic Buildings and Monuments Commission for England must be notified of any application in Greater London.

4 The application must be advertised in a local newspaper and a notice posted on or near the site.

5 The decision should be made within eight weeks from the receipt of the application or such extended periods as agreed with the applicant.

Results

The outcome of the application can be either:

- non-determination, i.e. deemed refusal
- refusal (reasons to be given)
- consent, with conditions (reasons to be given)
- consent.

The applicant can appeal to Secretary of State against the decision within six months of receipt of the decision notice or, in the case of non-determination, six months from the date the decision should have been made. If the applicant is aggrieved by any of the conditions, he can either appeal or apply to vary or discharge them (see Procedure 5).

4

Application for Approval of 'Conditions' on a Planning Permission

The 1990 Act gives the LPA wide powers to impose conditions on all types of planning permission. (A description of 'conditions' is given in note 3.) Some conditions, such as those requiring approval of additional information on, say, detailed design matters, require an application to the LPA to discharge them.

The condition must be within the terms of the original permission (i.e. same site size, etc.) but the LPA has discretion over minor changes.

Steps for the Applicant:

1 The application should be made in writing to the LPA with sufficient particulars to identify the original planning permission, e.g. reference number and date, and identifying the particular condition for which approval is sought. Form 4A is a suggested format for the application letter.

2 Include with the application suitably scaled plans and drawings as necessary to explain fully the scheme/proposal intended for approval. In the case of facing materials for approval, samples, if required, should be given a reference number and listed in Form 4A. The samples can be posted, but more probably delivered by hand, to the LPA, together with Form 4A.

3 The same number of copies of plans and drawings should be included with the application form as for the original application. In the case of facing material samples, only one sample per material, if any, is usually required, but check with the LPA.

4 No Article 7 Certificate is required.

Circ.31/92 **5** No fee is payable.

Relevant LPA Action:

1 Approval or refusal of the condition(s) must be notified in writing.

2 The decision should be made within eight weeks from the receipt of the application.

GPDO Art.20

Results

There is no appeal against a refusal but, if aggrieved, the applicant can either apply to vary or revoke the conditions (see Procedure 5 or 6, as appropriate) or, if the 6-month time period on the original planning decision has not elapsed, then the applicant can appeal against that decision. If it has elapsed, then the only other course open to the applicant is to submit a fresh planning application (and go to appeal on that decision if necessary).

FORM 4A
Application letter
Source: RMJM

* Delete where inappropriate.

Insert
(a) address of LPA
(b) agent's name, address and
    telephone number or, if no
    agent, then applicant's name,
    address and telephone number
(c) applicant's name, address and
    telephone number
(d) reference number on the
    notification of permission
(e) date of notification
(f) description of development as
    it appeared in the original
    application
(g) full address or location of the
    land to which the application is
    related
(h) quote condition(s) for which
    approval is sought
(i) list of drawings or sample
    materials
(j) number of copies as for the
    original application.

. . . . (a) . . . . (b) . . . . . .

Dear Sir,

Town and Country Planning Act 1990

APPLICATION FOR APPROVAL OF CONDITIONS

*We write on behalf of . . . . (c)

We refer to planning permission reference number . . . . (d)

and dated . . . . (e)

for development consisting of . . . . (f)

at . . . . (g)

The planning permission was granted subject to conditions, in particular

. . . . (h)

This application seeks to comply with the above condition(s) by reference to the
following *drawings/sample materials.

. . . . (i)

(j) . . . . sets of drawings are attached.

We trust these meet with your approval and discharge the above condition(s).

Signed (c) . . . . Date . . . .

s.19 LBCA
s.74 LBCA

Steps for the Applicant:

Application for Varying or Discharging Conditions Attached to Listed Building Consent or Conservation Area Consent

Applications for varying or discharging conditions can only be made by a person having an interest in the building, i.e. an owner, a leaseholder or an occupier.

This procedure enables an application to be made which relates simply to the conditions without reopening the question of whether consent should have been granted.

1 Obtain the appropriate application form from the LPA, or if it does not have one, Form 5A is a suggested format for the application letter.

2 Complete and sign the application form and make the appropriate number of copies as the LPA requires.

3 If not the sole owner of the building, the applicant must notify all other owners. For the form of notice, see Form 2A (Procedure 2). 'Owner' in this context means a person having a freehold interest or a leasehold interest the unexpired term of which is not less than seven years.

4 If the applicant is unable to notify any or all owners, then an advertisement is required in a local newspaper circulating in the area. For the form of advertisement, see Form 2B.

5 Complete only one of either Certificate A, B, C or D:

Certificate A
a certificate stating that 21 days before the date of the application, no person other than the applicant was the owner of the building to which the application relates; see Form 2C

Certificate B
a certificate stating that the applicant has given the requisite notice of the application to all persons who, 21 days before the date of the application, were owners of the building to which the application relates; see Form 2D

Certificate C
a certificate stating that the applicant is unable to issue either Certificate A or B, that he has given the requisite notice of the application to one or more owners, that he has taken such steps as are reasonably open to him to ascertain the names and addresses of the remainder of the owners and that he has been unable to do so; see Form 2E

Certificate D

> a certificate stating that the applicant has taken such steps as are reasonably open to him to ascertain the names and addresses of the owners and that he has been unable to do so; see Form 2F.

If Certificate C or D is appropriate, then a copy of the actual newspaper advertisement must be attached.

6 Two sets of the original consent drawings should accompany the application (or number as requested).

Circ.31/92

7 No fee is payable.

Relevant LPA Action:

SI 1990 No. 1519

1 On receipt of the application, the applicant should be notified. The application should be registered and available for public inspection.

2 Notify the Secretary of State of the application and wait 28 days before determining application.

s.73 LBCA

3 The application must be advertised in the local paper and a notice posted on or near the site for a period of not less than seven days.

4 The decision should be made within eight weeks from the receipt of the application, or such extended periods as agreed with the applicant.

Results

The LPA may vary or discharge the conditions attached to the consent, and it may add new conditions as a consequence of the variation or discharge, as it thinks fit.

If the applicant is aggrieved by the decision of the LPA, he may appeal within six months of receipt of the decision notice. Appeals must be made on a form which is obtainable from the DoE/Welsh Office.

FORM 5A
Application letter
Source: RMJM

* Delete where inappropriate.

(a) address of LPA
(b) agent's name, address and telephone number or, if no agent, then applicant's name, address and telephone number
(c) applicant's name, address and telephone number
(d) reference number on the notification of consent
(e) date of notification
(f) description of development as it appeared in the original application
(g) full address or location of the land to which the application is related
(h) date the consent lapses
(i) list in full the conditions to be varied or discharged
(j) in the case of variations, list proposed conditions.

. . . . (a) . . . . (b) . . . .

Dear Sir,

**PLANNING (LISTED BUILDINGS AND
CONSERVATION AREAS) ACT 1990**

*We write on behalf of . . . . (c)

We refer to *listed building/conservation area consent reference number

. . . . (d) and dated . . . . (e)

The consent is for development consisting of . . . . (f)

at . . . . (g)

The consent remains valid until . . . . (h)

We hereby apply, under section 19 and section 74 (3) of the Act, to *vary/discharge the following condition(s) attached to the consent:

. . . . (i) to . . . . (j)

Please find attached a certificate of ownership.

Signed . . . . Date . . . .

Applications to Vary or Revoke Conditions Attached to a Planning Permission

Section 73 of the 1990 Act allows an application to be made to the LPA for planning permission for the development of land without complying with the conditions which were attached to a previously granted planning permission. This can occur, for instance, when external factors change, such as a proposed new highway being abandoned. A section 73 application can be used to apply for an extension of the time for starting a development or for making a reserved matters application, but only if the original time period has not yet expired.

Steps for the Applicant:

1 Obtain from the LPA its application form for varying or revoking conditions. If it does not have a specific application form, then the application should be made in writing with sufficient information to identify the undisposed permission, e.g. its reference number and date of approval. Form 6A is a suggested format for the application letter.

2 Article 6 Notices

Section 65 of the 1990 Act (as amended) and Articles 6 and 7 of the GDPO deal with issues related to ownership of the site. If the land is not in sole ownership, then notice must be served on all the owners using a form of notice prescribed in Art. 6 and Sch. 2 Part 1 of the GDPO. The description of the development in the form should make it clear that this is an application under section 73 to vary or revoke a condition. The form is set out in Form 1C (Procedure 1).

If the land is part of an agricultural holding, then a similar Notice must be served on any person who was a tenant on the day 21 days before the application is made.

If none or only some of the owners can be given notice, then an advertisement must be put in a local paper. The form of advertisement is again as in Form 1C.

3 Article 7 Certificates

Complete only one of either Certificate A, B, C or D:

Certificate A
a certificate stating that 21 days before the date of the application, no person other than the applicant was the owner of any of the land to which the application relates; see Form 1D (Procedure 1)

Certificate B

a certificate stating that the applicant has given the requisite notice of the application to all persons who, 21 days before the date of the application, were owners of any of the land to which the application relates; see Form 1E

Certificate C

a certificate stating that the applicant is unable to issue either Certificate A or B, that he has given the requisite notice of the application to one or more owners, that he has taken such steps as are reasonably open to him to ascertain the names and addresses of the remainder of the owners and that he has been unable to do so; see Form 1F

Certificate D

a certificate stating that the applicant has taken such steps as are reasonably open to him to ascertain the names and addresses of the owners and that he has been unable to do so; see Form 1G

If Certificate C or D is appropriate, then a copy of the actual newspaper advertisement must be attached.

4 None of the original drawings or application forms need be sent with the application.

5 Minimum fees are usually payable (see Appendix C for scales).

Relevant LPA Action:

s. 73

1 The LPA should only consider the question of the conditions without reopening the entire issue of whether permission should have been granted in the first place.

Results

The LPA may vary or revoke the conditions attached to the permission, and it may add new conditions as a consequence as it thinks fit.

If an application is refused, or granted subject to unacceptable conditions, an applicant may appeal to the Secretary of State.

FORM 6A
Application letter
Source: RMJM

* Delete where inappropriate.

(a) address of LPA
(b) agent's name, address and telephone number or, if no agent, then name, address and telephone number of applicant
(c) name, address and telephone number of applicant
(d) reference number on the notification of permission
(e) date of notification
(f) description of development as it appeared in the original application
(g) full address or location of the land to which the application is related
(h) date permission lapses
(i) list in full the conditions to be varied or revoked
(j) in the case of variations, list proposed conditions
(k) correct fee.

...... (a) .... (b) ......

Dear Sir,

TOWN AND COUNTRY PLANNING ACT 1990

*We write on behalf of .... (c)

We refer to planning permission reference number

.... (d) and dated .... (e)

The permission is for development consisting of

.... (f) at .... (g)

The permission remains valid until .... (h)

We hereby apply, under section 73 of the Act, to *vary/revoke the following condition(s) attached to the permission:

.... (i) to .... (j)

Please find attached an Article 7 Certificate and a cheque for

the sum of .... (k) being the fee due under section 303 of the Act.

Signed .... Date ....

7

Application for a Certificate of Lawful Existing Use or Development (CLEUD)

CLEUDs (sometimes referred to as Lawful Development Certificates or LDCs) were introduced into the 1990 Act by the PCA and replace Established Use Certificates. They can be sought for existing buildings, engineering or mining operations, or the failure to comply with conditions on a planning permission. The application must be formulated in relation to a particular use: you must ask 'is this use lawful'? rather than 'what use is lawful on this land'? A CLEUD is the equivalent of a planning permission.

Steps for the Applicant:

GDPO Art. 24(1)

1 Obtain the appropriate application form from the LPA. There is no prescribed form, but Form 7A is based on a model set out in Appendix 1 of Annex 1 to Circ. 17/92.

Note, most LPA's will only accept as evidence sworn affidavits or statutory declarations together with copies of supporting material.

2 Enclose with the application form a site plan (at 1:1250 scale) to identify the site to which the application relates. The site should be edged in red.

3 The fee is the same as for an equivalent planning application.

Relevant LPA Action:

1 The LPA must acknowledge receipt and register the application and make it available for public inspection.

2 The LPA can ask the applicant in writing for specific further information.

3 The decision should be made within eight weeks from the receipt of the application, or such extended periods as agreed with the applicant.

Results

There are four possible outcomes to the application:

- non-determination, i.e., deemed refusal
- refusal (reasons to be given)
- part refusal (reasons to be given)
- CLEUD granted.

The applicant may appeal to the Secretary of State within six months of the decision notice (or as directed) on non-determination, refusal or part refusal.

FORM 7A
Application form
Source: Circ. 17/92

Town and Country Planning Act 1990: section 191
as amended by section 10 of the Planning and Compensation Act 1991
Town and Country Planning General Development (Amendment) Order 1992

APPLICATION FOR A CERTIFICATE OF LAWFULNESS FOR AN EXISTING USE OR OPERATION OR ACTIVITY IN BREACH OF A PLANNING CONDITION

Applicant

Name ....

Address .... Postcode ....

Telephone number ....

Agent (if any)

Name ....

Address .... Postcode ....

Telephone number ....

Specify the nature of the applicant's interest in the land, e.g. owner, lessee, occupier.

If you do not have an interest:

(a)   give the names and addresses of anyone you know who has an interest in the land:

Name ....

Address .... Postcode ....

Telephone number ....

(b)   state the nature of their interest, if known:

(c)   state whether they have been informed about this application: **YES/NO**

Address and exact location of the land to which this application relates.

(a)   Describe the land and enclose three copies of an OS-based plan showing the boundary of the land edged red.

(b)   Describe the use, operation or activity you are applying for.

This application is for:

an existing use
an existing operation
an existing use, operation or activity in breach of a condition, being a use, operation or activity subsisting on the date of this application
site area (ha) ...

If there is more than one subsisting use of, or operation or activity, on the land at the date of this application, describe fully each one of them and, where appropriate, show to which part of the land each use, operation or activity relates.

FORM 7A continued

When was the use or activity begun, or the operation substantially completed?

_____

Under what grounds is the certificate being sought?

(1)   The use began more than ten years before the date of the application.

(2)   The use, operation or activity in breach of a condition began more than ten years before the date of this application.

(3)   The use began within the last ten years, as a result of a change of use not requiring planning permission, and there has not been a change of use requiring planning permission in the last ten years.

(4)   The operations were substantially completed more than four years before the date of this application.

(5)   The use of a single dwellinghouse begun more than four years before the date of this application.

(6)   Other (_specify – this might include claims that the change of use or operation was not development, or that it benefited from planning permission granted under the Act or by the General Development Order_).

_____

If the certificate is sought for a use, operation or activity in breach of a condition or limitation, specify the condition or limitation which has not been complied with, and attach a copy of the relevant planning permission.

_____

Give any additional information you consider necessary to substantiate your claim.

_____

List here all the documents, drawings or plans which accompany this application.

_____

I/We hereby apply for a certificate of lawful use or development under section 191 of the 1990 Act in respect of the existing use, operations or activity described in this application and the documents, drawings and plans which accompany it. I/ We enclose the appropriate fee of £. . . . .

Signed: . . . .   Date: . . . .

On behalf of: . . . .
(_insert name of applicant if signed by agent_)

_____

Warning: The amended section 194 of the 1990 Act provides that it is an offence to furnish false or misleading information, or to withhold material information, with intent to deceive. Section 193(7) enables the Council to revoke, at any time, a certificate that may have been issued as a result of such false misleading information.

Application for Approval of Reserved Matters, Following an Outline Planning Permission

The reserved matters of an outline planning permission refer to one or more aspects relating to buildings: siting, design, landscaping, external appearance, means of access.

In principle, approval of all the reserved matters must be gained before development can commence. In practice, however, detailed matters of design and landscaping are often approved after site development has started. The LPA can grant approval of a reserved matters application with conditions that require subsequent approval of details, just as in the grant of a full planning permission. Applications for approval can be made for all reserved matters at once or as a series of applications but multiple applications can cost more than a single application (Circ. 31/92, sections 35–8).

Landscaping in this context means the treatment of land (other than buildings) in order to enhance or protect the amenities of the site and the area in which it is situated. It includes screening by fences, walls or other means, the planting of trees, hedges, shrubs or grass, formation of banks, terraces or other earthworks, laying out of gardens or courts, and other amenity features.

Application for approval of all reserved matters must be made within three years of the grant of outline permission and development must start either within five years of the outline permission or two years after the final approval of the last reserved matter (section 92 of the 1990 Act) unless otherwise specifically stated in the original permission.

Steps for the Applicant:

GPDO Art.4

1 Some LPAs have their own application forms and these should be obtained and completed. Where no such forms exist, a written application should be made. Form 8A is a suggested format.

2 Submit with the appropriate copies of forms whatever drawings and plans are necessary to illustrate fully the matters reserved in the outline planning permission.

3 The same number of copies of the drawings should be enclosed as were originally submitted with the outline application or as indicated in the application form.

4 Fees are payable at the same rate as for a full application, but with certain exceptions for phased developments and multiple applications (see Appendix C).

Circ.31/92

Relevant LPA Action:

1 Acknowledge receipt of the application using the prescribed form.

Art.12

2 The applicant should be informed if the application is to be determined by the county planning authority.

Art.20

3 The decision should be made within eight weeks from receipt of the application, or such extended periods as agreed with the applicant.

4 The applicant should be notified of the decision in writing using the prescribed form (if a refusal, then reasons must be given and appeal conditions etc. should be given).

Art.22

FORM 8A
Application letter
Source: RMJM

* Delete where inappropriate.

(a) address of LPA
(b) agent's name, address and telephone number or, if no agent, then the applicant's name, address and telephone number
(c) applicant's name, address and telephone number
(d) reference number on the notification of permission
(e) date of notification
(f) description of development as it appeared in the original application
(g) full address or location of the land to which the application is related
(h) quote matter(s) determined by the outline permission (i.e. siting, access, etc.)
(i) quote matter(s) for which approval is sought
(j) number of copies as for the original application
(k) list of drawings
(l) number as agreed with the LPA
(m) correct fee.

. . . . (a) . . . . (b) . . . .

Dear Sir,

TOWN AND COUNTRY PLANNING ACT 1990

*We write on behalf of . . . . (c)

We refer to outline planning permission reference number

. . . . (d) and dated . . . . (e)

for development consisting of . . . . (f) at . . . . (g)

The planning permission determined . . . . (h)

and was granted subject to approval of reserved matters, including

. . . . (i)

This application seeks approval of the above matter(s) by reference to the

following drawings, ... (j) sets of which are attached:

(k) . . . . *We also enclose (l) . . . .

copies of an Explanatory Statement.

We trust these meet with your approval and discharge the above reserved matters.

Please find attached a *cheque/money order in the sum of . . . . (m) being the fee due under section 303 of the T&CPA 1990.

Signed . . . . Date . . . .

Application for Winning or Working of Minerals and Determination of Conditions

The winning or working of minerals is classified as development and requires planning permission in the normal manner but with the following further requirements and modifications (see MPG2 for general guidance):

- Applications for outline permission cannot be made for the working or winning of minerals (MPG2, para 11). An applicant therefore needs to make a full application – see Procedure 1.
- The Environment Act 1995 introduced a new requirement for the periodic review of all mineral permissions every 15 years following an initial review and updating of old permissions. Following the review an owner of land with mineral interest must apply to the mineral planning authority (MPA) for the determination of conditions. In doing so the applicant proposes a set of conditions which the MPA then approves, adds to or modifies. If the MPA fails to determine the application within three months, the conditions are deemed to be approved. Where no application for determination is made to the MPA, the mineral permission ceases to have effect except insofar as restoration is concerned. The procedures are described in MPG14 which includes a standard application form at annex F (Form 9I).
- In 1995 the DETR issued a new set of minerals planning forms designed to speed up the application process. The forms are included here as an indication of the type of information required but, for the sake of space, we have excluded the extensive notes that accompany the forms. They consist of one application form (Form 9A) and five annexes dealing with mineral extraction and processing, mineral exploration, underground mining, surface disposal of mine or quarry waste, and oil and gas operations (Forms 9B–9F).
- Notices as specified in the GDPO Art. 6 and Sch. 2 Part 1 must be served on any person entitled to an interest in the minerals as well as owners and tenants (1990 Act).
- The prescribed Art. 7 certificate should be obtained.
- Special notices under Art. 6 should be posted on the site. The notices must be posted in at least one place in every parish or community directly affected by the application.
- In the case of land containing coal, gas, oil, silver or gold, the mineral planning authority must inform the Coal Authority (for coal), the Secretary of State for Trade and Industry (for gas or oil), or the Crown Estate Commissioners (for gold or silver) of all applications for extracting any mineral. For example, an application to extract gravel in an area with underlying coal deposits must be notified to the Coal Authority.

**Steps for the
Applicant:**

1 Application is made on the appropriate forms to the district or London borough who will then pass the application on to the appropriate mineral planning authority. Forms 9A–F act as a good checklist of topics to be covered.

2 Steps as for Procedure 1, including Special Art. 6 notices and Art. 7 certificates.

3 Post notices on the site, in every parish (Form 9G).

4 An advertisement is required in a local paper circulating in the area. The form of the advertisement is the same as Form 9H.

5 Submit a Certificate under Art. 7 of the GDPO (Forms 1D, 1E or 1F, Procedure 1).

6 In all probability an Environmental Assessment will be required see procedure 20.

7 Fees are payable. See Appendix C.

**Relevant LPA
Action:**

1 Acknowledge receipt of the application using the prescribed form.

2 The applicant should be informed that the application is to be determined by the mineral planning authority (usually the county).

3 The decision should be made within eight weeks from receipt of the application (16 weeks if an EA is involved), or such extended periods as agreed with the applicant.

4 The applicant should be notified of the decision in writing using the prescribed form (if a refusal, then reasons must be given and appeal conditions etc. should be given).

FORM 9A
Standard minerals application form

Applicants should read accompanying guidance notes before completing the minerals application form and annexes.

All applicants must complete questions 1–9 on this form as fully as possible.

Town and Country Planning Act 1990

APPLICATION TO CARRY OUT MINERAL WORKING AND ASSOCIATED DEVELOPMENT

1   Applicant   **Agent**

Name   Name

Address   Address

Tel no.   Tel no.

Fax no.   Fax no.

Name of Contact   Name of Contact

2   The Application Site

(i)   Location and address of the site   Grid Ref at site access
                                                  and/or centre of site:
                                                  (delete as appropriate)

(ii)   Present use(s) of the site

(iii) Last previous use of the site as far as known (if different from (ii) above)

(iv)   Total application area (as outlined in red on your site plans) . . . . ha

(v)   What is the applicant's interest in the site?

(vi)   What is the applicant's interest in the adjoining land (as outlined in blue on your site plans)?

3   Nature of Minerals Application

(i)   Is the application for: (Answer as many
                                                       as necessary)

       (a) New mineral extraction?   YES/NO
       (b) Extension to an existing site?   YES/NO
           If yes, give date and reference
           number of existing permission . . . .
       (c) Associated operations?   YES/NO
       (d) Other (please give details)? . . . .   YES/NO

           . . . .

(ii)   Previous permissions for mineral operations on the site (if known).

       MPAs Ref No(s) . . . .   Date(s) of Decision(s) . . . .

FORM 9A continued

See guidance note for
supplementary information
required.

4   Type of Development

(i)   Does this application include:

Surface mineral extraction?	YES/NO
Mineral processing?	YES/NO
Mineral exploration?	YES/NO
Underground mining?	YES/NO
Other buildings, plant or structures associated with minerals development?	YES/NO
Proposals involving major surface disposal of mine or quarry wastes?	YES/NO
Oil or gas operations?	YES/NO

(ii)   Please give a brief description of development

5   Plans and Drawings

List here the plans and drawings submitted with the application. Please refer to guidance notes for drawings which are required or would be advisable to accompany your application.

Reference Number	Title
. . . .	. . . .
. . . .	. . . .
. . . .	. . . .
. . . .	. . . .
. . . .	. . . .
. . . .	. . . .
. . . .	. . . .
. . . .	. . . .
. . . .	. . . .
. . . .	. . . .

6   Supporting Material

(i)   Is an Environmental Statement submitted with this application?   YES/NO

(ii)   Is the applicant willing to make additional copies of the application documents, including the Environmental Statement available for public inspection at locations other than the offices of the MPA?   YES/NO
If yes, please provide the address where information can be inspected.

Address

Please specify the price of the Environmental Statement and address where this can be obtained for purchase.

Address	Document Title	£

(iii)   Is a Supporting Statement submitted with this application?   YES/NO

FORM 9A continued

7 Certification

Town and Country Planning General Development Procedures Order 1995. Certificates under Article 7.

(i) Surface landowner(s)

Name

Address

(ii) Mineral owner(s) if different from (i)

Name

Address

(iii) Certification under Article 7 of the General Development Procedures Order 1995. Please specify certificates completed.

	Please tick
Certificate A	
Certificate B	
Certificate C	
Certificate D	
Agricultural Holdings Certificate	

Applicants should note that the Mineral Planning Authority cannot entertain an application unless it is accompanied by the appropriate certificates.

8 Fees

(i) What fee accompanies this application?   £

Applicants should note that the Mineral Planning Authority cannot entertain an application unless it is accompanied by the appropriate fee.

9 Declaration

(Delete as appropriate)

I/We hereby apply for permission to carry out the development described in this application and declare that, to the best of my/our knowledge, the information is correct; or

In the case of agents, that I am/we are fully authorised to submit this application on behalf of the applicant(s).

Signed

Dated

On behalf of (insert applicant's name if signed by an agent)

4

FORM 9B
Annex 1:
Mineral extraction and processing

Note: Applicants should complete all relevant questions concerning mineral extraction and processing.

Town and Country Planning Act 1990

APPLICATION TO CARRY OUT MINERAL WORKING AND ASSOCIATED DEVELOPMENT

Mineral Extraction

A1.1 Please state:

(i) Mineral(s) to be extracted

(ii) Total quantity of saleable minerals to be extracted . . . . tonnes

(iii) Area of excavation . . . . ha

(iv) Maximum depth of surface working . . . . m

(v) Proposed duration of mineral extraction

Duration of operations . . . . years

Start date . . . .   End date . . . .

(vi) End use (e.g. construction, industrial processes etc) and immediate proposed destination of mineral(s) products

(vii) The location of any off-site processing plant

A1.2 For surface mineral workings or deposit on land of mineral wastes, please provide the following information in connection with soils and overburden; and the grade of any agricultural land:

(i)

	Depth (mm)		Volume (m^3)
	(Average)	(Ranges)	
Topsoil existing on site			
Subsoil existing on site			
Overburden to be removed			

(ii) Please specify the area of agricultural land (ha) and grades affected under the Agricultural Land Classification by extraction

(iii) Summarise the provision to be made for the temporary or permanent storage of soils or overburden

A1.3 Summarise wastes which will result from extraction operations (types and quantities).

FORM 9B continued

A1.4 Summarise the evaluation procedures undertaken to assess the quantity and quality of the minerals and the results of these

A1.5 Summarise the proposed method of extraction and scheme of working including phasing

Mineral Processing

A1.6 Type and quantity of material to be processed on site

Type	Maximum tonnes per annum
. . . .	. . . .
. . . .	. . . .
. . . .	. . . .

A1.7 Mineral products from processing:

type (a) . . . .   Estimated annual production . . . . tonnes

type (b) . . . .   Estimated annual production . . . . tonnes

type (c) . . . .   Estimated annual production . . . . tonnes

A1.8 Summarise plant and machinery to be used in processing of minerals

A1.9

(i)   Maximum height of plant as measured from existing ground level . . . . . . m

(ii)   Maximum height of stockpiles or storage facilities for processed material as measured from existing ground level . . . . . m

A1.10 Plant capacity

	Tonnes per Hour	Tonnes per Year
Estimated normal capacity of processing plant		
Estimated maximum capacity of processing plant		

A1.11 Source of water (if any) to be used in processing:

4

FORM 9B continued

A1.12 Details of waste arising from processing:

    (i)   Nature of waste

    (ii)   Estimated annual quantity produced ...... m^3

    (iii) Please specify maximum height(s) of any
          waste/tip(s) as measured from existing ground level .... m

    (iv) Is it proposed for waste tips to be located within
          excavations?   YES/NO

    (v)   Is it proposed to dispose of any wastes at a separate site?   YES/NO

          If yes, please state the location ....

    (vi) Specify methods to be used to transport waste
          (e.g. pipeline, conveyor belt)

    (vii) Will the mineral processing involve tailing lagoons?   YES/NO

Other Buildings, Plant or Structures

A1.13 Describe briefly:

    (i)   Purpose of buildings

    (ii)   Size and appearance of buildings etc.

A1.14 Would any ancillary operations last beyond the period of
mineral extraction?   YES/NO

If yes, describe these operations

Traffic and Transport

A1.15 Summarise method(s) of transportation of processed materials

A1.16 Is it proposed to use an existing means of access to the
application site?   YES/NO

A1.17 Are new access arrangements to be constructed or alterations
to existing access proposed?   YES/NO

If yes, please summarise the proposals

FORM 9B continued

A1.18

	Average	Maximum
Estimated number of loaded vehicles likely to enter or leave the site daily		
Estimated capacity of loaded vehicles		

    (ii) Summarise routes to be used to the primary road network on leaving the application site

    (iv) Proposed methods to be used to control transport impacts

Environmental Effects of Development

A1.19 To the best of your knowledge is any part of the application site covered by statutory designations including habitats of protected species?   YES/NO

    If yes, specify these

A1.20 Proposed hours of operation of the site

	Time Periods (hours)	Days of Week
(i) Soil stripping and overburden removal		
(ii) Mineral working		
(iii) Mineral processing		
(iv) Vehicular movements		
(v) Other (specify)		

A1.21 Noise levels and proposed controls

    (i)   State existing background noise levels at site boundaries and/or nearest properties, where measured (delete as appropriate)

    (ii)   State predicted noise levels at site boundaries and/or nearest properties where assessed (delete as appropriate)

    (iii) Describe measures for controlling noise and methods for noise monitoring (as relevant)

FORM 9B continued

A1.22 Describe proposed measures for controlling and suppressing dust (including treatment of storage heaps) and minimising the spread of any minerals and waste onto the public highway

A1.23 Blasting (where relevant)

(i) Will mineral extraction require blasting? YES/NO

If yes, state predicted maximum blasting vibration levels at nearby properties.

(ii) State anticipated frequency and hours of blasting (weekdays; other)

(iii) Indicate proposed public warnings for blasting

(iv) Specify proposed methods for monitoring vibration from blasting

A1.24 Will any hazardous materials be used or stored on site? YES/NO

If yes, specify type and storage method

A1.25 Water

(i) Outline any proposed measures to control water pollution and drainage/flood control measures

(ii) If working is to take place below the natural water table, is the working to be (delete as appropriate) WET or DRY?

If dry, describe proposed methods of dewatering, proposed method of water disposal and any proposed mitigation measures.

(iii) State the measures to be taken to prevent the spillage or seepage of fuel oils during delivery, storage and handling on site.

A1.26 State whether any processes are to be registered under Part A and B of the Environmental Protection Act 1990 and describe the nature of these operations

A1.27 Does your proposal affect a public right of way? YES/NO

If yes, ensure proposed diversions and/or closures are indicated on a plan.

FORM 9B continued

A1.28 Outline any visual impact and landscaping proposals during working

A1.29 Outline any measures to ensure stability of working faces, tips and associated structures

Landfilling of Mineral Extraction Sites (to be completed where relevant)

A1.30 Does your proposal include landfilling with any imported wastes?   YES/NO

If yes, please specify:

(i)   Estimated maximum void space for filling . . . . m^3

(ii)   Proposed total area to be filled . . . . ha

A1.31 Nature of materials to be deposited and the estimated annual rate of disposal (excluding material for soil formation, cover and restoration), if known

	Quantity (m^3) per Annum	Nature	Proportion Inert	Source(s)
Household				
Industrial				
Commercial				
Other wastes (please specify)				

A1.32 State the nature of any built development within 250 metres of areas proposed to be landfilled with household, industrial or commercial wastes.

A1.33 Summarise proposed measures for monitoring and controlling:

(i)   landfill gas;

(ii)   leachates

Restoration, Aftercare and Afteruse

A1.34 (i)   Summarise the intended afteruse or uses:

Agricultural	YES/NO	Total area . . . . ha
Forestry	YES/NO	Total area . . . . ha
Amenity (specify)	YES/NO	Total area . . . . ha
Other (specify)	YES/NO	Total area . . . . ha

FORM 9B continued

(ii) Is restoration and aftercare to be phased?   YES/NO

If yes, please summarise number and duration of phases

A1.35 Give details of the proposed use of soil materials in restoration

	Total Amounts (m³)	Average Thickness to be Spread (mm)
Topsoil from site		
Subsoil from site		
Overburden/other soil making material		
Other soil sources (please state)		

A1.36 Summarise the methods and machinery to be used in stripping, restoring soils and formation of storage mounds.

A1.37 (i) Is any restoration work likely to take place within 12 months of the commencement of working?   YES/NO

If yes, describe the proposed aftercare.

(ii) If no, summarise the items proposed for inclusion in an aftercare scheme, to be agreed at a later date, including land management during the aftercare period and intended arrangements in the longer term.

(iii) Who would carry out the aftercare operations?

(iv) Are there any specific proposals or agreements for the management of the land following completion of 'aftercare'?   YES/NO

If yes, please summarise

Benefits of the Development

A1.38 Indicate the benefits of the proposals

FORM 9C
Annex 2:
Mineral exploration

This annex should be completed (in addition to the main minerals application form and any other relevant annexes) for proposals involving mineral exploration (excluding oil or gas) and requiring planning permission. **Please read the accompanying guidance notes before completing these questions.**

Town and Country Planning Act 1990

APPLICATION TO CARRY OUT MINERAL WORKING AND ASSOCIATED DEVELOPMENT

A2.1 Mineral(s) sought

A2.2 Exploration site area . . . . . . ha

A2.3 (i) Duration of operations . . . . Months . . . . Days

(ii) Hours of working

	Time of Day	Days of Week
Operational Periods		

A2.4 (i) Do the methods of exploration involve:

(a) boreholes or other
excavations? YES/NO If yes, complete (ii) below
(b) seismic methods? YES/NO If yes, complete (iii) and (iv) below

(ii) If exploration involves boreholes or other excavations, please state:

number . . . . depth . . . .

(iii) If the exploration involves seismic methods, state the route of the survey

(iv) If explosive charge will be used, state:

depth maximum
of charge . . . . instantaneous charge . . . .

ground vibrations expected proposed maximum and
at the nearest average number
affected properties . . . . of blasts per day . . . .

(v) Summarise measures to make the site safe after cessation of operations

A2.5 State restoration proposals

LLYFRGELL COLEG MENAI LIBRARY

FORM 9D
Annex 3:
Underground mining

This annex should be completed (in addition to the main minerals application form and any other relevant annexes) for proposals involving underground mining (excluding oil or gas) and requiring planning permission. **Please read the accompanying guidance notes before completing these questions.**

Town and Country Planning Act 1990

APPLICATION TO CARRY OUT MINERAL WORKING AND ASSOCIATED DEVELOPMENT

A3.1 Depth(s) of extraction

Minimum . . . .   Maximum . . . .

A3.2 Number(s) and/or names of seams or veins to be extracted

A3.3 (i) Method of mining to be used (e.g. longwall, shortwall, pillar and stall, solution or stope)

(ii) Summarise investigations on anticipated subsidence and likely areas to be affected by this application

(iii) Summarise any measures to prevent or reduce the occurrence of subsidence

A3.4 (i) Type of waste to be brought to the surface

. . . .

. . . .

(ii) Total volume of waste to be brought to the surface and the proportion of which is inert

Total volume of waste . . . . m^3 Proportion inert . . . . %

(iii) Summarise proposed methods to bring waste to the surface

(iv) Summarise proposed method and location for disposal of wastes

A3.5 Summarise proposed treatment of mine openings on the cessation of operations

FORM 9E
Annex 4:
Major surface disposal of mine or quarry wastes

This annex should be completed (in addition to the main minerals application form and any other relevant annexes) for proposals involving major surface disposal of mine and quarry wastes (excluding oil or gas) and requiring planning permission. **Please read the accompanying guidance notes before completing these questions.**

Please note: The restoration, aftercare and afteruse of waste tips should be included in your answers to A1.34–A1.37

Town and Country Planning Act 1990

APPLICATION TO CARRY OUT MINERAL WORKING AND ASSOCIATED DEVELOPMENT

A4.1 (i) Please state the total site area for proposed deposit of mine and quarry wastes ...... ha

A4.2 (i) What is/are the proposed construction method(s) of tips of solid wastes?

(ii) What are the total number of proposed tip(s) and estimated total amounts of materials for disposal?

No. of Tips .... Material for Disposal (m³) ....

(iii) Does the proposal involve tailing lagoons? YES/NO

If yes, how many?

A4.3 (i) Summarise the physical properties and characteristics of wastes from extraction

(ii) Summarise the chemical properties of wastes from extraction (if relevant)

A4.4 For temporary tip(s), specify date(s) of removal, by individual tip

FORM 9F
Annex 5:
Oil and gas operations

This annex should be completed for proposals involving oil or gas operations and requiring planning permission. **Please read the accompanying guidance notes before completing these questions.**

For **Exploration**, complete Questions A5.1, A5.4 and A5.5
For **Appraisal**, complete Questions A5.2, A5.4 and A5.5
For **Production**, complete Questions A5.3, A5.4 and A5.5

Town and Country Planning Act 1990

APPLICATION TO CARRY OUT MINERAL WORKING AND ASSOCIATED DEVELOPMENT

Exploration

A5.1 (i) Please state

(a) total area of exploration . . . . ha

(b) route(s) of any seismic survey(s) to be carried out during exploration

(ii) Does the seismic method to be employed use vibrosis methods? YES/NO

(iii) Does the seismic method to be employed use any explosive charge? YES/NO

If yes:

(a) what is the depth of charge and maximum instantaneous charge?

Depth . . . . Maximum Instantaneous Charge . . . .

(b) what is the average and maximum number of explosive charges to be used per day?

Average per day . . . . Maximum per day . . . .

(c) what will be the estimated level of ground vibration at the nearest affected properties?

(iv) Will the exploration method involve the drilling of wells? YES/NO

If yes:

(a) what criteria is being used for selecting the well site(s)?

(b) what is the expected number of wells to be drilled? . . . . . .

(c) what is the average depth of wells? . . . . . m

(d) what is the proposed method of disposal of drilling wastes?

(v) What equipment will be used for exploration?

(vi) What is the anticipated duration of operations?

Start Date . . . . Completion Date . . . .

FORM 9F continued

Appraisal

A5.2 (i) State:

    (a) appraisal site area . . . . ha

    (b) criteria to be used for the selection of well sites

    (c) equipment to be used to undertake the appraisal

    (d) methods to be used to undertake the appraisal

  (ii) If exploration well(s) site is to be used

    (a) what is the number of wells to be drilled? . . . .

    (b) what will the average depth of wells be? . . . . m

Production

A5.3 (i) Please state

    (a) anticipated maximum volume of oil/gas (delete as appropriate) to be extracted

       barrels/standard cubic feet (delete as appropriate) per day . . . .

       total per annum . . . .

    (b) total reserves anticipated from the field . . . . . . total

    (c) life of the field . . . . . . years

    (d) equipment and plant to be used

    (e) anticipated capacity for the plant

    (f) location of any off-site processing plant

  (ii) Please state the proposed method(s) of transport of oil and/or gas from well(s) to gathering, processing and storage facilities (e.g. pipelines, rail, road or shipping)

FORM 9F continued

Specific Environmental Effects of the Proposals

A5.4 (i) Please state oil spill contingency plans and measures for the protection of surface and groundwater

(ii) Please state measures taken to minimise atmospheric and noise emissions

(iii) Please state proposed methods to be used to dispose of drilling wastes and other operational waste arisings

A5.5 Summarise specific restoration proposals

FORM 9G
Site notice and newspaper advertisement

Source:
GDPO
Sch.2 Part 1

* Delete if inappropriate.

(a) address or location of the proposed development
(b) applicant's name
(c) name of LPA
(d) description of the proposed development
(e) address at which the application may be inspected (the applicant is responsible for making the application available for inspection within the area of the LPA)
(f) date giving a period of not less than 21 days, beginning with the date when the notice is posted
(g) address of LPA.

Town and Country Planning (General Development Procedure) Order 1995

NOTICE UNDER ARTICLE 6

Proposed development at . . . . (a)

I give notice that . . . . (b) is applying to

the . . . . (c) Council for permission to . . . . (d)

Members of the public may inspect copies of:

• the application
• the plans
• and other documents submitted with it

at . . . . (e)

during all reasonable hours until . . . . (f)

Anyone who wishes to make representations about this application should write to

the Council at . . . . (g) by . . . . (f)

Signed . . . . *On behalf of . . . . (b)

Date . . . .

Form 9H
Certificate
Source:
GDPO
Sch.2 Part 2

Town and Country Planning (General Development Procedure) Order 1995

CERTIFICATE UNDER ARTICLE 7

I certify that:

*   I have/The applicant has* given the required notice to the persons specified below being persons who, at the beginning of the period of 21 days ending with the date of the accompanying application, were owners of any part of the land to which the application relates.

Owner's name	Address at which notice was served	Date on which notice was served
....	....	....

*   There is no person (other than me/the applicant*) who at the beginning of the period of 21 days ending with the date of the accompanying application was the owner of any part of the land to which this application relates, whom I/the applicant* know/s* to be such a person and whose name and address is known to me/the applicant* but to whom I have/the applicant has* not given the required notice.

*   I have/The applicant has* posted the required notice, sited and displayed in such a way as to be easily visible and legible by members of the public, in at least one place in every parish or community within which there is situated any part of the land to which the accompanying application relates, as listed below.

Parish/community	Address at which notice was served	Date on which notice was served
....	....	....

*   Save as specified below, this/these* notice/s* was/were* left in position for not less than seven days in the period of 21 days immediately preceding the making of the application.

*   The following notice(s)* was/were*, however, left in position for less than seven days in the period of not more than 21 days immediately preceding the making of the application.

Parish/community	Address at which notice was served	Date on which notice was served
....	....	....

This happened because it/they* was/were* removed/obscured/defaced* before seven days had passed during the period of 21 days mentioned above. This was not my/the applicant's fault or intent.

I/The applicant* took the following steps to protect and replace the notice:

.... (a)

Notice of the application, as attached to this certificate, has been published in the

.... (b) on .... (c)

continues

FORM 9H continued

*Delete as inappropriate.

(a) description of steps taken
(b) name of local newspaper circulating in the area where the land is situated
(c) date of publication (which must be not earlier than the beginning of the period of 21 days ending with the date of the application)
(d) applicant's name.

---

* None of the land to which the application relates is, or is part of, an agricultural holding, or

* I have/The applicant has* given the required notice to every person other than my/him/her* self who, at the beginning of the period of 21 days ending with the date of the application, was a tenant of an agricultural holding on all or part of the land to which the application relates, as follows:

Tenant's name	Address at which notice was serviced	Date on which notice was served
. . . .	. . . .	. . . .

Signed . . . .   *On behalf of . . . . (d)

Date . . . .

FORM 9I
Official form for application for determination of conditions to which a mineral site/mining site is to be subject
Source:
MPG14
Annex F

Environment Act 1995
(Section 96 and paragraph 9 of Schedule 13/paragraph 6 of Schedule 14)

**APPLICATION FOR DETERMINATION OF CONDITIONS FOR
MINERAL SITE/MINING SITE**

Name of mineral planning authority . . . .

Three copies of the completed form and accompanying plans, documents and

certificates should be returned to . . . .

. . . . *(address of mineral planning authority)*

Section 1.   The Applicant and the Owners

1.1   Applicant

Name . . . .

Address . . . .

Tel. no. . . . .

1.2   Agent (if any) to whom all letters are sent

Name . . . .

Address . . . .

Tel. no. . . . .

1.3   Please specify the land or minerals comprised in the site of which the applicant is the owner or in which the applicant is entitled to an interest.

1.4   Please identify, and give the address for, each person that the applicant knows or, after reasonable inquiry, has cause to believe to be an owner of the land, or entitled to an interest in any mineral, comprised in the site.

1.4.1   The surface land owners

Name . . . .

Address . . . .

Tel. no. . . . .

FORM 9I continued

1.4.2   The mineral owners

Name ....

Address ....

Tel. no. ....

1.5   Address/location of site to which the application relates
(ATTACH: OS base plans showing location of the site and distinguishing the area(s) to which each permission relates)

1.6   Type of application
Please state whether this application is made in connection with an initial review or a periodic review. If made in connection with a periodic review, please state which review – i.e. first, second, third, etc.

1.7   Planning permission relating to the site
Please list all planning permissions for development consisting of the winning and working of minerals or involving the depositing of mineral waste.

Section 2.   Current use of the land covered by the permission(s)

2.1   Please give a general description of the land covered by the permissions:

2.2.1   Total area of the land covered by the permission(s) (in ha): ....

2.2.2   Total area to be excavated (in ha): ....

2.2.3   Total area to be used for the depositing of mineral waste (in ha): ....

2.3   Please describe the present uses of the land: ....

Section 3.   Details of any land adjoining the permission area owned or controlled by the applicant.

3.1   Give the particulars of the applicant's interest in adjoining land (outline in blue on OS base plan)

3.2   Give details of any other planning permission relating to the land covered by the permission or to any land specified in 3.1 above:

Please give planning permission reference number(s):

FORM 9I continued

Section 4.   Nature of intended future development at site

Give details of any intended:

4.1   Lateral extension of existing working:

4.2   Deepening of existing working:

4.3   Extensions of existing operations for depositing mineral waste:

4.4   Re-opening of disused working:

4.5   Re-activation of operations for the depositing of mineral waste:

Section 5.   Proposed conditions

5.1   Please set out in an attached schedule, the conditions to which you propose the permission(s) should be subject. The conditions should cover:

- duration of the permission(s);
- access, traffic and protection of then public highway;
- working programme;
- environmental protection;
- landscaping;
- restoration;
- after-use;
- aftercare (where appropriate).

Section 6.   Plans and drawings

In addition to the location plan, plan showing the area of the permission(s) (and adjoining areas in the applicant's ownership or control, where appropriate), attach plans showing the following:

6.1   The existing surface levels over the area of extraction and/or depositing and land in the immediate vicinity.

6.2   The general method of working, including details of direction and phasing.

6.3   The proposed final levels of the worked out areas prior to restoration.

6.4   The proposed surface area, height and location of mineral stockpiles; topsoil; subsoil; overburden mounds; and, mineral waste deposits.

6.5   Details of the access to the site, parking, loading, unloading areas etc.

6.6   Details of landscape and restoration including the final levels of the restored site.

6.7   Details of services crossing or adjacent to the site – e.g. drainage, gas or electricity supplies.

6.8   Details of land to remain unworked within the area of the application.

FORM 9I continued

Section 7. Voluntary agreements

7.1   Please indicate the need for any agreements to achieve environmental acceptability and after-use identified in pre-application discussions.

(ATTACH outline or draft agreements)

Section 8. Notification and certification of application

The application must be accompanied by the appropriate certificates and notices required by the Town and Country Planning Act 1990, as if it were an application for planning permission.

(ATTACH appropriate certificates and notices)

I/We hereby apply for approval of the conditions as described in the application and accompanying schedule and plans.

Signed . . . .   Date . . . .

On behalf of . . . .   (insert applicant's name if signed by agent)

NOW CHECK that you have enclosed:

(i)   Three copies of the location plan with the permission area(s) accurately marked (and, where relevant, showing any areas of adjoining land owned or under the control of the applicant accurately marked in blue);
(ii)   Three copies of the plans specified in section 7 of the application form;
(iii) Three copies of the schedule of proposed operating and restoration conditions;
(iv) Three copies of the appropriate certifictes and notices required

and that all forms and certificates are signed and dated.

Application for Express Consent to Display an Advertisement

Under section 220 and 221 of the 1990 Act all outdoor advertisements, with certain exceptions, require consent. Precisely what type of advertisement needs consent, and the procedure for obtaining consent, is contained in the Town and Country Planning (Control of Advertisements) Regulations 1992 (SI 1992 No. 666) and Amendment SI 1994 No. 2351. Circs. 5/92 and 15/94 give additional guidance. The criteria as to whether a particular advertisement needs consent to be displayed, or whether it has deemed consent, are very complex and detailed. Appendix F summarises the situation, but if in doubt, refer to the SIs or consult with the LPA.

Special provisions apply to advertisements in conservation areas, National Parks, AONBs, areas of special advertisement control and experimental areas. All these areas are considered to merit protection on amenity grounds and applications will be treated more strictly. There is a presumption in such areas against commercial or illuminated advertisements. The procedure for applying for express consent in these environmentally sensitive areas, however, is the same as for other areas.

s.220, 221

Except for statutory notices, no advertisement can be displayed without the permission of the owner of the land or building.

An offence is committed if an advertisement which needs consent is displayed without consent, unless the owner of the land or the person to whom the advertisement gives publicity (his goods, trade, business or other concerns) can prove it was displayed without his knowledge or consent.

s.224

Unless specifically excluded, normal controls of advertising apply in UDCs, EZs and SPZs.

If the advertisement is displayed on a listed building, then in addition to obtaining express consent under the 1992 Regulations, listed building consent is required and Procedure 2 should be followed. Both applications should be submitted simultaneously.

> Special note: The display of advertisements does not of itself constitute development, but the use of any external part of a building not normally used for that purpose is a material change of use (see note 24). However, section 222 of the 1990 Act provides that where the display of an advertisement is in accordance with the regulations, the planning permission for the change of use shall be deemed to have been granted. If, however, the advertisement involves a special construction (e.g. hoarding, flagpole), then further planning permissions may be necessary.

Steps for the Applicant:

1 Obtain from the LPA the appropriate application form. If it does not have its own, then use the format shown in Form 10A derived from Circ. 5/92. Determine how many copies of the application the LPA wants.

2 If the applicant does not own the land or building on which the advertisement is to be displayed, then permission must be obtained from the owner or other person entitled to grant permission. Some LPAs may ask for written evidence that permission has been obtained. Form 10B is a suggested format for such a document.

3 Prepare the number of copies, as required, of the application form, a site plan at 1:1250 scale, and appropriately scaled drawings to illustrate the nature of the advertisement. Include details of colour, lettering, materials and means of illumination, if any.

4 A fee is payable (see Appendix C).

Relevant LPA Action:

1 The application must be registered and available for public inspection.

2 The LPA is entitled to request further information.

3 Each application must be considered on its merits. Reasons for refusals must be clearly stated and explicit. The power of the LPA to control advertisements may be exercised only in the interest of 'amenity' and 'public safety'.

4 The decision should be made within eight weeks from the receipt of the application, or such extended periods as agreed with the applicant.

Results

The outcome of the application can be either:

- non-determination, i.e. deemed refusal
- refusal (reasons to be given)
- consent, subject to conditions (reasons to be given)
- consent.

The applicant can appeal to the Secretary of State against the decision, but only within six months of the receipt of the decision notice or, in the case of non-determination, six months from the date the decision should have been made.

Consent is normally granted for five years.

Section 225 of the 1990 Act gives the LPA power to remove or obliterate placards and posters which, in its opinion, are displayed in contravention to the advertisement regulations.

An LPA can refuse to determine similar applications within two years of a refusal by the Secretary of State on appeal. This is intended to prevent delaying tactics on the part of an applicant. There is no right of appeal against such action.

FORM 10A
Application Form
Source:
Circular 5/92

APPLICATION FOR CONSENT TO DISPLAY AN ADVERTISEMENT

Town and Country Planning Act 1990
The Town and Country Planning (Control of Advertisements) Regulations 1992

1 Applicant
Full Name (Block capitals) . . . .

Address . . . . Tel. no. . . . .

2 Agent (if any)
Full Name (Block capitals) . . . .

Address . . . . Tel. no. . . . .

3 Full postal address or location of the land on which the advertisement is to be

displayed . . . .

4 State the purpose for which the land or building is now used

. . . .

5 (a) Has the applicant an interest in the land?   *YES/NO*
    (b) If NO, has the permission of the owner, or of any other person
        entitled to give permission for the display of the advertisement
        been obtained?   *YES/NO*

6 (a) State the nature of the advertisement (e.g.: hoarding, shop sign, projecting
        sign, etc.)

. . . .

    (b) Is the advertisement already being displayed?   *YES/NO*

7 Description of advertisement   Size (m)   Illumination type
    (i)

    (ii)

    Continue on separate sheet if necessary.

8 Period for which consent is sought.

I enclose a *cheque/money order for the appropriate fee of £. . . . .

Signed . . . . (a) Date . . . .

---

* Delete where inappropriate.

(a) Applicant or agent.

FORM 10B
Consent of owner
Source: RMJM

* Delete where inappropriate.

(a) address of building or land on which the advertisement(s) are to be displayed
(b) name of owner
(c) address at which owner can be contacted
(d) signature of the owner.

TOWN AND COUNTRY PLANNING ACT 1990

**Town and Country Planning
(Control of Advertisements) Regulations 1992**

As owner of . . . . (a)

I, ... (b)

of . . . . (c), hereby give consent

as required under the above Regulations, for the display of *an advertisement/
advertisements on the above *land/building.

Signed . . . . (d)   Date . . . .

11

Application for Hazardous Substances Consent

Planning consent must be gained before specified controlled quantities, or above, of certain hazardous substances are permitted on, over or under land. The relevant powers are the Planning (Hazardous Substances) Act 1990 (HSA) and the Planning (Hazardous Substances) Regulations 1992 (SI 1992 No. 656). Schedule 1 of the Regulations specifies these substances and the controlled quantities. The schedule contains 71 substances in three categories: (A) toxic substances; (B) highly reactive and explosive substances; and (C) flammable substances not specified in (A) or (B). Appendix H contains the list of substances and their controlled quantities.

Regulation 4 specifies various exemptions including: during transportation, the temporary presence of substances being transferred from one means of transport to another, the presence of substances in aerosol containers of one litre or less; the presence of substances in an exempt pipeline; substances unloaded from a vessel during an emergency; additional quantities of ammonium nitrate-based fertilisers in certain circumstances.

Application is made to the relevant Hazardous Substances Authority (*HSA* to distinguish it from HSA, the Act). This is generally the district council or London borough, but the county council is the *HSA* if the land is in a national park (unless the park authority has been granted planning powers) or if the land is used for working minerals or waste disposal. A UDC is the *HSA* if it has been granted full planning powers and the relevant Minister is the *HSA* for operational land of statutory undertakers who are authorised to carry on harbour undertakings.

s.17 to 21, HSA

The consent is only applicable to the particular person(s) having an interest in the land. The consent is revoked if there is a change of person in control of the part of the land to which it relates.

Where there is a change of person in control, an application for the continuation of the consent must be made to the *HSA*. The form of such an application must be sought from the authority.

There are three classes of hazardous substance consents:

(a) deemed consents by virtue of an established presence (section 11 of HSA);
(b) deemed consents granted by a government department (section 12 of HSA);
(c) express consent for any other circumstance (section 6 of HSA).

(a) Deemed consents by virtue of an established presence:
A claim for an established presence could only be made to the *HSA* if a hazardous substance was present on, over or under the land for 12 months prior to 1 June 1992 and if an application was made in the transitional period which ended in December 1992.

(b) Deemed consents granted by government departments:
If a development authorised by a government department involves the presence of hazardous substances requiring a consent, the department may, on granting authorisation, direct that the hazardous substance consent is deemed to be granted. This is the case with consents under section 36 of the Electricity Act 1989. In such cases the department must consult the Health and Safety Commission.

(c) Express consent procedures:
The procedure for express consent is set out in Part III of the Regulations.

Steps for the Applicant

1 Contact the LPA, determine who is the *HSA*, obtain and complete the relevant forms: Form 11A.

2 Provide a site map and a substance location plan at a scale not less than 1:2500. This must identify areas of storage, manufacture or other industrial processes, the location of major plant involved in the process and the access point to and from the land.

3 Publish Regulation 6 notices (in the local press and on the site: Form 11B) and provide a certificate A, B or C to say it has been done or attempted (Form 11C).

4 Notify all owners with Form 11D and provide a Regulation 7(1) certificate A, B, C or D (regarding ownership of the site) to say it has been done or attempted: Form 11E.

5 A fee is payable.

Relevant LPA Action:
2.9,10 HSA

1 The authority may grant consent, either unconditionally or subject to such conditions as it thinks fit, or may refuse consent.

2 If the application relates to more than one hazardous substance, the authority may make different determinations in relation to each.

3 The consent must include a statement of the maximum quantity of hazardous substance permitted any one time.

FORM 11A
General application for hazardous substances consent
Source:
SI 1992 No.656 Sch.2

PLANNING (HAZARDOUS SUBSTANCES) ACT 1990–SECTION 7(1)

PLANNING (HAZARDOUS SUBSTANCES) REGULATIONS 1992, REGULATION 5

General application for Hazardous Substances Consent

1 Applicant . . . .

    Address . . . .

    Tel no. . . . .

    Agent (if any) to whom correspondence should be sent*

    Name . . . .

    Address . . . .

    Tel no. . . . .

    Contact . . . .

2 Address of application site . . . .

3 Substance(s) covered by application

Name	Entry number in Schedule 1 to the 1992 Regulations	Maximum quantity proposed to be present (in tonnes)#

\# or kilograms in the case of substances with entry numbers 21, 26 or 34

4 Manner in which substance(s) is/are to be kept and used
    Provide the following information for each substance covered by the application (referring to the substance location plan where appropriate)

    (a) Tick one box below to show whether the substance will be present for storage only or will be stored and involved in a manufacturing, treatment or other industrial process:

Substance entry number	Storage only	Stored **and** involved in industrial process

    (b) For each vessel to be used for **storing** the substance(s), give the following information:

Vessel No.	Entry No. of substance(s) to be stored in vessel	Installed above ground (yes#/no)	Buried (yes/no)	Mounded (yes/no)	Max capacity (cu. m.)	Highest vessel design temp. (°C)	Highest vessel design pressure (bar absolute)

\# if 'yes', specify whether or not it will be provided with full secondary containment

FORM 11A continued

(c) State for each substance the largest size (capacity in cu. m.) of any **moveable** container to be used for that substance:

(d) Where the substance is to be used in a **manufacturing, treatment or other industrial process(es)**, give a general description of the process(es), describe the major items of plant which will contain the substances; and state the maximum quantity (in tonnes) which is liable to be present in the major items of the plant, and the maximum temperature (°C) and pressure (bar absolute) at which the substance is liable to be present:

Substance entry No.	Description of process(es)	Major items of plant	Max quantity (tonnes)	Max temp (°C)	Max pressure (bar absolute)

5   Additional information

(a) Has any application for hazardous substance consent or planning permission relating to the application site been made which has not yet been determined?   **YES/NO**

(b) Will any such application be submitted at the same time as this application?   **YES/NO**

If you have answered **YES** to either of the preceding questions, give sufficient details to enable the application(s) to be identified.

(c) **Plans**. Please list the maps or plans or any explanatory scale drawings of plant/buildings submitted with this application.

I/we* hereby apply for hazardous substance consent in accordance with the proposals described in the application

Signed . . . .

On behalf of* . . . . (insert applicant's name if signed by agent)*

Date . . . .

* Delete where inappropriate.

FORM 1B
Site and press notice
Source: Planning (Hazardous
Substances) Regulations
1992, Sch.2

* Delete where inappropriate.

(a) Applicant's name
(b) name of Council or other body
    to whom the application is to be
    made
(c) brief details of the consent
    being sought
(d) address or location of the
    application site
(e) address at which the
    application may be inspected (it
    must be available for inspection
    within the locality of the
    application site)
(f) date giving a period of not less
    than 21 days beginning with the
    date the notice is published or
    first displayed on the site
(g) address of Council or other
    body to whom application is
    being made.

PLANNING (HAZARDOUS SUBSTANCES) ACT 1990

PLANNING (HAZARDOUS SUBSTANCES) REGULATIONS 1992, REGULATION 6

Notice of Application for Hazardous Substances Consent

I GIVE NOTICE THAT . . . . (a) is applying to the . . . . (b)

for hazardous substances consent . . . . (c) at . . . . (d)

Members of the public may inspect a copy of the application at . . . . (e)

during reasonable hours until . . . . (f).

Anyone who wishes to make representations about the application should write to

the . . . . (b) at . . . . (g) by . . . . (f).

Signed . . . .

On behalf of* . . . .

Date . . . .

FORM 11C
Certificate of posting notice
Source: Planning (Hazardous Substances) Regulations 1992, Sch.2

PLANNING (HAZARDOUS SUBSTANCES) ACT 1990

PLANNING (HAZARDOUS SUBSTANCES) REGULATIONS 1992, REGULATION 6

Posting of Notice of Application Certificate

Certificate A

I certify that:

- I/The applicant* posted the Notice required by section 6(1)(b) of the above Regulations on the land which is the subject of the accompanying application.

- The Notice was left in position for a period of not less than seven days during the 21 day period preceding the application.

or

Certificate B

I certify that

- I have/The applicant has* been unable to post the Notice required by section 6(1)(b) of the above Regulations on the land which is the subject of the accompanying application because I have/the applicant has* no right of access or other rights in respect of the land that would enable me/the applicant* to do so.

- I have/The applicant has* taken the following steps to acquire those rights, but have/has* been unsuccessful:

. . . . (a)

or

Certificate C

I certify that

- I/The applicant* posted the Notice required by section 6(1)(b) of the above Regulations on the land which is the subject of the accompanying application.

- It was, however, left in position for less than seven days during the 21 day period preceding the application.

- This happened because it was removed/obscured/defaced* before seven days had elapsed.

- This was not my/the applicant's fault or intention.

- I/The applicant* took the following steps to protect and replace the Notice:

. . . . (b)

Signed . . . .

On behalf of* . . . .

Date . . . .

---

* Delete where inappropriate.

(a) description of steps taken to acquire right of access
(b) details of steps taken to replace notice.

FORM 11D
Notice to owners

Source: Planning (Hazardous
Substances) Regulations
1992, Sch.2

(a) Applicant's name
(b) name of Council or other body
to whom the application is to be
made
(c) brief details of the consent
being sought
(d) address or location of the
application site
(e) address at which the
application may be inspected (it
must be available for inspection
within the locality of the
application site)
(f) address of Council or other
body to whom application is
being made.

PLANNING (HAZARDOUS SUBSTANCES) ACT 1990

PLANNING (HAZARDOUS SUBSTANCES) REGULATIONS 1992

Notice of Application for Hazardous Substances Consent

To be served on an owner

I GIVE NOTICE THAT . . . . (a) is applying to the . . . . (b)

for hazardous substances consent . . . . (c) at . . . . (d).

You may inspect a copy of the application at . . . . (e)

within 21 days of the service of this Notice.

If you wish to make representations about the application you should write to the

. . . . (b) at . . . . (f)

within 21 days of the service of this Notice.

Signed . . . .

On behalf of* . . . .

Date . . . .

FORM 11E
Certificate of ownership
Source: Planning (Hazardous Substances) Regulations 1992, Sch.2

PLANNING (HAZARDOUS SUBSTANCES) ACT 1990

PLANNING (HAZARDOUS SUBSTANCES) REGULATIONS 1992

Certificates under Regulation 7(1)

Certificate A

I certify that:

- At the beginning of the period of 21 days ending with the date of the accompanying application nobody, except the applicant, was the owner of any part of the land to which the application relates.

or

Certificate B

I certify that:

- I have/The applicant has* given the requisite notice to everyone else who, at the beginning of the period of 21 days ending with the date of the accompanying application, was the owner of any part of the land to which the application relates, as listed below:

Owner's name	Address at which notice was served	Date on which notice was served

or

Certificate C

I certify that:

- I/The applicant* cannot issue a certificate A or B in respect of the accompanying application.

- I/The applicant* has given the required notice to the persons specified below, being persons who at the beginning of the period of 21 days ending with the date of the application, were owners of any part of the land to which the application relates.

Owner's name	Address at which notice was served	Date on which notice was serviced

- I have/The applicant* has taken all reasonable steps open to me/the applicant* to find out the names and addresses of the remaining owners of the land, or of a part of it, but have/has* been unable to do so. These steps were as follows:

.... (a).

or

Certificate D

- I/The applicant* cannot issue a certificate A or B in respect of the accompanying application.

- I have/The applicant* has taken all reasonable steps open to me/the applicant* to find out the names and addresses of everyone else who, at the beginning of the period of 21 days ending with the date of the application was the owner of any part of the land to which the application relates, but have/has* been unable to do so. These steps were as follows:

.... (a).

Signed ....

On behalf of* ....

Date ....

---

* Delete where inappropriate.

(a) details of steps taken.

12

Application for a Certificate of Lawfulness of Proposed Use or Development (CLOPUD)

The old procedure for determining whether planning consent is required under section 64 of the 1990 Act has been replaced (by virtue of section 10 of the PCA) by a CLOPUD under section 192 of the 1990 Act which provides a firmer legal basis. It can be used to determine a proposed use, multiple uses, change of use or building/engineering/mining operation.

Steps for the Applicant:

1 Obtain forms from the LPA if it has them. There is no prescribed form but Form 12A is based on a model set out as Appendix 2 to Annex 1 to Circ. 17/92.

2 Attach copies of a plan (usually 1:1250) showing the site edged in red.

3 No Art. 6 notices or Art. 7 certificates are required.

4 The current application fee is half that for the equivalent planning application (Appendix C).

Relevant LPA Action:
GDPO
Art.24

1 The LPA is entitled to ask for further information.

2 The application must be registered and available for inspection.

3 The decision should be made within eight weeks from receipt of the application, or such extended periods as agreed with the applicant.

Results

The outcome of the application can be either:

- non-determination, i.e. deemed refusal
- refusal or part refusal
- approval and issue of certificate.

The applicant can appeal to the Secretary of State against the decision, but only within six months of receipt of the decision notice or, in the case of non-determination, six months from the date the decision should have been made.

FORM 12A
Application form
Source: Circ.17/92

For the Council's use only

Application No . . . .

Date received . . . .

. . . . Council

Town and Country Planning Act 1990: section 192, as amended by section 10 of the Planning and Compensation Act 1991

Town and Country Planning General Development (Amendment) Order 1992

APPLICATION FOR A CERTIFICATE OF LAWFULNESS FOR A *PROPOSED* USE OR DEVELOPMENT

1. Applicant (in block capitals)

    Name . . . .

    Address . . . .

    Post Code . . . .

    Tel. No. . . . .

2. Agent (if any)

    Name . . . .

    Address . . . .

    Post Code . . . .

    Tel. No. . . . .

3. (1) Nature of applicant's interest in the land, e.g. owner, lessee, occupier.

    (2) If you do not have an interest:

      (a) give name(s) and address(es) of anyone you know who has an interest in the land;

      (b) state the nature of their interest (if known);

      (c) state whether they have been informed about this application.
      YES/NO

4. Address or exact location of the land to which this application relates:

    Describe here and enclose (. . .) copies of an OS plan showing the boundary of the land edged red.

FORM 12A continued

5. Has the proposal been started?   **YES/NO**

6. If the proposal consists of, or includes, carrying out building or other operations give a detailed description of **all*** such operations and attach plans or drawings as are necessary to show their precise nature.

   (In the case of a proposed building the plans should indicate its precise siting and exact dimensions)

   * Includes the need to describe any proposal to alter or create a new access, lay out any new street, construct an associated hardstandings, means of enclosure or means of draining the land/buildings.

7. If any of the proposal relates to a change of use of the land/buildings:

   (1) give full description of the scale and nature of the proposed use, including the processes to be carried on, any machinery to be installed, and the hours the proposed use will be carried on;

   (2) fully describe the existing use or the last known use, with the date when this ceased.

8. Briefly describe why you think that the existing, or last, use of the land is lawful, or why you consider that any existing buildings which it is proposed to alter or extend are lawful (you can use section 12 of this application to state your case more fully).

   Specify the supporting documentary evidence (such as planning permission) which accompanies this application.

9. If you consider that the *existing* or last use is within a 'use class' in the Town and Country Planning (Use Classes) Order 1987, state which one.

10. If you consider that the *proposed* use is within a 'use class' in the Town and Country Planning (Use Classes) Order 1987, state which one.

11. Is the proposed operation or use temporary or permanent? If temporary, give details.

FORM 12A continued

12. State why you think that a Lawful Development Certificate should be granted for this proposal.

(Continue on a separate sheet if necessary)

I/We hereby apply for a lawful use or development certificate under section 192 of the 1990 Act in respect of the proposed use, operation or activity described in this application and the documents, drawings and plans which accompany it. I/We enclose the appropriate fee of £ . . . .

Signed . . . .   Date . . . .

On behalf of . . . .   (insert name of applicant if signed by an agent)

Warning: The amended section 194 of the 1990 Act provides that it is an offence to furnish false or misleading information or to withhold material information with intent to deceive. Section 193(7) enables the Council to revoke, at any time, a certificate they may have issued as a result of such false or misleading information.

13

Application for Scheduled Monument Consent

The consolidating Act relating to ancient monuments is the Ancient Monuments and Archaeological Areas Act 1979, and all references in this Procedure are to that Act, unless otherwise stated. A scheduled monument is defined in note 31.

Subject to the exceptions listed below, consent is required for any works to a scheduled monument or to any part of it:

- which will result in its demolition, destruction or damage
- for the purpose of removing, repairing or making any alterations or additions
- involving any flooding or tipping operations on land where there is a scheduled monument.

Assuming scheduled monument consent is applied for, neither listed building consent nor conservation area consent need be obtained if the monument is also either a listed building and/or in a conservation area.

Scheduled monument consent is not required for the execution of any of the following works as set out in the Ancient Monuments (Class Consents) Order (SI 1994 No. 1381):

Class I
    Agricultural, horticultural or forestry works, if they are the same kind as previously executed in the same field or location since 1964; but not including on ploughed land, (a) any works likely to be deeper than previous ploughing; (b) on other land, any works deeper than 300 mm; (c) sub-soiling, drainage works, uprooting trees, hedges or shrubs, the stripping of top soil, tipping or the commercial cutting of turf; (d) the demolition, alteration or disturbance of any building or structure; (e) the erection of any building or structure; (f) the laying of paths, hardstandings or foundations or the erection of fences or other barriers.

Class II
    Works executed more than 10 m below ground level by any licensed operator (within the meaning of the Coal Industry Act 1994), the British Coal Corporation, or any person acting pursuant to a licence granted by the Corporation.

Class III
    Works executed by the British Waterways Board in relation to land owned or occupied by them, being: works of repair or maintenance not involving a material alteration to a monument; or which are essential for the purpose of ensuring the functioning of a canal.

Class IV

> Works for the repair or maintenance of machinery, if they do not involve a material alteration to a monument.

Class V

> Works which are essential for the purpose of health or safety, provided that such works are the minimum necessary and notice and justification in writing are given to the Secretary of State as soon as possible.

Class VI

> Works executed by English Heritage.

Class VII

> Works of archaeological evaluation by or on behalf of persons who applied for consent under section 2, being works to supply information for the determination of that application, under the supervision of a person approved by the Secretary of State or English Heritage, and in accordance with an approved written specification.

Class VIII

> Works for the maintenance or preservation of a scheduled ancient monument as agreed under section 17 of the Act.

Class IX

> Works for the preservation, maintenance or management of a monument in accordance with section 24.

Class X

> Works consisting of the placing of survey markers to a depth of less than 300 mm for the purpose of surveying of visible remains.

The procedure for applications is prescribed in the Ancient Monuments (Applications for Scheduled Monument Consent) Regulations 1981 (SI 1981, No. 1301).

Steps for the Applicant:

1 Apply to the Secretary of State using the form shown in Form 13A.

2 If the applicant is not the sole owner, then he must notify all owners and occupiers. For the form of notice, see Form 13B. Note that in this context 'owner' includes a person entitled to a tenancy of the monument granted or extended for a term of which not less than seven years remain unexpired.

3   Complete only one of either Certificate A, B, C or D:

Certificate A
a certificate stating that 21 days before the date of the application, no person other than the applicant was the owner of the monument; see Form 13C

Certificate B
a certificate stating that the applicant has given the requisite notice of the application to all persons who, 21 days before that period were owners of the monument; see Form 13D

Certificate C
a certificate stating that the applicant is unable to issue either Certificate A or B, that he has given the requisite notice of the application to one or more owners, that he has taken such steps as are reasonably open to him to ascertain the names and addresses of the remainder of the owners and that he has been unable to do so; see Form 13E

Certificate D
a certificate stating that the applicant has taken such steps as are reasonably open to him to ascertain the names and addresses of the owners and that he has been unable to do so; see Form 13F.

4   The application should be accompanied by a plan of the site (at 1:1250 scale) edged in red, and 'before' and 'after' drawings at an appropriate scale to give a clear picture of the works proposed.

5   No fee is payable.

6   Four copies of the application form and drawings should be sent to the Secretary of State, plus one copy of the appropriate ownership certificate. The address to which the application should be sent is:

Buildings, Monuments and Sites Division
Department for Culture, Media and Sport
2–4 Cockspur Street
London SW1Y 5DH

or, for Wales,

Cadw: Welsh Historic Monuments
Brunel House
2 Fitzalan Road
Cardiff CF2 1UY

**Relevant Action
by the Secretary
of State:**
c.2(11)

1   The procedure on applications is similar to that on the applications called in under the 1971 Act.

Results
s.2(4)

Scheduled monument consent may be granted either unconditionally or subject to conditions.

Consent is usually for five years, unless otherwise stated, the Secretary of State's decision being final.

s.55

The only grounds for appeal are on the validity of the decision. A challenge can be made to the High Court within six weeks of the decision.

FORM 13A
Application letter
Source:
Ancient Monuments
(Applications for Scheduled
Monument Consent)
Regulations 1981
(SI 1981, No. 1301)
Regulation 2(1), Schedule 1

APPLICATION FOR SCHEDULED MONUMENT CONSENT

Ancient Monuments and Archaeological Areas Act 1979 (as amended), s.2

1. Applicant

Name .... Address ....

Post Code .... Tel. no. ....

2. Occupier of monument – if not the applicant

Name .... Address ....

Post Code .... Tel. no. ....

3. Monument to which application relates

Name (if any) of monument .... Address or Location ....

County Monument Number .... National Grid Reference ....

4. Description of proposed works

....

....

5. List of plans and drawings accompanying application

....

....

6. Any other information relevant to application

....

....

I/We hereby apply for scheduled monument consent for the works described in this application and shown on the accompanying plans and drawings.

Signature .... Date ....

*On behalf of ....

*Name of agent .... Address of agent ....

Post Code .... Tel. no. ....

---

* Delete if inappropriate.

FORM 13B
Application notice

Source:
Ancient Monuments
(Applications for Scheduled
Monument Consent)
Regulations 1981
Regulation 3, Schedule 2,
Part II

* Delete where inappropriate.

(a) address or location of the
monument, and the name (if
any)
(b) name and address of the
applicant
(c) brief description of the
proposed works.

ANCIENT MONUMENTS AND ARCHAEOLOGICAL AREAS ACT 1979

Notice of application for scheduled monument consent

This notice relates to the ancient monument at . . . . (a)

An application is to be made *by/on behalf of . . . . (b)

to the Secretary of State for *the Environment/Wales for scheduled monument
consent under the Ancient Monuments and Archaeological Areas Act 1979 to carry
out the following works:

. . . . (c)

An opportunity to make representations with respect to the application will be
afforded by the Secretary of State before the application is determined.

Signature . . . . Date . . . .

FORM 13C
Certificate A

Source:
Ancient Monuments
(Applications for Scheduled
Monument Consent)
Regulations 1981
Regulation 3, Schedule 2,
Part I

ANCIENT MONUMENTS AND ARCHAEOLOGICAL AREAS ACT 1979

Certificate in accordance with paragraph 2(1)(a)

It is hereby certified that no person other than the applicant was the owner of the
monument to which the accompanying application relates at the beginning of the
period of 21 days which ended on the date of the application.

Signature . . . . Date . . . .

FORM 13D
Certificate B

Source:
Ancient Monuments
(Applications for Scheduled
Monument Consent)
Regulations 1981
Regulation 3, Schedule 2,
Part II

(a) Insert names and addresses.

ANCIENT MONUMENTS AND ARCHAEOLOGICAL AREAS ACT 1979

Certificate in accordance with paragraph 2(1)(b)

It is hereby certified that the applicant has given the requisite notice of the
accompanying application to all the persons other than the applicant who, at the
beginning of the period of 21 days which ended on the date of the application, were
owners of the monument to which the application relates, namely

. . . . (a)

Signature . . . . Date . . . .

FORM 13E
Certificate C

Source:
Ancient Monuments
(Applications for Scheduled
Monument Consent)
Regulations 1981
Regulation 3, Schedule 2,
Part I

ANCIENT MONUMENTS AND ARCHAEOLOGICAL AREAS ACT 1979

Certificate in accordance with paragraph 2(1)(c)

It is hereby certified

(1) that the applicant is unable to issue a certificate in accordance with either paragraph 2(1)*(a)* or *(b)* of Schedule 1 to the Ancient Monuments and Archaeological Areas Act 1979;

(2) that the applicant has given the requisite notice of the accompanying application to the following persons who, at the beginning of 21 days which ended on the date of the application, were owners of the monument to which the application relates, namely

. . . . (a) and,

(3) that the applicant has taken such steps as are reasonably open to him to ascertain the names and addresses of the remainder of the persons who at the beginning of that period were owners of that monument and has been unable to do so.

Signature . . . . Date . . . .

(a) Insert names and addresses of all the owners notified.

FORM 13F
Certificate D

Source:
Ancient Monuments
(Applications for Scheduled
Monument Consent)
Regulations 1981
Regulation 3, Schedule 2,
Part I

ANCIENT MONUMENTS AND ARCHAEOLOGICAL AREAS ACT 1979

Certificate in accordance with paragraph 2(1)(d)

It is hereby certified that the applicant is unable to issue a certificate in accordance with paragraph 2(1)*(a)* of Schedule 1 to the Ancient Monuments and Archaeological Areas Act 1979, but has taken such steps as are reasonably open to him to ascertain the names and addresses of the other persons who, at the beginning of the period of twenty-one days which ended on the date of the accompanying application, were owners of the monument to which the application relates and has been unable to do so.

Signature . . . . Date . . . .

14

s.9(1)

Application to Fell a Tree Covered by the Forestry Act 1967

Some parts of Great Britain are devoted to forestry under agreements with the Forestry Commissioners (the Commissioners). Under the Forestry Act 1967, the Commissioners have power to control the felling of trees. References below relate to that Act.

s.9(1)

If the land is under the Act, then a licence granted by the Commissioners is required to fell any growing tree, with the following exceptions:

s.9(2) and s.9(3)

s.9(2)

s.9(3)
s.14
s.9(4)(c)

s.9(4)(b)

s.9(4)

- trees with a trunk diameter of less than 80 mm (or less than 150 mm in the case of coppice or underwood, or 100 mm where felling is carried out to improve the growth of other trees)
- trees in an orchard, garden, churchyard, public open space or Inner London Borough
- if the aggregate cubic content of the trees which are felled by the occupier or tenant to the land in any quarter year does not exceed five cubic metres
- if felling is part of an agreed plan of operations
- when carried out by an electricity operator
- when carried out by a statutory undertaker if the tree(s) are on its land and they interfere with operations or maintenance
- if the felling is required for the purpose of carrying out development that has planning permission or is 'permitted development'.

s.10

An application for a felling licence can only be made by a person having an interest in the land on which the trees are growing.

The topping or lopping of trees and the trimming or laying of hedges does not need a licence, but if the trees are subject to a TPO, then TPO consent is required (see Procedure 15).

s.10

When a licence is applied for in the case of felling a tree subject to a TPO, a separate application for TPO consent is not needed.

Steps for the Applicant:

1   The application for a licence must be on a form which is obtainable from the Commission's local Conservator of Forests. The relevant address can be obtained from:

> The Forestry Commission
> 231 Corstorphine Road
> Edinburgh, EH12 7AT
> Tel: Edinburgh (0131) 334 0303.

s.10(1)

2   The completed form should be submitted in duplicate or, if the trees are also subject to TPOs, in triplicate.

Sch. 2, Reg. 4

3 No fee is payable.

4 The licence must be received before felling commences.

Relevant Actions by the Commissioner:

s.10(2)

1 The licence can be granted, or granted subject to conditions, or refused. If refused, a written statement on the grounds of the refusal must be supplied to the applicant.

s.13(1)

2 Failure by the Commissioners to give notice of a decision within three months (or longer if agreed) should be treated as a refusal.

s.10(5)

3 In the case of a refusal of a licence, the Commissioners have the power to review the refusal and to offer to grant a licence if a further application is made.

Results

A person aggrieved by a refusal or condition on a licence can request the Minister of Agriculture, Fisheries and Food (in Wales, the Secretary of State) to refer the matter to a committee appointed under section 27. After considering the committee's report, the Minister can confirm, reverse or modify the Commissioner's decision.

15

Application to Fell or Lop a Tree Subject to a Tree Preservation Order

Under section 198 of the 1990 Act, consent is required to fell or lop a tree if it is either subject to an individual TPO or if it forms part of a group subject to a TPO.

The definition of 'tree' is wide, and includes saplings (see note 28). Bushes and shrubs within a TPO group do not need consent for their removal or cutting back.

Root pruning of TPO trees needs consent (see note 42).

The felling or lopping of trees which are dead, dying or dangerous does not need consent. However, it is prudent to inform the LPA of the proposed work so that they have an opportunity to check and confirm the condition of the tree(s).

Steps for the Applicant:

1 Obtain from the LPA the appropriate application forms if it has them. If the LPA does not have its own forms, then application must be made in writing, stating the reason for the work. The application must include:

- location plan (at 1:1250 scale)
- detailed plan showing location of tree(s) to be worked on
- species, height and spread of tree(s)
- specification of work to be carried out on a tree-by-tree basis
- the reasons for making the application: why it is necessary or desirable to lop or fell the trees.

Form 15A is a suggested format for the application letter.

Circ.31/92

2 No fee is payable.

Relevant LPA Action:

1 Applications must be registered and available for public inspection.

2 A certificate under Article 5 may accompany a refusal or a conditional consent. This excludes the applicant from the opportunity of claiming compensation.

3 The decision should be made within eight weeks from receipt of the application, or such extended periods as agreed with the applicant.

Results

The LPA may grant unconditional or conditional consent or refusal. Non-determination is deemed refusal.

The applicant can appeal to the Secretary of State within 28 days of receiving the decision notice, or within 28 days of the date the decision should have been made.

FORM 15A
Application letter
Source:
RMJM

* Delete where inappropriate.

(a) address of LPA

(b) agent's name, address and telephone number or, if no agent, then the applicant's name, address and telephone number

(c) applicant's name, address and telephone number

(d) address or location where tree(s) are situated

(e) reference number of location plan

(f) reference number of detailed plan

(g) insert reason for work (e.g. to prevent further rot, increase light to dwelling, etc.).

. . . . . . (a) . . . . (b) . . . . . .

Dear Sir,

Town and Country Planning Act 1990

**APPLICATION FOR CONSENT TO *FELL/LOP* A TREE
SUBJECT TO A TREE PRESERVATION ORDER**

*We write on behalf of . . . . (c)

We hereby apply for consent to do work to tree(s) subject to a tree preservation order.

The trees in question are situated at . . . . (d)

Plan . . . . (e) attached illustrates the location of the site.

Plan . . . . (f) shows the detailed location of the tree(s).

Information on the tree(s) is as follows:

Tree Ref . . . .   Species . . . .

Height (m) . . . .   Spread (m) . . . .

Work to be carried out . . . .

The reason(s) for the work *is/are . . . . (g)

Signed . . . .   Date . . . .

117

s.211

Notification to Fell or Lop a Tree in a Conservation Area

The LPA must be given six weeks notice of intention to do work on trees in a conservation area when the tree(s) are not protected by a Tree Preservation Order (TPO). Within this time period the LPA may issue a TPO.

The term 'work on trees' includes cutting down, topping, lopping, root pruning, uprooting, wilfully damaging or wilfully destroying any tree (see note 42).

It can be argued that no notification need be made to the LPA if the trees in question are dead, dying or dangerous as trees in that state would not be made the subject of a TPO. However, it is difficult to prove after the event that the tree was either dead, dying or dangerous and therefore it is prudent to inform the LPA anyway.

SI 1975 No. 148

Certain cases are exempt. These include:

- the cutting down of a tree in accordance with a felling licence granted by the Forestry Commissioners
- the cutting down, uprooting, topping or lopping of a tree on land in the occupation of an LA when it is done by or with the consent of that authority
- the cutting down, uprooting, topping or lopping of a tree with a diameter not exceeding 75 mm, or the cutting down or uprooting of a tree with a diameter not exceeding 100 mm where it is done to improve the growth of other trees.
('Diameter' is measured over the bark, at a point 1.5 m above ground level.)

Steps for the Applicant:

1 Notify the LPA in writing of the works to be carried out and the reason for the works. Include details on:

- species, height and spread of tree(s)
- specification of the work to be carried out
- reasons for lopping or felling.

Form 16A is a suggested format for the notification letter.

2 Plans should accompany the letter of notification and should show:

- location plan (at 1:1250 scale)
- detailed plan showing location and spread of the tree(s) to be worked on (cross-referenced to the letter).

3 No fee is payable.

**Relevant LPA
Action:**

1 The notification must be registered and available for public inspection.

2 The LPA has six weeks in which to inspect the tree(s) and initiate a TPO. If the LPA states it does not want to issue a TPO, or the six weeks elapse and no action is taken, then deemed consent to carry out the work can be assumed. The applicant has two years to complete the work or a further notice is needed.

3 If the LPA serves a TPO, then the applicant must complete Procedure 15.

**FORM 16A
Notification letter**
Source: RMJM

* Delete if inappropriate.

(a) address of LPA
(b) agent's name, address and telephone number or, if no agent, then applicant's name, address and telephone number
(c) applicant's name, address and telephone number
(d) address or location where tree(s) are situated
(e) reference number of location plan
(f) reference number of detailed plan
(g) reason for work (e.g. to prevent further rot, increase light to dwelling, etc.).

...... (a) .... (b) ......

Dear Sir,

Town and Country Planning Act 1990

NOTIFICATION OF WORK TO TREES IN A CONSERVATION AREA

*We write on behalf of .... (c)

TAKE NOTICE that work is proposed to a tree/trees not subject to a tree preservation order but in a conservation area.

The tree/trees in question *is/are situated at .... (d)

Plan .... (e) attached illustrates the location of the site.

Plan .... (f) shows the detailed location of the tree(s).

Information on the tree(s) is as follows:

Tree Ref .... Species ....

Height .... Spread ....

Work to be carried out ....

The reason(s) for the work *is/are .... (g)

If within six weeks *I/we have received no written response to this notice, *I/we will assume deemed consent for the works specified.

Signed .... Date ....

17

Steps for the developing department:

Notification under Circular 18/84 for Crown or Local Authority Development

The Crown includes the Crown Estate, government departments, the Duchies of Lancaster and Cornwall and all other bodies entitled to Crown exemption from planning legislation such as the Metropolitan Police. All these bodies follow the procedures set out in Circ. 18/84 when developing for their own purposes. The premise behind the Circular is that, while the Crown does not require planning permission, it must consult the LPA before proceeding with any proposal which would otherwise need planning permission.

1 Developing departments are advised by the Circular to consult informally with the LPA as early as possible.

2 The formal stage entails sending the LPA four copies of a statement of the proposal marked 'Notice of Proposed Development by (Department)' giving sufficient details of the proposal and four copies of a location plan. The proposal will make it clear whether it is 'outline' or contains all relevant details, and in the former case, which reserved matters are included (see note 6).

3 If the Crown does not own all the land, the developing department must issue notices to owners and agricultural tenants, as in section 65 procedure.

4 An Environmental Statement must accompany the Notice if one has been requested by the LPA.

5 No fee is payable.

6 The Notice may be accompanied by a request for further information as set out in Annex A of Circ. 18/84.

Relevant LPA Action:

1 Deal with the Notice as if it were a statutory planning application, including an entry in a non-statutory addendum to the Register, Part 2.

2 Consult with the county on appropriate issues.

3 Reply to request made under Annex A of Circ. 18/84.

4 LPA views should be sent to the developing department within eight weeks, including any objections to the Notice.

5 The LPA can approve the proposal, suggest conditions which would make it acceptable, or object to it (giving clear reasons). In the latter case the Secretary of State for the Environment acts as referee and arbiter.

Development by a Local Authority

The process by which a local authority obtains planning permission for development it proposes to carry out is set out in section 316 of the 1990 Act as amended by the PCA and the Town and Country Planning General Regulations 1992. In principle the LPA applies for planning consent for development on its own land, or for joint development with others involving its own land (Regulation 3), in the same way as any other developer. But the permission is tied to the LPA and does not run with the land.

In cases where the LPA's interest in a joint development is not significant from a financial point of view, or if it has no interest in the development, the application will be determined by another body under Regulation 4. This means that a county decides for a district or vice versa or the application is called in by the Secretary of State. In these cases the permission runs with the land.

LPAs can also make and determine outline and reserved matters applications on their own land but not listed building consents.

**Local Authority
Action:**

1 In the case of a Regulation 3 development, pass a resolution to seek permission.

2 Serve notices on owners/tenants.

3 Carry out any other publicity which would be required by the statutory provision for a normal application.

4 Place a copy of the resolution and details of the proposal on the Register.

5 Refer to the Secretary of State if in conflict with the approved development plan.

6 After the statutory periods for objections, if the Secretary of State has not required the authority to refer the application to him, pass a second resolution.

7 Note: the permission enures only for the benefit of the authority, not for the benefit of the land.

If the authority wishes to obtain deemed planning permission for development of land it controls but does not wish to carry out the development itself, it can do so under Regulation 4. The procedure is similar to the above except that the second resolution must specifically include a condition requiring the LPA's approval to the siting, design, external appearance, means of access and landscaping of the site. Such a deemed permission enures to the benefit of the land.

MPG2

GDPO
Art.3

Application for Outline Planning Permission to Develop Land

Outline planning applications are only relevant where the proposal involves, or will involve, the erection of new buildings. 'Building' in this instance does not include plant or machinery. Outline applications are not accepted if they only relate to extensions, alterations or change of use of existing buildings. Outline applications for advertisements or for the mining or working of minerals are not possible.

The applicant can apply for outline planning permission only if the LPA agrees that the application can be considered separately from the siting or design or external appearance or means of access or landscaping. These are termed 'reserved matters' (see note 6). Landscaping, in this context, is defined in Procedure 8.

Outline applications relating to development in conservation areas are rarely accepted. Similarly, development proposals that affect the setting of a scheduled ancient monument, or the setting of a listed building, will require an application for full planning permission and not an outline application.

It is prudent to check with the LPA at an early stage as to what type of application will be entertained and what information is needed if an application for outline permission is acceptable.

Steps for the Applicant:

1 The procedure for applying for outline planning permission is identical to Procedure 1 except for the amount of information needed to describe the proposed development. This can be limited to just a plan identifying the site and a written description of the development.

2 An application for outline planning permission needs a section 65 Certificate as for an application for full planning permission.

3 The applicant can submit details of any of the 'reserved matters' as part of an outline application, in which case the LPA must treat them as part of the development and cannot reserve them for subsequent approval.

4 If the applicant wants to show details to help the LPA, but wants to reserve the right to change them subsequently, they must be clearly labelled as being for illustrative purposes only.

5 A fee is payable, see Appendix C.

**Relevant LPA
Action:**

GDPO Art. 3

1 The application is treated in the same way as a full application but the LPA has discretion to ask for whatever additional information it deems necessary to determine the application. The LPA has one month to specify what further illustrative and other material is needed (if necessary).

2 If the applicant, for whatever reason, does not want to give the additional information asked for, he can appeal to the Secretary of State within six months of the request for the information.

3 Circulate copies of the application form(s) and plans and drawings to consultees.

4 A notice of the application is issued to immediate neighbours (and other neighbours if the proposal is thought likely to affect their amenity).

5 The decision should be made within eight weeks from the receipt of the application, or such extended periods as agreed with the applicant.

Results

The outcome of the application can be either:

- non-determination, i.e. deemed refusal
- refusal (reasons to be given)
- permission, subject to condition (reasons to be given) and approval of reserved matters
- permission subject to approval of reserved matters.

The applicant can appeal to the Secretary of State against the decision, but only within six months of receipt of the decision notice or, in the case of non-determination, six months from the date the decision should have been made.

19

Application for a Certificate of Immunity from Listing

Under section 6 of the LBCA, any person who is seeking, or has been granted, planning permission for any development involving the alteration, extension or demolition of a building, may apply to the Secretary of State for a certificate stating that it is not intended to list the building shown in the application plans. There is no immunity from listing in Scotland.

If the building in question is assessed as being of special architectural or historic interest, it will be listed and no certificate issued. The normal range of listed building controls will apply.

If a certificate of immunity is issued, then this gives a statutory guarantee that the building named in it will not be listed or made the subject of a building preservation notice for a period of five years from the date of issue of the certificate. Even if a certificate of immunity is granted, consent for demolition will still be required, see note 34.

s.6 LBCA

Steps for the Applicant:

1 There is no prescribed application form, but Form 18A is a suggested format.

2 A plan at 1:1250 scale with the position of the building(s) marked on it should be submitted with the application form, together with photographs of each elevation and of any notable interior features. The photographs should be labelled to identify the particular elevation and internal feature.

Circ.8/87

3 The application should be sent to DCMS (Department for Culture Media and Sport), Listing Branch, 2–4 Cockspur Street, London SW1Y 5DH.

4 No fee is payable.

5 At the same time as submitting the application, notice must be sent to the LPA. Form 18B is a suggested format for this notice.

s.6 LBCA

6 If the building is in Greater London, notice must also be given to English Heritage, Fortress Ho., 23 Savile Row, London W1X 2HE.

Relevant Action by the Secretary of State

1 The building(s) for which an application for a certificate is made is completely reassessed under section 6 of the LBCA.

2 When a certificate is issued, the Department will notify both the District and County Council (in Greater London, the Borough Council, LDDC, and the London Division of the Commission).

FORM 19A
Application letter
Source: RMJM

. . . . . . (a) . . . . (b) . . . . . .

Dear Sir,

Planning (Listed Buildings and Conservation Areas) Act 1990

APPLICATION FOR A CERTIFICATE OF IMMUNITY FROM LISTING

*We write on behalf of . . . . (c)

We hereby apply, under section 6 of the above Act, for a certificate of immunity from listing for building(s) situated at

. . . . (d)

Attached are photographs of the external elevations, *no internal features are notable/and notable internal feature(s).

The approximate date of construction was . . . . (e)

The architect(s) of the building *was/were . . . . (f) is/are unknown.

Information about the architectural or historic interest of the building(s) *is unknown to the applicant/is as follows:

. . . . (g)

We *are applying for/have recently received planning permission to/from

. . . . (h)

We confirm that notice of this application has been given to the *district council/ London borough above. *Notice has also been given to the Historic Buildings and Monuments Commission for England.

Signed . . . .   Date . . . .

* Delete where inappropriate.

(a) address of the Listing Branch (see step 3)
(b) agent's name, address and telephone number or, if no agent, then applicant's name, address and telephone number
(c) applicant's name, address and telephone number
(d) address of building(s) to which the application relates
(e) year of construction (or decade if exact date unknown)
(f) name of architect or firm of architects
(g) relevant information on historic or architectural interest
(h) name and address of LPA.

FORM 19B
Notice of application
Source: RMJM

PLANNED (LISTED BUILDINGS AND CONSERVATION AREAS) ACT 1990

Take notice that under section 6 of the above Act, ... (a)

has applied to the Secretary of State for a certificate of immunity from listing for

building(s) situated at . . . . (b)

Signed . . . .   *On behalf of . . . .

Date . . . .

* Delete if inappropriate.

(a) name and address of the applicant
(b) address of building(s) to which the application relates.

20

Determination of the Need for an Environmental Assessment

Appendix G gives the general background to environmental assessments (EA) and environmental statements (ES). The legislation under SI 1988 No. 1199 (with amendments in SI 1992 No. 1494 and SI 1994 No. 667) introduces four related types of procedure which are set out below and illustrated in the flow charts (adapted from *Environmental Assessment, A Guide To Procedures*, HMSO 1989):

(a) pre-application determination by LPA
(b) pre-application direction by Secretary of State
(c) post-application direction by Secretary of State
(d) procedures in preparing and submitting an ES

(a) Pre-application determination by LPA
Before making a planning application, it is advisable to check whether an EA is needed. An applicant can ask the relevant planning authority (which may be the County in the case of minerals or waste disposal) for its opinion at any time prior to the application (Flowchart 20a).

Steps for the Applicant:

1 Request to LPA consisting of:

- letter asking for LPA opinion (Form 20A)
- plans to identify the land
- brief description of the nature and purpose of the proposed development and its possible effects on the environment
- any other relevant information.

Reg.5, SI 1988 No. 1199

2 No fee is payable.

Relevant LPA Action:

1 Notify the applicant within three weeks either:

- that more information is required
- that an EA is not required
- that an EA is required, specifying full reasons for conclusion.

2 LPA puts details of conclusions on public record.

(b) Pre-application direction (Regulation 6) by Secretary of State
If the LPA fails to respond within three weeks, or if its opinion is that an EA is necessary, the applicant may apply to the Secretary of State for a direction (Flowchart 20b).

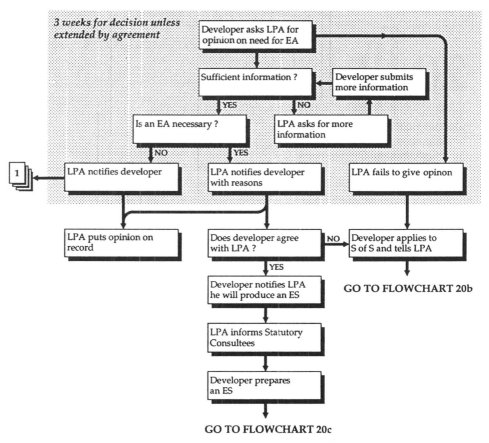

Flowchart 20a
Pre-application request for LPA opinion

Steps for the Applicant:

1 Application to the Regional Office of the DETR consisting of:

- letter asking for direction (Form 20B)
- copy of request to LPA under Regulation 5(1) together with documents which accompanied it
- copy of LPA requests for more information (if any) under Regulation 5(3)
- copy of any opinion given by LPA and accompanying statement of reasons
- any representations the applicant wishes to make.

2 Copy of all the above to the LPA.

3 No fee is payable.

Steps for the Secretary of State:

1 He shall notify the applicant and the LPA of any points on which he needs more information.

2 He shall issue a direction within three weeks of the application or a such longer period as he may reasonably require.

3 He shall send a copy to the LPA and if he directs that an EA is required, he shall send a written statement giving full reasons for his conclusion.

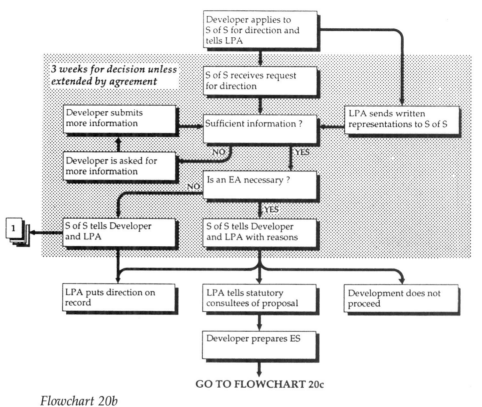

GO TO FLOWCHART 20c

Flowchart 20b
Request for direction by Secretary of State

(c) Post-application direction (Regulation 9) by Secretary of State

If the LPA receives an application without an ES which, in its opinion, is a Schedule 1 or 2 proposal requiring an ES, it must tell the applicant within three weeks of the application giving full reasons. The applicant must then reply in writing to the LPA within three weeks either accepting their view or saying that he is applying to the Secretary of State for direction. If the applicant fails to write within three weeks, planning permission will be deemed refused without right of appeal (Flowchart 20c).

If the applicant wishes to appeal under Regulation 9, the procedure is as follows (similar to that for Regulation 6):

Steps for the Applicant:

1 Appeal to the Regional Office of the DETR consisting of:

- letter appealing under Regulation 9
- copy of application for planning permission
- all documents sent to the LPA as part of the application
- all relevant correspondence with the LPA.

2 If the Secretary of State replies saying that an ES is needed, the applicant must write within three weeks to the Secretary of State to inform him that he proposes to provide an ES.

3 No fee is payable.

Steps for the Secretary of State:

1 He shall notify the applicant, and the LPA, within three weeks of receiving the appeal (or such longer period as he may reasonably require) whether an ES is required and, if so, give full reasons (Regulation 10).

2 If, after having been notified of the need for an ES, the applicant fails to reply within three weeks saying that he will provide one, the Secretary of State will tell the applicant that no further action will be taken on his application. In other words, planning permission will be refused.

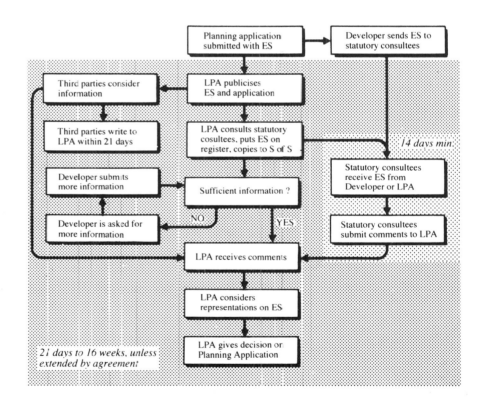

Flowchart 20c
ES Procedures

(d) Procedures in preparing and submitting an ES

One purpose of an EA is to bring together professional views of all relevant environmental effects. This means that at least all parties who have a statutory duty to comment on the ES should be consulted during its preparation. When an LPA asks for an EA it has to tell the statutory consultees that it has done so and must also tell the applicant the names and addresses of the consultees. The consultees are obliged to provide any relevant data that they possess to the applicant on request but are not required to set up surveys etc. to obtain more data. They may make a 'reasonable charge' for making this information available (Regulation 20).

There is no set form for an ES but it must contain the information specified in paragraph 2 of Schedule 3 (see Appendix G). Some items in Schedule 3 will have more relevance than others for a particular proposal and there may be other issues that should be addressed. It is therefore wise to consult the LPA in advance about the critical issues and the depth to which their environmental effects should be studied. But this pre-ES consultation cannot be definitive: the applicant can still be required to provide further information after the ES has been submitted (Regulation 21).

At the end of the process, the ES becomes a public document: copies must be made available to public bodies and to the public, and this fact must be advertised. It must thus be capable of being read and understood by a non-technical reader. It becomes a vital part of the public perception of the proposal and not just a technical appendix.

Steps for the Applicant:

1 Pre-EA consultation with LPA to determine scope of ES.

2 Consultation with statutory consultees and exchange of data during production of ES. It is not necessary to state the views of statutory consultees in the ES (they usually respond direct to the LPA) but it helps if the applicant can report on his discussions and on any agreed measures to reduce or remedy adverse environmental effects.

3 Publicity: in the case of an ES being submitted at the same time as a planning application, the LPA must publicise the application and the ES on the site and in the local press in accordance with the GDPO Art. 8. The form of the notice is set out in the GDPO, Sch. 3. In addition to the normal section 65 Notice contents, the Notice must state where the ES can be inspected and from what address, and at what price, copies may be obtained (see Form 20C). The charge must be reasonable and reflect printing and distribution costs. The number of copies is open to negotiation with the LPA but in our experience a minimum of 50 is required. In the case of a post-application ES, the applicant is responsible for the publicity.

4 If necessary, provide further publicity material such as a non-technical summary or an exhibition.

5 On submission of the planning application, in addition to the normal forms, certificates and drawings, send:

- Certificates under section 65
- two copies of ES (one for the LPA, and one for the Secretary of State)
- send copies of ES to all statutory consultees
- note of the name of everybody to whom the applicant has sent an ES
- or send extra copies of ES to the LPA for onward transmission to statutory consultees (this process can waste time).

6 The normal planning application fee applies.

Steps for the LPA: 1 On receipt of planning application with ES etc., send copy to the Secretary of State, and consult statutory consultees.

2 Inform applicant if any further information is required to amplify or verify his ES. There is no stated time period for making such a request other than, by implication, it should be well within the 16 week period set down as the maximum for a decision.

FORM 20A
Application letter to LPA
Source: RMJM

* Delete where inappropriate.

(a) address of LPA and/or Mineral Planning Authority etc.
(b) applicant's/agent's name and address
(c) location of site and identity of proposal.

...... (a) .... (b) ......

Dear Sir,

The Town and Country Planning
(Assessment of Environmental Effects) Regulations 1988

APPLICATION UNDER REGULATION 6(1) TO ESTABLISH THE NEED FOR
AN ENVIRONMENTAL ASSESSMENT

Site: .... (c)

*On behalf of .... (b)

We intend to submit a planning application for the above site and need to know if, in your opinion, an Environmental Assessment is required. We enclose:

- plan showing location of the site
- statement of nature of the proposal and possible environmental effects
- other explanatory material.

Signed .... Date ....

FORM 20B
Application letter to DETR

Source: RMJM

* Delete where inappropriate.

(a) address of Regional Office of DETR
(b) applicant's/agent's name and address
(c) location of site and identity of proposal
(d) applicant's name
(e) name of LPA.

...... (a) .... (b) ......

Dear Sir,

**The Town and Country Planning
(Assessment of Environmental Effects) Regulations 1988**

**APPLICATION UNDER REGULATION 6(1) TO ESTABLISH THE NEED FOR
AN ENVIRONMENTAL ASSESSMENT**

Site: .... (c)

*On behalf of .... (b)

The local planning authority (..................................... (e))
have given their opinion that the above proposed development is within the
definition of Schedule 1 (or Schedule 2) of the Regulations and requires an
environmental assessment (or have failed to give an opinion within three weeks of
our request).*

We disagree with the opinion and hereby seek a direction from the Secretary of
State. We enclose the following:

- copy of request to LPA under regulation 5(1) together with documents which
  accompanied it
- copy of notification by LPA under regulation 5(3) asking for further information,
  and our response
- copy of the opinion given by the LPA and their reasons
- a statement of our case that the proposal does not require an EA.

Signed .... Date ....

FORM 20C
Site notice and advertisement in newspaper
Source: GDPO Sch. 3

NOTICE OF APPLICATION FOR PLANNING PERMISSION

Town and Country Planning (General Development Procedure) Order 1995

NOTICE UNDER ARTICLE 8 OF APPLICATION FOR PLANNING PERMISSION ACCOMPANIED BY AN ENVIRONMENTAL STATEMENT

Proposed development at . . . . (a)

I give notice that . . . . (b)

is applying to the . . . . (c) Council

for planning permission to . . . . (d)
and that the application is accompanied by an environmental statement.

The proposed development does not accord with the provisions of the development plan in force in the area in which the land to which the application relates is situated.*

Members of the public may inspect copies of:

- the application
- the plans
- the environmental statement
- and other documents submitted with the application

at . . . . (e)

during all reasonable hours until . . . . (f)

Members of the public may obtain copies of the environmental statement from:

. . . . (g)

so long as stocks last, at a charge of . . . . (h).

Anyone who wishes to make representations about this application should write to

the Council at . . . . (i) by . . . . (f)

Signed . . . . *On behalf of . . . . (b)

Date . . . .

---

* Delete where inappropriate.

(a) location of development
(b) applicant's name
(c) name of Council
(d) description of proposed development
(e) address at which it may be inspected, usually LPA offices
(f) date not less than 21 days from publication/posting of notice
(g) address of applicant, agent or LPA by agreement
(h) reasonable price to cover copying and distribution
(i) address of Council.

21

Application for Renewal of a Planning Permission

Application can be made for the renewal of a planning permission which has not been implemented so long as its original time period has not expired. There are two possible routes: first, the simple renewal of the permission as a whole, and second, a variation of the time condition under section 73. Recent cases seem to suggest that the result is the same in both instances: the LPA will be empowered to review the whole case and not be confined, in the second method, to the time condition alone. It is therefore open to the LPA to reconsider the principle of the development and to impose new conditions if it sees fit. Once the time limit of a permission has elapsed, a completely new application is required.

Para 60 of Circ. 11/95 gives guidance on the determination of renewal applications. As a general rule such applications should only be refused where there has been some material change in planning circumstances (e.g. a change in relevant planning policy at local or government level, or a change in highway considerations); or if continued failure to start development would contribute to unacceptable uncertainty; or if the application is premature because it still has a reasonable time to run.

Para 1.18 of PPG6 suggests that LPAs should have in mind the need to revitalise town centres when they are asked to renew unimplemented permissions for town centre uses in out of centre locations.

Steps for the Applicant:

1 Apply in writing to the LPA, identifying the original permission. There is no special form but Form 21A is a suggested format.

2 The requirements of section 65 of the 1990 Act and Arts. 6 and 7 of the GDPO apply, which means that the applicant must notify all owners and tenants using Form 1C (Procedure 1).

3 The applicant must certify that he has notified all owners and tenants or has tried to do so by use of one of Forms 1D to 1G (Procedure 1).

4 A standard fee is payable for all renewal applications.

5 An explanatory note may be helpful, explaining why it has not been possible to implement the permission in the prescribed time.

Steps for the LPA:

1 Acknowledge receipt of the application.

2 Register and publicise the application as required by Art. 25 and Art. 8 of the GDPO.

3 Circulate copies of the application to consultees.

4 Ask for further information if needed.

5 The application should be determined within eight weeks.

6 The applicant has a right of appeal on refusal or non-determination.

FORM 21A
Application letter
Source: RMJM

(a) address of LPA
(b) address of agent or applicant
(c) name of applicant
(d) Ref. number of original planning permission
(e) name of LPA
(f) date of grant of permission
(g) description of proposed development
(h) address or location of proposed development
(i) agent or applicant
(j) date
(k) applicant.

...... (a) .... (b) ......

Dear Sir,

Town and Country Planning Act 1990

APPLICATION FOR RENEWAL OF PLANNING PERMISSION

On behalf of .... (c) we apply for the renewal of the

planning permission ref. .... (d) granted by .... (e) Council

on .... (f) for .... (g) at .... (h)

We enclose an explanatory note giving reasons for our request and enclose a

cheque for £ .... being the application fee under the relevant Regulations.

Signed .... (i)   Date .... (j)

on behalf of .... (k)

22

Application for Prior Approval for Demolition

Demolition, or the building operation involved in demolition, was brought into the definition of development requiring planning permission by the PCA (section 13 (1)) only to be partially exempted by section 13 (2) and Part 31 of the GPDO as permitted development, and further modified by the Town and Country Planning (Demolition – Description of Buildings) Direction 1995.

Several categories of building are excluded from the definition of demolition as development. Listed buildings, those in conservation areas and scheduled monuments are excluded because their demolition is controlled by other legislation. Buildings of less than 50 m³ are excluded, as are gates, fences, walls or other means of enclosure (so long as they are not in conservation areas). But, most significantly, any building which is not a dwelling or adjoining a dwelling is excluded. In other words, offices, factories and churches can be demolished without prior approval under the planning act. Partial demolition of any building is regarded as structural alteration and is thus a building operation that requires planning consent in the normal way.

The net effect is that anyone wanting to demolish a dwelling or a building adjoining a dwelling must first apply to the LPA for a determination as to whether prior approval of the authority will be required as to the method of demolition and the proposed restoration of the site.

Exemptions include buildings that are affected by a planning permission for redevelopment and buildings affected by obligations under section 106 agreements.

Steps for the Applicant

1 Apply to the LPA in writing with a description of the proposed development and a statement that a site notice has been posted (Form 22A).

2 Display a site notice for not less than 21 days in the period 28 days after the application was submitted.

3 A fee is payable.

4 Demolition shall not begin until:

(a) written notice from the LPA that prior approval is not required
(b) the granting of approval within 28 days of the application
(c) the expiry of 28 days without notification.

5 Demolition shall be in accordance with the terms of approval or the terms of application if there is no approval.

6 Demolition shall be carried out within five years of the date of approval or the date of application if there was no approval.

7 **NB.** 6 weeks' notice must be given to the local authority, adjoining occupiers, the gas and electricity suppliers of the intention to demolish **any** building under section 80 of the Building Act 1984. The LA must respond with a section 81 Notice which may give details of safety measures for adjoining buildings and services.

Relevant LPA Action:

1 The LPA should acknowledge receipt of the application.

2 The LPA must respond within 28 days to the application stating whether or not prior notice is required.

3 LPAs are urged to make prompt decisions and resolve any problems.

**FORM 22A
Application letter**
Source: RMJM

. . . . . . (a) . . . . (b) . . . . . .

Dear Sir,

Town and Country Planning (General Permitted Development) Order 1995, Part 31, A2:

APPLICATION FOR PRIOR APPROVAL FOR DEMOLITION

On behalf of . . . . (c) we apply for a determination

as to whether the prior approval of the . . . . (d)

Council will be required for the demolition of . . . . (e)

We enclose a written description of the development, stating the method of demolition and the proposed restoration of the site.

We declare that a site notice has been posted on or near the land on which the building to be demolished is sited and that it will be left in place for 21 days in the period of 28 days starting with the date of this application.

Signed . . . . (f)   Date . . . . (g)

on behalf of . . . . (h)

(a) address of LPA
(b) address of agent or applicant
(c) name of applicant
(d) name of LPA
(e) address or location of the building
(f) agent or applicant
(g) date
(h) applicant.

SUMMARY OF PROCEDURES

		Applicant must have 'interest' in the land	Source of application form	Section 65 notices or certificates	Site plan required (site edged in red)	Illustrative plans and drawings	Explanatory note	Environmental statement	Fee required
1	Application for full planning permission to develop land	✗	LPA	✓	✓	✓	✓	Maybe	✓
2	Application for listed building consent	✗	LPA	✓	✓	✓	✓	✗	✗
3	Application for conservation area consent	✗	LPA	✓	✓	✓	✓	✗	✗
4	Application for approval of 'conditions' on a planning permission	✓	Form 4A	✗	✗	Only if relevant	✓	✗	✗
5	Application to vary or discharge conditions attached to listed building or conservation area consent	✓	LPA (if none, Form 5A)	✓	✗	✗	✓	✗	✗
6	Application to vary or revoke conditions attached to a planning permission	✗	LPA (if none, Form 6A)	✓	✗	✗	✓	✗	✓
7	Application for a Certificate of Lawful Existing Use or Development	✓	LPA (if none, Form 7A)	✓	✓	Only if relevant	✓	✗	✓
8	Application for approval of reserved matters, following an outline planning permission	✓	LPA (if none, Form 8A)	✗	✗	✓	✓	✗	✓
9	Application for winning or working of minerals	✗	LPA	✓ and s.67	✓	✓	✓	✓	✓
10	Application for express consent to display an advertisement	✗	LPA (if none, Form 10A)	✗	✓	✓	Maybe	✗	✓
11	Application for hazardous substances consent	✓	LPA	✓	✓	Check with LPA	✓	Maybe	✓
12	Application for a Certificate of Lawfulness of Proposed Use or Development	✗	LPA	✗	✓	✓	Only if complex	✗	✓
13	Application for scheduled monument consent	✓	Form 13A	✓	✓	✓	✓	✗	✗
14	Application to fell or lop a tree covered by the Forestry Act 1967	✓	Forestry Commission	✗	✓	✗	✗	✗	✗
15	Application to fell a tree subject to a tree preservation order	✗	LPA (if none, Form 15A)	✗	✓	✓	Maybe	✗	✗
16	Notification to fell or lop a tree in a conservation area	✗	Form 16A	✗	✓	✓	✗	✗	✗
17	Notification under Circular 18/84 for Crown or local authority development	✗ ✓	Procedure 17	✓	✓	✓	✓	Maybe	✗
18	Application for outline planning permission to develop land	✗	LPA	✓	✓	Maybe	✓	Maybe	✓
19	Application for a certificate of immunity from listing	✓	Form 19A	✗	✓	✗	✗	✗	✗
20	Determination of the need for an environmental assessment	✗	Procedure 20	✓	✓	✓	✓	✓	No extra fee
21	Application for renewal of planning permission	✗	Procedure 21	✓	✓	✗	✓	✗	✓
22	Application for prior approval for demolition	✗	Form 22A	✓	✓	✓	✓	✗	✓

Miscellaneous definitions from the 1990 Act

'aerodrome'	means any area of land or water designed, equipped, set apart or commonly used for the landing or departure of aircraft. Includes a helicopter landing pad, whether on the ground, on the roof of a building, or elsewhere.
'area of outstanding natural beauty'	an area designated as such by an order made under section 87 of the National Parks and Access to the Countryside Act 1949.
'building'	includes any structure or erection and any part of a building as so defined, but not including plant or machinery.
'building or works'	includes waste materials, refuse and other matters deposited on land.
'caravan'	means any structure (but not a tent or railway carriage) designed or adapted for human habitation which is capable of being moved (and including a motor vehicle so designed or adopted) provided its dimensions do not exceed 18.3m in length, 6.1m in width and 3.0m in overall height of living accommodation.
'caravan site'	means land on which a caravan is stationed for the purpose of human habitation.
'cemetery'	includes a burial ground or any other place of interment for the dead.
'development'	means the carrying out of building, engineering, mining or other operations in, on, over or under land, or the making of any material change in the use of any buildings or other land. For the purposes of the Act 'Building operations' includes (a) demolition, (b) rebuilding, (c) structural alterations or additions to a building, (d) other operations normally undertaken by persons carrying on business as a builder.
'erection'	in relation to buildings includes extension, alteration and re-erection.
'existing'	in relation to any building or other structure, means existing immediately before the carrying out of development.
'felling'	includes wilfully destroying by any means.
'flat'	means a separate, self-contained set of premises constructed for use as a dwelling and part of a building from some other part of which it is divided horizontally.
'forestry'	means the growing of a utilisable crop of timber.
'general development order'	means a development order applicable to all land in England and Wales (subject to specified exceptions).
'glasshouse'	means a building which has not less than three-quarters of its total external area comprised of glass or other translucent material, is designed for the production of horticultural procedure and is used, or is to be used, solely for agriculture.
'height'	height of a building is construed as meaning height when measured from ground level. Ground level in this context means the level of the surface of the ground immediately adjacent to the building in question or, where the level is not uniform, the level of the highest part of the surface of the ground adjacent to the building.

'interest'	in relation to land includes any estate in land and any right over land, whether by virtue of ownership, licence or agreement.
'land'	includes buildings, and land covered with water.
'means of access'	includes any means of access, private or public, for vehicles or pedestrians.
'minerals'	includes all minerals and substances in or under land, but not including peat cut for purposes other than sale.
'mining operations'	means the winning and working of minerals in, on or under land, whether by surface or underground working.
'occupier'	means in relation to land or buildings, a person who, by virtue of an estate or interest held by him, is entitled to possession of the land or building.
'office'	includes a bank, estate agent, building society or employment agency, car hire or driving school offices, but not including a post office or betting office.
'original'	means, in relation to a building existing on 1 July 1948, as existing on that date; for a building constructed later than that, as the building was originally constructed.
'painting'	includes any application of colour.
'post office'	does not include any building used primarily for sorting mail or administration.
'private way'	means a highway or footpath which is not maintainable at the public expense.
'satellite antenna'	means apparatus designed for transmitting microwave radio energy to satellites or receiving it from them, and includes any mountings or brackets attached to such apparatus.
'shop'	means a building used for carrying on of any retail trade or retail business, as categorised in Class A1 of the use class order.
'site'	means the whole area of land within a single unit of occupation.
'site of special scientific interest'	means land to which section 28(1) of the Wildlife and Countryside Act 1981 applies.
'terraced house'	means a dwellinghouse (see note 14) that is: • situated in a row of three or more dwellinghouses and, • sharing a party wall with the dwellinghouse on either side of it, but including the dwellinghouses at each end of a row.
'unadopted street'	means a street (as defined by the Public Health Act 1936) not maintainable at the public expense.
'warehouse'	means a building used for storage or distribution purposes.
'wholesale warehouse'	means a building where wholesale business is transacted and goods are stored or displayed, but only incidentally to the transaction of that business.

Supporting Material

Planning applications for all but the smallest developments should be accompanied by some form of written explanation and usually by extra illustrative material. The Explanatory Statement 'supporting information to the planning application', or Planning Statement as it is sometimes called, should be directed to the planning officer and the planning committee and should address the issue of how the proposal satisfies the relevant planning policies. The Explanatory Statement is part of the application, and therefore in the public domain and available for inspection, but it does not form part of the planning consent were it to be granted, unless specifically referred to in the conditions attached to the consent.

One purpose of the Explanatory Statement is to describe to the planning authority, as objectively as possible, the content of the proposed development and the effect it will have on the site and its surroundings. It should therefore contain a description of the existing site, the activities on it and the surrounding area, followed by a description of the proposals and how they will affect the existing situation. The planning officer may well use extracts from the report to prepare his own report to the planning committee.

The degree of detail and the range of topics covered in the Explanatory Statement will obviously depend on the nature and scale of the proposed development, the type of application, and the planning policies being addressed. Below is a checklist of topics that may need to be covered. It is unlikely that all the topics would need to be covered in any one application.

Contents of a typical Explanatory Statement

General introduction: Site location; type of application (full/outline/listed building/ reserved matter, etc.); brief description of the development; reasons for the development; the authors of the report and their professional standing.

The applicant: The interest of the applicant in the site (owner, option holder, etc.); extent and current use of adjoining land/buildings if owned by the applicant; any future plans for both the site and the adjoining land; and previous experience of similar developments (if applicable).

Description of the application site: Site area, boundary, configuration, orientation, topography and geology; general condition; vehicular and pedestrian access to the site; description and areas of existing use(s); buildings and infrastructure on the site including number of parking spaces etc; site drainage; microclimate; landscape features and other notable natural features. Use photographs to illustrate the site (see Additional Illustrative Material below).

APPENDIX B

Physical context of the site:

Surrounding land uses; proximity to existing residential areas; proximity to transport facilities and other infrastructure; significant views, landmarks and natural features; visibility from surrounding areas.

Statutory influences on and around the site:

Planning policy context; land use designation; special policies in the development plan relating to the site; relevant supplementary planning guidance; conservation areas, listed buildings, TPOs, AONBs, SSSIs, areas of archaeological importance, scheduled ancient monuments, contamination, Green Belts, National Parks, areas of special advertisement control, Article 4 directions, public rights of way, etc.

Site selection:

Other sites investigated (if applicable), criteria used to select site, suitability of the selected site.

Proposed development

The general design and size of the project (gross external floor areas by land use); site access (vehicular and pedestrian); site formation/preparation works (including demolition work); site services; parking and service provision; activities to be carried out on the site and number of people to be employed/accommodated; estimated traffic generation (during and after construction) of HGVs and cars; trees to be felled/retained; proposed landscaping or restoration of the site (if applicable); phasing of the development; hours of operation (during construction and use); special licences required; disposal of sewage and waste; special features.

Impact studies (if appropriate)

- Traffic: estimated traffic impact on surrounding network (during and after construction) of HGVs and cars; effect on public transport facilities;
- Retail: type of goods to be sold and impact on existing competing retail centres;
- Environmental issues: nature conservation issues, archaeological desk study, contamination studies, noise/dust pollution, etc.

Other issues:

Loss of existing use(s) and natural resources (e.g. agricultural land); future expansion plans; special measures to deal with contamination; proposed changes to public rights of way, road closures, etc.; heads of terms for the section 106 and/or section 278 agreements (if required); acceptable planning conditions (if appropriate).

Consultations:

Measures taken to consult with the local authority and statutory and other consultees, and general response; measures taken to inform the public, adjoining owners and local amenity groups, of the proposed development, and response to the consultation.

Summary:

Short description of the development and a summary of its positive and negative impacts (compared to a do-nothing scenario).

It is important in an Explanatory Statement to explain that the site does *not* contain elements that might have a bearing on the planning situation, i.e. it should be stated, for example: 'the site has no listed buildings, nor is in, nor borders, a conservation area, and there are no trees with tree preservation orders'. As regards impacts, the same advice applies, if no change occurs to some particular aspect as a result of the development, such as traffic generation, it needs to be pointed out.

The objective is that by the time the planning officer has reached the end of the Explanatory Statement, he or she has an accurate picture of the site and is in no doubt about the content of the proposed development and the extent of the impacts (both positive and negative) that the proposals are likely to have. In particular, it will be clear that the proposal does not contravene the relevant development plan policies, or if it does, that the impacts have been satisfactorily ameliorated.

Planning description

The wording of the description of the proposed development should include all the different land uses proposed, including, where appropriate, reference to site formation works, internal roads, landscaping and car parking. Where floor areas are quoted, then these should be total gross external areas, in square metres (square feet are no longer accepted). A description accompanying an outline application can include words such as 'up to' or 'approximately' and the description can be very broad such as 'A university campus' or 'Industrial estate for B2 use'. In a detailed application, the description needs to be exact.

Application site boundary

Careful consideration needs to given to the planning application boundary, the so-called 'red line drawing'. It should be remembered that the red line should encompass all the development, as described in the planning description (see above). It is a common mistake to draw the application boundary too tightly (in order to minimise the planning application fees) and to exclude parts of the site which, whilst not needed for actual building work, are used for additional or displaced car parking, for example, which in turn is necessary for the rest of the proposal to function properly.

It is also better to draw the red line larger so as to include areas around the periphery that will be landscaped and areas that are likely to be occupied during the construction period by the contractor's huts and parking/storage areas. Although soft landscape does not require planning permission, it should still be included within the planning application boundary and may form an important planning consideration. There is no reason why the 'red line' cannot be a series of defined areas, or islands, so long as the significance of each area is explained.

It should be noted that where an application includes works to a trunk road, the road itself should not be within the red-line boundary. Works to other categories of road, with the exception of 'white-lining', however, should be included.

Obviously, where the red line encloses land outside the control of the applicant, ie., the applicant is not the 'owner', then formal notice needs to be served on the owner, whether private or public, including the local authority determining the application.

With the increased use of Computer Aided Design (CAD), more and more 'red-line drawings' are being prepared on computers. It should be remembered that the red line should lie *inside* the boundary line and not on it or outside it. Calculation of the site area by computer should be carried out on a separate drawing, where the line is actually on top of the boundary. If this is not done then the site will be under-sized by half the thickness of the line around the entire length of the boundary.

Adjoining land in the control of the applicant

The planning application must include a plan showing the extent of the land adjoining the application site that is in the control of the applicant. This is usually illustrated as a 'blue line' on the application site plan. Only if the 'blue line' land actually adjoins the application site need it be shown on the plan. As with the red line, the blue line should be drawn so as to lie inside the boundary line.

Additional illustrative material

Drawings

The type of drawing needed for planning application purposes is not the same as that needed for tendering purposes, for example. Planning officers are very rarely architects and therefore the drawings should be kept clear of extraneous description and be easy to understand. Needless to say, they should be accurate, complete and drawn to a recognisable scale. In the case of in-fill sites, care is needed in drawing the adjoining buildings accurately. Additional drawings to those requested in the application forms should only be included if they add to the understanding of the proposed scheme. Coloured-up elevations can be helpful for the planning committee to visualise the proposals.

Photographs

Photographs of the site and its surroundings can be informative and are recommended to be included in an Explanatory Statement. A plan showing where each photograph was taken from must be provided.

Models

Experience has shown that models do not always help the planning case. Viewing the scheme from above, a bird's eye view, misrepresents how the proposed development will actually be seen which is more likely to be from ground level. The effect of the type of model employed also needs to be assessed — for example, a block model can only illustrate certain basic aspects of a scheme and consequently could be misinterpreted by a lay audience.

Perspective sketches	Perspective sketches have become somewhat devalued as a means of illustrating development proposals. Accuracy is essential because 'artistic licence' can be mistaken for deliberate misrepresentation.
Photomontages	Computer-generated photomontages taken from ground level are by far the most informative illustrative material to include in an Explanatory Statement. Coupled with 'before' photographs of the site, the changes to the site are not only accurately portrayed but are taken from a viewpoint that passers-by will have and therefore relevant to an assessment of visual impact.
Video fly-bys	Simulated views of the proposed development, in fly-by form, can be very effective if the viewpoint taken is at passer-by level and on a route that is actually possible. Aerial views, however, can be counter-productive, as described above under Models.
Samples of facing materials	At some stage in the approval process there is a need for the facing materials of proposed buildings to be approved by the local planning authority. Although external materials are usually made a planning condition, there are advantages if at the original application stage samples of the proposed facing materials are included. If bricks are used, then the mortar colour should be included in the sample. Illustrating the various materials is best done by mounting them all on a titled panel, rather than having them loose.

APPENDIX C

Scale of Fees

Section 87 of the Local Government, Planning and Land Act 1980 gives the Secretary of State power to prescribe fees for most types of application under the planning legislation. General guidance on the provisions of the fees scheme is given in Circ. 31/92.

Fees are required for:

- full and outline applications, including retrospective applications where development has already taken place (Procedures 1 and 18) renewals (Procedure 21) and applications to vary or remove conditions (Procedure 16)
- applications for approval of reserved matters (Procedure 8)
- applications for consent to display advertisements (Procedure 10)
- applications for certificates of lawfulness of existing or proposed use or development (CLEUDS and CLOPUDs, Procedures 7 and 12)
- applications for prior approval determination for permitted development (Procedure 22)

Cheques or money orders should be made payable to the LPA. Calculating the correct fee can be complicated and for all but straightforward cases Circ. 31/92 should be referred to. If an application is submitted with the wrong fee, or with a faulty or dishonoured cheque, processing the application will cease until the correct fee is received. In most cases the application will start again at the beginning of the process, as if it had just been received. Thus, an error over the fee could result in considerable delay. Fees are increased every two years or so. The fees set out below came into force in October 1997 under SI 1997 No. 37 and it is therefore sensible to check with the LPA on the latest situation. Most LPAs send out a schedule of charges with planning application forms but in order to minimise delays it is prudent to check with the LPA before submitting a cheque. Note the following definitions:

'site area' — this should be taken as the land to which the application relates shown edged in red on the plan accompanying the application.

'floor space' — wherever a fee is based on floor space, this should be taken as the gross amount (all storeys) to be created by the development, calculated by external measurement.

'... or part thereof' — where the floor space or site area of the proposal is not an exact multiple of the unit of measurement provided by the fees scale, the amount remaining is taken to be a whole unit for fee purposes.

'dwellinghouses'
for fee purposes. dwellinghouse is defined as a building or part of a building which is used as a single private dwellinghouse and for no other purpose. Note that this differs from the GPDO definition (see note 14) and includes flats, maisonettes, and houses in multiple occupation. Check with the LPA if in any doubt.

Outline applications

Erection of dwellings.
£190 per dwellinghouse. Maximum £9,500.

Erection of agricultural buildings.
£190 per 0.1 ha. Maximum £4,750 (= 2.5 ha).

Other outline applications.
£190 per 0.1 ha (or part thereof) of site area. Maximum £4,750 (= 2.5 ha).

Full applications and 'reserved matters'

Alterations, extensions etc. to private dwellings.
£90 per dwellinghouse. Maximum £190.

Erection of dwellings.
£190 per dwellinghouse created. Maximum £9,500 (= 50 dwellings).

Erection of buildings other than dwellings, glasshouses, or plant and machinery.
Works not creating more than 40 m^2 of additional floor space – £95. More than 40 m^2 but not more than 75 m^2 of additional floor space – £190. Each additional 75 m^2 (or part thereof) – £190. Maximum £9,500 (= 3,750 m^2).

Erection of agricultural buildings up to 465 m^2 (not including dwellings).
£35.

Erection of agricultural buildings above 465 m^2 (not including dwellings or glasshouses).
Works creating more than 465 m^2 and up to 540 m^2 – £190. Each additional 75 m^2 (or part thereof) – £190. Maximum £9,500 (= 4,215 m^2).

Erection of glasshouses and polytunnels.
Works creating more than 465 m^2 – £1,085 (otherwise £35).

Erection, alteration or replacement of plant and machinery.
£190 per 0.1 ha (or part thereof) of site area. Maximum £9,500 (= 5 ha).

Approval of reserved matters where flat rate (below) does not apply.
The fee is based on floor space/numbers of dwellinghouses involved. In principle this fee is the same as for full application but the rules can be complicated. Refer to Circ. 31/92 and SI 1997 No. 37 or its successor. Consult LPA if in doubt.

Other applications

Exploratory drilling for oil or natural gas.
£190 per 0.1 ha (or part thereof) of site area. Maximum £14,250 (= 7.5 ha).

Winning, working, storage of minerals, etc. and waste disposal.
£95 per 0.1 ha (or part thereof) of site area. Maximum £14,250 (= 15 ha).

Car parks, service roads or other accesses.
£95 (serving existing uses only).

Other operations on land.
£95 per 0.1 ha (or part thereof) of site area. Maximum £950 (= 1 ha).

For non-compliance with conditions including retention of temporary buildings, etc.	£95 (if not exempt as a revision).
Change of use to or sub-division of dwellings.	£190 per additional dwelling created. Maximum £9,500.
Other changes of use except waste or minerals.	£190.
Buildings on the site of demolished buildings.	The fee due is calculated on total floor space created by the new development, regardless of whether an existing building stood on the site or not.
Mixed category applications with residential use.	The fee for an application having a mix of uses, including residential use, is calculated by adding together the fees appropriate for each development. This applies whether the two types are combined or in separate buildings. Shared areas, e.g. foyers, are allocated *pro rata* to the floor of each type of development. For outline applications in this category, the fee is simply derived from the total site area.
Mixed category applications not including residential uses.	Where an application relates to two or more categories, but not including residential uses, only the highest of the fees calculated under those categories is charged.
Determination of prior approval for demolition, agricultural buildings or telecommunications works.	£35.
Variation or removal of a condition.	£95.
Renewal of temporary conditions.	£95.
Renewal of permission where work has not started and time limit not expired.	£95.

Certificate of Lawful Development for:
    existing use or development (CLEUD)
    proposed use or development (CLOPUD)
	
	Same fee as equivalent planning application.
	Half fee of equivalent planning application.

Hazardous Substance Consents

no one substance exceeds the controlled quantity	£250.
in excess of twice the controlled quantity	£400.
removal of a condition on a consent	£200.
continuation upon partial change in ownership	£200.

Advertisements

Relating to the business on the premises.	£50.
Advance signs directing the public to a business.	£50.
Other advertisements.	£190.

Concessionary fees and exemptions

Works to improve the disabled person's access to a public building or to improve his access, safety, health or comfort at his dwellinghouse.	No fee.

Applications by parish, etc. councils (applies also to advertisement applications).	Half the normal fee.
Applications required because of the removal of permitted development rights by a condition or by an Article 4 direction.	No fee.
Playing fields (for sports clubs, etc.).	£190.
A revised or fresh application for development (or advertisement) of the same character or description within 12 months of refusal, or of the making of the earlier application if withdrawn, or within 12 months of expiry of the statutory eight week period where the applicant has appealed to the Secretary of State on the grounds of non-determination.	No fee.
A revised or fresh application for development of the same character or description within 12 months of receiving permission.	No fee.
Duplicate applications made by the same applicant.	Normal fee for both applications.
Alternative applications for one site.	Highest of the fees applicable for each alternative, plus a sum equal to half the fees applicable to all the other applications.
Development crossing planning authority boundaries, requiring more than one application.	Only one fee, paid to the authority having the larger proportion of the site but calculated for the whole scheme, and subject to a special ceiling. Calculating the fee is complex and beyond the scope of this guide. Refer either to Circ. 31/92, or the LPA to whom the fee is payable.

The fee is always determined on the basis of the application as made. Even if permission is granted for a development of a different size, or if the application is adjusted in the course of discussions, there is no provision for adjustment to the fee payable, either in the form of refunds or additional charges.

Planning fees are always calculated so as to round up to the nearest whole multiple of an area rate, so that the fee on an outline application for 1.05 ha would be rounded up to 11 × £190 = £2090.

If there is an unresolved disagreement between the applicant and the LPA about the amount of the fee payable, there is no special disputes procedure. However, if the applicant appeals against non-determination, the Secretary of State will take a view on whether the fee requirements have been met (as part of the process of determining whether the eight-week period has elapsed and he has jurisdiction). Only in the context of a non-determination appeal has the Secretary of State power to rule on the correctness of the fee for a particular application.

APPENDIX D

Use classes

A use class order, made under section 55 of the 1990 Act by the Secretary of State, specifies particular groups of uses within which a change of use from one purpose to another does not constitute development (and does not therefore need permission).

The current order is the Town and Country Planning (Use Classes) Order 1987. A use omitted from the list is treated as a one-off, or *sui generis*. It should be noted that these use classes do not apply in Scotland, check with the LPA.

The Order divides uses into four parts; Part A, uses generally found in a shopping area; Part B, a business and industrial use class; Part C, a residential class; and Part D, non-residential institutions and leisure class. The details are as follows:

PART A, Class A1
Shops

Use for all or any of the following purposes:

(a) for the retail sale of goods other than hot food
(b) as a post office
(c) for the sale of tickets or as a travel agency
(d) for the sale of sandwiches or other cold food for consumption off the premises
(e) for hairdressing
(f) for the direction of funerals
(g) for the display of goods for sale
(h) for the hiring out of domestic or personal goods or articles
(i) for the washing or cleaning of clothes or fabrics on the premises
(j) for the reception of goods to be washed, cleaned or repaired,

where the sale, display or service is to members of the public.
Note: warehouse clubs are treated as retail businesses.

Class A2
Financial and professional services

Use for the provision of:

(a) financial services, or
(b) professional services (other than health or medical), or
(c) any other services (including use as a betting office) which is appropriate to a shopping area,

where the services are provided principally to visiting members of the public. A solicitor's office catering principally for visiting members of the public has been held to qualify as A2.

Class A3
Food and drink

Use for the sale of food or drink for consumption on the premises or of hot food for consumption off the premises.

PART B, Class B1
Business

Use for all or any of the following purposes:

(a) as an office other than a use within class A2 (financial and professional services), or
(b) for research and development of products or processes, or
(c) for any industrial process,

being a use which can be carried out in any residential area without detriment to the amenity of that area by reason of noise, vibration, smell, fumes, smoke, soot, ash, dust or grit.

Class B2
General industrial

Use for the carrying on of an industrial process other than one falling within class B1 above.

Classes B3 to B7
(deleted)

Special industry groups were deleted from the Use Classes Order 1987 by the Town and Country Planning (Use Classes) (Amendments) Order 1995. The five special industry groups dealt with works under the Alkali Regulations (B3); metal smelting, refining, forging and finishing (B4); the getting, dressing and treatment of inorganic minerals (B5); the distilling, processing and recovery etc. of organic oils and chemicals (B6); and the processing of animal products (B7).

Class B8
Storage or distribution

Use for storage or as a distribution centre.

Part C, Class C1
Hotels

Use as a hotel, boarding or guest house where, in each case, no significant element of care is provided.

Note: hostels were excluded from Class C1 by the Town and Country Planning (Use Classes) (Amendment) Order 1994, and are now a *sui generis* use.

Class C2
Residential institutions

Use for the provision of residential accommodation and care to people in need of care (other than a use within Class C3):

- use as a hospital or nursing home
- use as a residential school, college or training centre.

Class C3
Dwellinghouses

Use as a dwellinghouse (whether or not sole or main residence):

(a) by a single person or by people living together as a family, or
(b) by not more than six residents living together as a single household (including a household where care is provided).

APPENDIX D

PART D, Class D1
Non-residential institutions

Any use not including a residential use:

(a) providing any medical or health services except the use of premises attached to a residence of a consultant or practitioner
(b) as a crêche, day nursery or day centre
(c) for the provision of education
(d) for the display of works of art (other than for sale or hire)
(e) as a museum
(f) as a public library or public reading room
(g) as a public hall or exhibition hall
(h) for, or related to, public worship or religious instruction.

Class D2
Assembly and leisure

Use as:

(a) a cinema,
(b) concert hall
(c) bingo hall or casino
(d) dance hall or
(e) a swimming bath, skating rink, gymnasium or area for other indoor or outdoor sports or recreations, not involving motorised vehicles or firearms.

Notable *sui generis* uses

These are uses for which no classes are specified (not exhaustive):

- theatre, amusement arcade or centre, or fun fair
- for the washing or cleaning of clothes or fabrics in coin operated machines or on premises at which the goods to be cleaned are received direct from the visiting public
- for the sale of fuel or display for sale of motor vehicles
- for a taxi business or business for the hire of motor vehicles
- as a scrapyard, or a yard for the storage or distribution of minerals or the breaking of motor vehicles
- prisons or remand centres.

Permitted development

Some types of development are automatically permitted without the need to seek planning consent. Permission is granted under development orders made by the Secretary of State under sections 59–61 of the 1990 Act. Development orders may be either general orders (GDOs) applicable to all land (subject to any specified exception), or special orders (SDOs) applying only to certain specified land.

Both GDOs and SDOs are subject to change and it is important to check the current situation with the LPA before proceeding with development. The basis of the GDOs is the Town and Country Planning (General Permitted Development) Order 1995 (SI 1995 No. 418).

There are 35 categories (called 'Parts') of permitted development with each 'Part' divided into 'Classes'. For the sake of brevity, only Part 1 has been covered in full, the majority of the other 32 Parts have only been summarised.

Note that where enlargements to buildings are involved, the permitted allowance is granted on the basis of the original size of the building, or its size in 1948, not in relation to any subsequent enlargements.

Definitions of the various terms in this appendix are contained in Appendix A.

PART 1
Development within the curtilage of a single dwellinghouse

Dwellinghouse in this context has the meaning given in note 14. More stringent conditions apply to permitted development in the case of dwellinghouses within so-called 'article 1(5) land', e.g. conservation areas, National Parks and AONBs. Note, 'the original dwellinghouse' means the house as first built, or as it stood on 1 July 1948 if built before then.

Class A

The enlargement, improvement or other alteration (including extensions) of a dwellinghouse is permitted development so long as the cubic content of the original dwellinghouse (by external measurement) is not exceeded by more than 70 m^3, or 15% subject to a maximum of 115 m^3, whichever is the greater. In the case of terraced houses (including 'end-of-terrace' houses) and houses within 'article 1(5) land', this is reduced to 50 m^3 or 10% respectively, still with a maximum of 115 m^3.

All the above are subject to important restrictions:

(i)   the height of the enlarged, improved or altered building not to exceed the highest part of the roof of the original dwelling

(ii)   no part of the building to project beyond the forward most part of the original dwellinghouse fronting a highway, unless more than 20 m from the highway

(iii)   any extension within 2 m of the boundary must not exceed 4 m in height

(iv)   the total area of ground covered by buildings (other than the original dwellinghouse) does not exceed 50% of the total area of the curtilage excluding the ground area of the original dwellinghouse

(v)   the development does not consist of or include the installation, alteration or replacement of a satellite antenna

(vi)   development is not within the curtilage of a listed building

(vii) the development does not consist of or include an alteration to any part of the roof

(viii) in the case of a dwelling on article 1(5) land, development is not permitted if it consists of or includes cladding of part of the exterior with stone, artificial stone, timber, plastic or tiles.

Any building greater than 10 m^3 should be treated as the enlargement of the dwellinghouse for all purposes, including calculating cubic content, where the dwellinghouse is on article 1(5) land, or would be within 5 m of any part of the dwellinghouse. Also, where any part of the dwellinghouse would be within 5 m of an existing building within the same curtilage, that building shall be treated as forming part of the resulting building for the purpose of calculating the cubic content.

Class B

The enlargement of a dwellinghouse consisting of an addition or alteration to its roof is permitted development, so long as:

(i)   the height of the highest part of the existing roof is not exceeded

(ii)   no part of the addition extends beyond the plane of any existing roof slope which fronts any highway

(iii) the increase in the cubic content of the dwellinghouse would be less than 40 m^3 in the case of a terraced house, or 50 m^3 in any other case

(iv) the cubic content of the resulting building would not exceed that of the original dwellinghouse

     (a) in the case of a terrace house by more than 50 m^3 or 10%, whichever is the greater,

     (b) in any other case, by more than 70 m^3 or 15%, whichever is the greater, or

     (c) in any case, by more than 115 m^3.

(v)   the dwellinghouse is not on article 1(5) land.

Class C

Any other alteration to the roof of a dwellinghouse is permitted development, so long as it would not result in a material alteration to the shape of the dwellinghouse.

Class D

The erection or construction of a porch outside any external door of a dwellinghouse is permitted development, so long as:

(i) the ground area (measured externally) of the structure would not exceed 3 m^2

(ii) any part of the structure would be no more than 3 m above ground level, or

(iii) the structure would not be within 2 m of any boundary of the curtilage of the dwellinghouse with a highway.

Class E

The provision is permitted within the curtilage of a dwellinghouse of any building or enclosure, swimming or other pool required for a purpose incidental to the enjoyment of the dwellinghouse as such, or the maintenance, improvement or other alteration of such a building or enclosure.

However, development is not permitted by Class E if:

(i) it relates to a dwelling or a satellite antenna

(ii) any part of the building or enclosure to be constructed would be nearer to any highway which bounds the curtilage than

(a) the part of the original dwellinghouse nearest to that highway, or

(b) 20 m – whichever is nearer to the highway

(iii) where the building to be constructed would be greater than 10 m^3, any part of it would be within 5 m of any part of the dwellinghouse

(iv) the height of that building or enclosure would exceed

(a) 4 m, in the case of a building with a ridged roof, or

(b) 3 m, in any other case

(v) the total area of ground covered by buildings or enclosures within the curtilage (other than the original dwellinghouse) would exceed 50% of the total area of the curtilage (excluding the ground area of the original dwellinghouse) or

(vi) in the case of any article 1(5) land or land within the curtilage of a listed building, it would consist of the provision, alteration or improvement of a building with a cubic content greater than 10 m^3.

For the purposes of Class E, 'purpose incidental to the enjoyment of the dwellinghouse' includes the keeping of poultry, bees, pet animals, birds or other livestock for the domestic needs or personal enjoyment of the occupants of the dwellinghouse.

Class F

The provision within the curtilage of a dwellinghouse of a hard surface for any purpose incidental to the enjoyment of the dwellinghouse as such is permitted development.

APPENDIX E

Class G

The erection or provision within the curtilage of a dwellinghouse of a container for the storage of oil for domestic heating is permitted development so long as:

(i) the capacity of the container would not exceed 3500 litres,
(ii) no part of the container would be more than 3 m above ground level, or
(iii) no part of the container would be nearer to any highway which bounds the curtilage than:

(a) the part of the original building nearest to that highway, or
(b) 20 m, whichever is nearer.

Class H

The installation, alteration or replacement of a satellite antenna on a dwellinghouse or within the curtilage of a dwellinghouse is permitted development.

Development is not permitted by Class H if:

(i) the size of the antenna (excluding any projecting feed element) when measured in any dimension exceeds 45 cm if installed on a chimney; 90 cm on or within the curtilage other than on the chimney; 70 cm in any other case;
(ii) the highest part of the antenna on a roof or a chimney would be higher than the roof or the chimney respectively;
(iii) there is any other satellite antenna on the dwellinghouse or within its curtilage
(iv) in the case of Article 1(5) land the antenna is on a chimney; a building which is higher than 15 m; or on a roof slope which faces a waterway in the Broads or a highway elsewhere.

For the purposes of Part 1:
'resulting building' means the dwellinghouse as enlarged, improved or altered, taking into account any enlargement improvement or alteration to the original dwellinghouse, whether permitted by this Part or not.

PART 2
Minor operations
Class A

The erection, construction, maintenance, improvement or alteration of a gate, fence, wall or other means of enclosure is permitted, so long as:

(i) its height, if constructed adjacent to a highway would not exceed one metre above ground level
(ii) the height of any other gate, fence, wall or means of enclosure would not exceed two metres above ground level;
(iii) the height of any improved or altered means of enclosure does not exceed its former height or the heights referred to above;
(iv) it would not involve development within the curtilage of, or to a gate, fence, wall or other means of enclosure surrounding, a listed building.

Class B	The formation, laying out and construction of a means of access to a highway which is not a trunk road or a classified road, is permitted, where that access is required in connection with development permitted by any Class in Schedule 2 of the GPDO (other than by Class A of this Part).
Class C	The painting of the exterior of any building or work is permitted, except where the painting is for the purpose of advertisement, announcement or direction.

PART 3
Changes of use

Class A	Development is permitted consisting of a change of the use of a building to a use falling within Class A1 (shops) from a use falling within Class A3 (food and drink) or from a use for the sale, or display for sale, of motor vehicles.
Class B	Development is permitted consisting of a change of the use of a building

(i) to a use falling within Class B1 (business) from any use falling within Class B2 (general industrial) or B8 (storage and distribution), where the floor space does not exceed 235 m^2

(ii) to a use falling within Class B8 (storage and distribution) from any use falling within Class B1 (business) or B2 (general industrial), where the floor space does not exceed 235 m^2.

Class C	Development is permitted consisting of a change of use to a use falling within Class A2 (financial and professional services) from a use falling within Class A3 (food and drink).
Class D	Development is permitted consisting of change of use of any premises with a display window at ground floor level to a use falling within Class A1 (shops) from a use falling within Class A2 (financial and professional services).
Class E	Development is permitted consisting of change in the use of any building or other land from a use permitted by a planning permission granted on an application, to another use which that permission would have specifically authorised when it was granted.
Class F	Change of use is permitted to a mix of Class A1 or Class A2 and a single flat from Class A1 or Class A2 so long as some or all of the Class A1/A2 premises is below the flat. Change of use is also permitted in building with a display window to a mix of Class A2 and single flat from Class A2 so long as the ground floor with the display window is not used for the flat.
Class G	Change of use is permitted to Class A1 or Class A2 from a mix of those uses with a single flat, or, in buildings with a display window,

APPENDIX E

to Class A1 from a mix of A2 and a single flat, but not if the part occupied by the flat was used for Class A1 or A2 immediately prior to being so used.

PART 4
Temporary buildings and uses
Class A

Permitted development includes the provision on land of buildings, moveable structures, works, plant or machinery required temporarily in connection with and for the duration of operations (with the exception of mining operations) being or to be carried out on, in, under or over that or adjoining land.

Class B

The use of any land, but not a caravan site nor land within the curtilage of a building, is permitted for any purpose for not more than 28 days in total in any calendar year, and the provision on the land of any moveable structure for the purposes of the permitted use. Not more than 14 days in total may be for the holding of a market or for motor car and motorcycle racing.

PART 5
Caravan sites
Class A

Permitted development includes the use of land, other than a building, as a caravan site in the circumstances specified in paragraphs 2 to 10 of Schedule 1 to the Caravan Sites and Control of Development Act 1960.

Class B

Development required by the conditions of a site licence for the time being in force under the 1960 Act is permitted.

PART 6
Agricultural buildings and operations
Class A

Permitted development includes the carrying out on agricultural land comprised in an agricultural unit of 5 ha or more:

(i) works for the erection, extension or alteration of a building; or
(ii) any excavation or engineering operations, which are reasonably necessary for the purposes of agriculture within the unit.

In the GPDO there follows an extensive list of exceptions including the erection of a dwelling; the erection, significant extension or alteration of any other building; the formation or alteration of a private right of way; excavations for the deposit of waste; and the proximity of buildings, slurry storage or livestock structures to major roads, aerodromes and protected buildings. The overall effect is that, for many types of development, it is necessary to apply to the LPA for a determination as to whether prior approval is required. This procedure is described, in relation to demolition, in Procedure 22.

158

Class B

On agricultural units between 0.4 ha and 5 ha, permitted development includes:

(i) The extension or alteration of agricultural buildings provided that: dwellings cannot be constructed, extended or altered within the definition; it is more than 5m from the boundary; the increase in volume is less than 10% taken together with other buildings within its curtilage; its height is not increased; if its agricultural use ceases within ten years, then planning consent must be obtained for an alternative use, or the building must be removed.

(ii) The installation of additional or replacement plant or machinery provided that: its height is not greater than that which it replaces; if it is within 3 km of an aerodrome, its height is less than 3 m or 12 m if beyond 3 km; its area is less than 465 m^2.

(iii) The provision, rearrangement or replacement of a sewer, main, pipe, cable or other apparatus.

(iv) The provision, rearrangement or replacement of a private right of way.

(v) The provision of a hard surface of less than 465 m^2.

(vi) The deposit of waste so long as it is not imported for any purpose other than the provision of buildings, rights of way, hard surfaces etc. and so long as the surface of the land is not materially increased.

(vii) The carrying out of various operations connected with fish farming, such as repairing ponds, installation of aeration machinery and the replacement of tanks.

Again, there are many general restrictions which mean that the LPA needs to be consulted, and in all but the most simple cases an application for prior approval will be necessary.

Class C

Mineral working for agricultural purposes is permitted so long as excavation is more than 25 m from a highway, and the excavated minerals are only used on the same agricultural unit for agricultural purposes.

PART 7
Forestry buildings and operations
Class A

The carrying out on land used for the purposes of forestry, including afforestation, is permitted for development reasonably necessary for those purposes consisting of:

(i) works for the erection, extension or alteration of a building (but not a dwelling)

(ii) the formation, alteration or maintenance of private ways

(iii) operations on that land to obtain the materials required for the formation, alteration or maintenance of such ways

(iv) other operations (not including engineering or mining operations), so long as:

(a) the height of any building or works within 3 km of the perimeter of an aerodrome would not exceed 3 m

(b) any part of the development would not be within 25 m of a trunk or classified road.

PART 8
Industrial and warehouse development
Class A

The extension or alteration of an industrial building or a warehouse is permitted, so long as its use remains unchanged and:

(i) the height of the building as extended or altered would not exceed the height of the original building;

(ii) the cubic content of the original building would not be exceeded by more than:
(a) 10% in respect of development on any article 1(5) land
(b) 25% in any other case;

(iii) the floorspace of the original building would not be exceeded by more than
(a) 500 m^2 in respect of development on any article 1(5) land, or
(b) 1000 m^2 in any other case;

(iv) the external appearance of the premises concerned would not be materially affected;

(v) the development would be more than 5 m from any boundary of the curtilage of the premises;

(vi) the development would lead to a reduction in the space available for the parking or turning of vehicles.

Class B

Development on industrial land consisting of:

(i) the installation of additional or replacement plant or machinery,

(ii) the provision, rearrangement or replacement of a sewer, main, pipe, cable or other apparatus, or

(iii) the provision, rearrangement or replacement of a private way, private railway, siding or conveyor is permitted as long as any plant or machinery would not exceed 15 m in height or the height of anything replaced, whichever is the greater.

Class C

The creation of a hard surface within the curtilage of an industrial building or warehouse to be used for the purpose of the undertaking concerned is permitted development.

Class D

Permitted development includes the deposit of waste material resulting from an industrial process on any land used for that purpose on 1 July 1948 whether or not the superficial area or the height of the deposit is extended as a result.

PART 9
Repairs to unadopted streets and private ways
Class A

The carrying out on land within the boundaries of an unadopted street or private way of works required for the maintenance or improvement of the street or way is permitted.

PART 10
Repairs to services
Class A

The carrying out of any works for the purposes of inspecting, repairing or renewing any sewer, main, pipe, cable or other apparatus, including breaking open any land for that purpose is permitted.

PART 11
Development under local or private Acts or orders
Class A

Permitted development includes development authorised by:

(i)   a local or private Act of Parliament;
(ii) an order approved by both Houses of Parliament; or
(iii) any order made under section 14 or 16 of the Harbours Act 1964;

which designates specifically the nature of the development authorised and the land upon which it may be carried out.

PART 12
Development by local authorities
Class A

Permitted development includes the erection or construction and the maintenance, improvement or other alteration by a local authority or by an urban development corporation of:

(i)   any small ancillary building, works or equipment on land belonging to or maintained by them required for the purposes of any function exercised by them on that land otherwise than as statutory undertakers;
(ii) lamp standards, information kiosks, passenger shelters, public shelters and seats, telephone boxes, fire alarms, public drinking fountains, horse-troughs, refuse bins or baskets, barriers, etc.

Class B

The deposit by a local authority of waste material on any land used for that purpose on 1 July 1948 whether or not the superficial area or the height of the deposit is extended as a result is permitted.

PART 13
Development by local highway authorities
Class A

The carrying out by a local highway authority on land outside but adjoining the boundary of an existing highway of works required for or incidental to the maintenance or improvement of the highway is permitted.

APPENDIX E

PART 14
Development by
drainage bodies
Class A

Development by a drainage body in, on or under a watercourse or land drainage works in connection with the improvement, maintenance or repair of the watercourse or works, is permitted development.

PART 15
Development by the
Environment Agency
Class A

Development by the Environment Agency for the purposes of their functions is permitted development.

PART 16
Development by
sewerage undertakers
Class A

Development by or on behalf of a sewerage undertaker is permitted development.

PART 17
Development by
statutory undertakers
Class A

The following are permitted developments:

Development by railway undertakers on their operational land, required in connection with the movement of traffic by rail.

Class B

Development on operational land by statutory undertakes or their lessees in respect of dock, pier, harbour, water transport, or canal or inland navigation undertakings.

Class C

The improvement, maintenance or repair of an inland waterway (other than a commercial waterway or cruising waterway) to which section 104 of the Transport Act 1968 applies.

Class D

The use of any land by statutory undertakers for the spreading of any dredged material.

Class E

Development for the purposes of their undertaking by statutory undertakers for the supply of water or hydraulic power.

Class F

Development by a public gas supplier required for the purposes of its undertaking.

Class G

Development by statutory undertakers for the supply of electricity for the purposes of their undertaking.

Class H

Development required for the purposes of the carrying on of any tramway or road transport undertaking.

Class I

Development required for the purposes of the functions of a general or local lighthouse authority.

Class J	Development required for the purposes of the Post Office consisting of:

(i) the installation of posting boxes or self-service machines,
(ii) any other development carried out in, on, over or under the operational land of the undertaking.

PART 18
Aviation development
Class A

The carrying out on operational land by a relevant airport operator or its agent of development (including the erection or alteration of an operational building) in connection with the provision of services and facilities at a relevant airport.

Class B

Air navigation development at an airport.

Class C

Air navigation development near an airport.

Class D

Development by Civil Aviation Authority within an airport.

Class E

Development by Civil Aviation Authority on its operational land for air traffic control and navigation.

Class F

Development by Civil Aviation Authority in an emergency.

Class G

Temporary development by Civil Aviation Authority for air traffic control etc.

Class H

Development by Civil Aviation Authority for surveys etc.

Class I

Use of airport buildings managed by relevant airport operators.

PART 19
Development ancillary to
mining operations
Class A–C

Permitted development includes the carrying out of operations for the erection, extension, installation, rearrangement, replacement, repair or other alteration of any:

(i)   plant or machinery,
(ii)   buildings,
(iii) private ways or private railways or sidings, or
(iv) sewers, mains, pipes, cables or other similar apparatus, on land used as a mine.

PART 20
Coal Authority
mining development
Class A–E

The winning and working underground by the Coal Authority, their lessees or licensees and any development required for the purposes of a mine is permitted development.

APPENDIX E

PART 21
Waste tipping at a mine
Class A & B

The deposit of waste derived from the winning and working of minerals at a mine is permitted.

PART 22
Mineral exploration
Class A & B

Development is permitted on any land during a specified period consisting of:

(i)   the drilling of bore holes,
(ii) the carrying out of seismic surveys, or
(iii) the making of other excavations,

for the purpose of mineral exploration, and the provision or assembly on that land or adjoining land of any structure required in connection with any of those operations.

PART 23
Removal of material from mineral working deposits
Class A & B

The removal of material of any description from a mineral working deposit is permitted development.

PART 24
Development by telecommunications code system operators
Class A

Permitted development includes development by or on behalf of a telecommunications code system operator for the purpose of the operator's telecommunication system in, on, over or under land controlled by that operator or in accordance with his licence.

PART 25
Other telecommunications development
Class A & B

The installation, alteration or replacement on any building or other structure of a microwave antenna and any structure intended for the support of a microwave antenna, so long as the building is not a dwellinghouse or the building or structure is more than 15m in height, is permitted development.

PART 26
Development by or on behalf of the Historic Buildings and Monuments Commission for England
Class A

Development by or on behalf of the Historic Buildings and Monuments Commission for England, consisting of:

(i)   the maintenance, repair or restoration of any building or monument;
(ii) the erection of screens, fences or covers designed or intended to protect or safeguard any building or monument; or
(iii) the carrying out of works to stabilise ground conditions by any cliff, watercourse or the coastline;

where such works are required for the purpose of securing the preservation of any building or monument, is permitted development.

164

PART 27
Use by members of certain recreational organisations
Class A

The use of land by members of recreational organisation for the purposes of recreation or instruction, and the erection or placing of tents on the land for the purposes of the use, is permitted.

PART 28
Development at amusement parks
Class A

Development is permitted on land used as an amusement park consisting of:

(i) the erection of booths or stalls or the installation of plant or machinery to be used for or in connection with the entertainment of the public within the amusement park; or
(ii) the extension, alteration or replacement of any existing booths or stalls, plant or machinery so used.

In both cases above, the building should not exceed 5m in height.

PART 29
Driver information systems

The installation, alteration or replacement of system apparatus by or on behalf of a driver information systems operator.

PART 30
Toll road facilities

Development consisting of the setting up and the maintenance, improvement or other alterations of the facilities for the collection of tolls and the provision of hardstanding for vehicles.

PART 31
Demolition of buildings

Any building operation consisting of the demolition of a building, with the exception of buildings that have been rendered unsafe by the action or inaction of anyone with an interest in the land and which it is practicable to repair or make safe.

All (but see Note below) demolition, however, is subject to the following conditions:

(i) where demolition is urgently necessary in the interests of health or safety the developer shall give the LPA a written justification as soon as reasonably practicable;
(ii) in all other cases the developer shall apply to the LPA for a determination as to whether prior approval will be required to the method of demolition and any proposed restoration of the site.

Note: Under the Town and Country Planning (Demolition – Description of Buildings) Direction 1995 several categories of building are excluded from the definition of development for the purposes of this Part. Listed buildings, those in conservation areas and scheduled monuments are excluded because their demolition is proscribed by other legislation. Buildings of less than 50 m³ are excluded, and, most significantly, **any building which is not a dwelling or adjoining a dwelling**. In other words, offices, factories and churches can be demolished without prior approval under the planning act.

Buildings that are the subject of a planning application for their redevelopment or which are to be demolished under an agreement such as a section 106 agreement do not require prior approval.

Prior approval is not required for the demolition of gates, fences, walls or other means of enclosure except in conservation areas.

PART 32
Schools, colleges, universities, hospitals

The erection on the site of any school, college, university or hospital of any building required for use as part of, or for a purpose incidental to the use of, the school, college, university or hospital provided that:

(i)   the cumulative floorspace would not exceed 10% of the original;
(ii) the volume would not exceed 250 m³;
(iii) the addition would not be within 20 m of the site boundary;
(iv) it would not result in the loss of a playing field;
(v) on article 1(5) land building materials shall match the existing buildings.

PART 33
Closed circuit television cameras

The installation, alteration or replacement on a building of a closed circuit television camera to be used for security purposes.

Advertisement control

What constitutes an advertisement is relatively straightforward (see note 22), but whether the advertisement needs no consent, has deemed consent or needs express consent, is far more difficult to determine. Circs. 5/92 and 15/94 provide further guides to advertisement control. The Town and Country Planning (Control of Advertisements) Regulations 1992 and the (Amendment) Regulations 1994 give very detailed criteria for the many different types of advertisement. The following is a condensed summary which gives a broad indication of the categories and conditions. The way the Regulation is drafted makes it impracticable to state what the circumstances are that would result in a need for an application for express consent – that decision can only be determined by a process of elimination. Relevant definitions are given at the end of this appendix.

The Regulations deal with advertisements in three ways:

1. Advertisements exempted from control (Schedule 2 of the Regulations).

There are ten classes of advertisement that are exempt from all control:

Class A
Tethered balloon

Advertisements displayed on, or consisting of, a balloon not more than 60 m above ground level (provided the site is not used for such purpose on more than 10 days in total in any calendar year, the site is not in a National Park, the Broads, an AONB, a conservation area, or an area of special control, and only one such balloon is displayed).

Class B
On enclosed land

Advertisements displayed on enclosed land and not readily visible from any place to which the public have right of access; bus and railway stations are regarded as 'enclosed land'.

Class C
On a vehicle

Advertisements displayed on or in a vehicle, including a vessel on any inland waterway, provided the vehicle is not used primarily for advertising.

Class D
Part of the fabric of the building

Advertisements incorporated in the fabric of a building (not merely fixed to or painted on the building).

Class E
On articles for sale

Advertisements displayed on articles for sale or on pumps etc., provided they are not illuminated and do not exceed 0.1 m^2.

Class F
Election notices

Election notices (on condition they are removed within 14 days after the close of the poll).

APPENDIX F

Class G	Statutory notices/advertisements.
Class H **Traffic signs**	Illuminated or non-illuminated traffic signs, provided the signs are displayed by, or with the permission of a local highway, traffic or police authority.
Class I **National flag**	The national flag of any country, displayed on a single vertical flagstaff.
Class J **Within a building**	Advertisements displayed within a building, provided they are not illuminated and not within 1 m of any external door or window through which it is visible from outside.

2. Advertisements which may be displayed with deemed consent (Schedule 3 of the Regulations)

Class 1 **Functional advertisements**	**A** Functional advertisements of local authorities, statutory undertakers and public transport undertakers; the advertisements shall not be illuminated unless reasonably required.
	B Advertisements displayed by LPAs on land in their area.
Class 2 **Sign boards on buildings**	**A** Direction or warning signs not exceeding 0.3 m^2 in area.
	B Advertisements relating to a person, partnership or company at the premises where they are displayed (limited to one advertisement, not exceeding 0.3 m^2 in area per road frontage).
	C Advertisements relating to any institutions (e.g. educational, medical), hotels, hostels, public house, flats, clubs etc. (limited to one advertisement for each premises per road frontage, and not exceeding 1.2 m^2 in area).
	Note: All advertisements specified under Class 2 shall not contain characters or symbols of a height exceeding 0.75 m (or 0.3 m in areas of special control) and no part of the advertisement shall be more than 4.6 m above ground level (or 3.6 m in areas of special control). Illumination is not permitted except for advertisements relating to medical services or supplies under Class 2B and 2C.
Class 3 **Temporary advertisements**	**A** Estate agents' boards, relating to the sale or letting, for residential, agricultural, industrial or commercial use, of the land or premises on which the advertisement is displayed (only one advertisement may be displayed at any time on the land or premises), on condition that:

168

- No advertisement may indicate that the land or premises have been sold or let, other than by adding a statement that a sale or letting has been agreed, or that the land or premises have been sold or let, subject to contract.
- The advertisement shall be removed within 14 days after the sale is completed or a tenancy is granted.
- The boards shall not exceed 0.5 m² (or 0.6 m² for two joined boards) for advertisements relating to residential use, and 2 m² (or 2.3 m² for two joined boards) for other uses.
- Where the advertisement is displayed on a building, any projection from the face of the building shall not exceed 1 m.

B Temporary advertisements announcing sales of goods or livestock not exceeding 1.2 m² in area; only one advertisement may be displayed at any one time on the land where the goods or livestock are situated or where the sale is held, provided that:

- The advertisement shall not be displayed earlier than 28 days before the day on which the sale is due to take place and shall be removed within 14 days after the sale is completed.

C Temporary advertisements relating to the carrying out of building or similar work on land on which they are displayed; limited to one advertisement per road frontage, per separate development project, and shall be displayed only for the period that the works are in progress, on condition that:

- Where the advertisement is displayed closer than 10 m from a highway, it shall not exceed 2 m² in area in the case of an advertisement referring to one person, or for more than one person, an additional 0.4 m² for each additional person.
- Where the advertisement is displayed further than 10 m from a highway, it shall not exceed 3 m² for one person and for more than one person, an additional 0.6 m² for each additional person.
- In either of the above cases, 0.2 m² of the permitted area may be added for the name of the development project.
- Subcontractors and others not referred to on the main advertisement may display a separate advertisement not exceeding 0.5 m² on each frontage of the land for a maximum period of three months.

D Temporary advertisements announcing a local event or activity not promoted or carried on for commercial purposes on condition that:

- The advertisement (limited to 0.6 m² in area) shall not be displayed earlier than 28 days before the day on which the event is due to take place and shall be removed within 14 days after the end of the event.

E Advertisements relating to any demonstration of agricultural methods or processes provided that:

- The maximum area of display is limited to 1.2 m^2 in area and each advertisement within the display shall not exceed 0.4 m^2, with the maximum period of displaying being six months in any period of 12 months.
- The advertisement shall not be displayed earlier than 28 days before the day on which the demonstration is due to take place and shall be removed within 14 days after the end of the demonstration.

F Temporary advertisement relating to the visit of a travelling circus, fair or similar travelling entertainment provided that:

- The advertisement (limited to 0.6 m^2 in area) shall not be displayed earlier than 14 days before the opening of the entertainment and shall be removed within seven days after the closing of the entertainment.
- No part of the advertisement shall be more than 3.6 m above ground level.
- At least 14 days before the advertisement is first displayed, the LPA are to be notified in writing of the first date on which, and of the site at which, it is to be displayed.

Note: All Class 3 advertisements shall not be illuminated or contain characters or symbols of a height exceeding 0.75 m (or 0.3 m in areas of special control). Excluding Class 3F, no part of the advertisement shall be more than 4.6 m above ground level (or 3.6 m in areas of special control).

Class 4
Illuminated signs on business premises

A Illuminated advertisement displayed on the frontage of premises within a retail park, which overlook or face on to a communal car park wholly bound by the retail park; in case of projecting advertisement, the surface is limited to 1 m^2 in area, it shall not project more than 1 m from the wall and shall not be more than 1.5 m in height.

B Other illuminated advertisements on business premises; in case of projecting advertisement, the surface is limited to 0.75 m^2 in area, it shall not project more than 1 m from the wall or 2/3 of the width of any footway or pavement below whichever is less, and shall not be more than 1 m in height or project over any carriageway.

For both Class 4A and 4B, the following apply:

- No such advertisement is permitted within a conservation area, an AONB, a National Park or the Broads unless it is displayed on the date of designation of the relevant area, in which case it may continue to be displayed for a period of five years from that date.

- Only one such advertisement parallel to a wall and one projecting at right angles from such a wall is permitted and the advertisement may only be displayed on a wall containing a shop window.
- Only characters of the advertisement but no part of the background is to be illuminated from within and no such advertisement may include any intermittent light source, moving feature, exposed cold cathode tubing, animation or reflective material (limits on luminance are specified in Part II of Schedule 3).
- In case of any advertisement containing a light source, the face of the advertisement shall not be more than 0.25 m from any wall parallel to which it is displayed.
- No character or symbol on the advertisement may be more than 0.75 m in height.
- The lowest part of the advertisement must be at least 2.5 m above ground level and no part of the advertisement may be higher than 4.6 m above ground level or above the bottom level of any first floor window in the wall on which it is displayed, whichever is the lower.

Class 5
Advertisements on business premises

Other advertisements on business premises which are not illuminated except for advertisements relating to medical services or supplies, provided that:

- The advertisements may only be displayed on a wall containing a shop window and no part of the advertisement may be higher than 4.6 m above ground level (or 3.6 m in areas of special control) or above the bottom level of any first floor window in the wall on which it is displayed, whichever is the lower.
- No character or symbol on the advertisement may be more than 0.75 m in height (or 0.3 m in areas of special control).
- In areas of special control, the space occupied by the advertisement may not exceed 0.1 m^2 of the overall area of the face of the building on which it is displayed, up to a height of 3.6 m from ground level.

Class 6
Forecourt signs

Non-illuminated advertisements displayed in the forecourts of business premises; limited to 4.5 m^2 in area with no character or symbol exceeding 0.75 m in height (or 0.3 m in areas of special control) and no part of the advertisement may be more than 4.6 m above ground level (or 3.6 m in areas of special control).

Class 7
Flag advertisements

A Flag advertisements attached to a single flagpole projecting vertically from the roof of a building which bears no inscription or emblem other than the name or device of any person occupying the building or refers only to a specific event of limited duration which is taking place in the building. No character or symbol on the flag may be more than 0.75 m in height (or 0.3 m in areas of special control).

B Flag advertisements attached to a single vertical flagstaff on a site with planning permission for residential development, on which work is in progress or at least one house remains unsold. One flagstaff for 10 houses; two for up to 100; three for more than 100: flagstaff no higher than 4.6 m nor flag larger than 2 m^2, nor displayed for more than a year after substantial completion.

Class 8
Advertisements on hoardings around building sites

Advertisements on hoardings enclosing, either wholly or in part, land on which building operations are taking place or are about to take place, provided the building operations are in accordance with a planning consent granted for commercial, industrial or business development, and provided

- No such advertisement is permitted within a conservation area, an AONB, a National Park or the Broads unless it is displayed on the date of designation of the relevant area, in which case it may continue to be displayed for a period of one year from that date or two years from the commencement of the display, whichever is the later.
- The advertisement shall not be displayed earlier than three months before the commencement of the building operations and for no more than three years.
- The advertisement shall be at least 1.5 m high and 1 m long but not more than 3.1 m high and 12.1 m long.
- At least 14 days before the advertisement is first displayed, the LPA are to be notified in writing of the first date on which it is to be displayed and a copy of the site's relevant planning permission shall be sent.
- Illumination is permitted in a manner and to an extent reasonably required to achieve the purpose of the advertisement.

Class 9
Advertisements on highway structures

Four-sheet panel advertisements displayed on certain purpose built highway structures authorised under section 115E (1) of the Highways Act 1980 (a); limited to 2.16 m^2 in area with no part of the advertisement exceeding 4.6 m above ground level (or 3.6 m in areas of special control) and no character or symbol exceeding 0.75 m in height (or 0.3 m in areas of special control); illumination is not permitted.

Class 10
Neighbourhood Watch signs

Outdoor advertisements not exceeding 0.2 m^2 in area for approved Neighbourhood Watch schemes and similar schemes. The highest part of the advertisement must not exceed 3.6 m above ground level. No character or symbol on the advertisement may be more than 0.75 m in height (or 0.3 m in areas of special control) and no illumination is permitted.

- At least 14 days before any sign is first displayed, the LPA must be told where it is to be displayed and formally notified that:

(a) the Watch scheme has been properly established;

(b) the local police authority has agreed to the display of the sign;
(c) if the sign is on highway land, the highway authority has granted consent for its display.

- The advertisement shall be removed within 14 days after:

(a) the scheme ceases to operate;
(b) the scheme ceases to be approved by the police authority;
(c) the highway authority withdraws consent for its display.

Class 11
Directional
advertisements

Directional advertisements not exceeding $0.15\ m^2$ in area on a single flat surface directing potential buyers and others to a residential development site, provided that:

- No part of the advertisement may be of a reflective material and illumination is not permitted.
- The design of the advertisement may not be similar to that of a traffic sign and the display shall not be within 50 m of a traffic sign.
- The advertisement shall not be displayed at a distance exceeding two miles from the main entrance of the site.
- Any character or symbol on the advertisement shall be at least 0.04 m and not more than 0.25 m in height.
- No part of the advertisement shall be more than 4.6 m above ground level (or 3.6 m in areas of special control).
- At least 14 days before the advertisement is first displayed, the LPA are to be notified in writing of the first date on which and the place at which it will be displayed.
- The advertisement shall not be displayed after the development is completed or, in any event, for more than two years.

Class 12

Advertisements displayed inside a building which do not fall within Class J in Schedule 2 above.

Class 13

Advertisements on sites used for the display of advertisements on and continually since 1st April 1974.

Class 14

Advertisements displayed continually after the expiration of express consent.

3. Advertisements requiring express consent

These include all advertisements not covered by the categories above, and advertisements that come under a Regulation 7 direction. If in any doubt, then discuss the matter with the LPA.

APPENDIX F

Definitions in Relation to Advertisements:

'area of special control' means an area designated by an order approved in accordance with Sch.2 of the Regulations.

'article' includes gas or liquid.

'balloon' means a tethered balloon or similar object.

'building' includes any structure or erection, and any part of a building as so defined.

'business premises' means any building normally used for the purpose of any professional, commercial or industrial undertaking, or for providing a service to the public. Includes restaurants, licensed premises and places of public entertainment.

'enclosed land' means land which is wholly or for the most part enclosed within a hedge, fence or wall or similar screen or structure. Included within the definition are railway stations (and their yards), and bus stations (and their forecourts, whether enclosed or not). Specifically excluded is land for the use of enjoyment of the public (e.g. public parks and public gardens) or land used for the carriage of passengers or goods by rail.

'experimental area' means an area designated under section 220/221 of the 1990 Act which for a prescribed period is subject to an assessment of the effect on amenity or public safety of advertisements of a prescribed description.

'illuminated advertisement' means an advertisement which is designed or adapted to be illuminated by artificial lighting, directly or by reflection.

'land' includes buildings, and land covered with water.

'local authority' means the council of a county or district, the Common Council (in the case of the City of London), the council of a London borough and any other authority within the meaning of the Local Loans Act 1875.

'National Park' has the meaning assigned to it by section 5 of the National Parks and Access to the Countryside Act 1949.

'site' means any land or any building on which an advertisement is displayed.

'statutory undertakers' means persons authorised by any enactment to carry on any railway, light railway, tramway, road transport, water transport, canal, inland navigation, dock, harbour, pier or lighthouse undertaking; or any undertaking for the supply of electricity, gas, hydraulic power or water. Also includes the Civil Aviation Authority, the British Airports Authority, the British Coal Corporation, the Post Office and companies deemed to be statutory undertakers by virtue of section 141(2) of the Transport Act 1968.

Environmental Assessments

Legislation was enacted in July 1988 that requires certain categories of development to be the subject of environmental assessments. This was partly the result of the European Community Directive (No. 85/337) to assess the impacts of certain public and private projects on the environment. The specific legislation in England and Wales is the Town and Country Planning (Assessment of Environmental Effects) Regulations 1988, (The Regulations) as amended by the T&CP (Assessment of Environmental Effects) (Amendment) Regulations 1992 and 1994 and the T&CP (Environmental Assessment and Permitted Development) Regulations 1995. The Regulations are explained in Circular 15/88. The Regulations, the Circular and DETR document *Environmental Assessment: a Guide to the Procedures* (HMSO 1989) and *Preparation of Environmental Statements for Planning Projects that Require Environmental Assessments: a Good Practice Guide* (DoE 1995) are essential reading for anyone involved in EAs: what follows is only a summary. The procedures are set out above in more detail in Section 3: Procedure 20; the diagram below is an overview of the process:

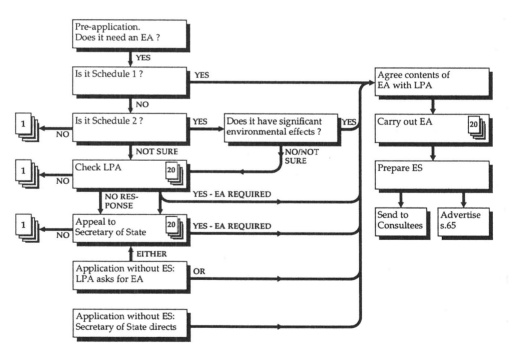

Environmental assessment flowchart

The Circular introduces three terms which are given specific definitions: **Environmental Assessment** (EA) is the name given to the whole process required to reach a decision, including **Environmental Information** (EI) from a number of sources such as the developer and statutory consultees. The specific information put forward by the developer with his planning application is referred to as the **Environmental Statement** (ES).

APPENDIX G

What developments require environmental assessment?

In the first instance the relevant planning authority decides whether an EA is required with reference to Schedule 1 and Schedule 2 of the Regulations.

Schedule 1 projects require EA in every case; planning permission cannot be granted unless the LPA has taken account of environmental information (Regulation 4). Schedule 1 contains ten types of project. They are (in summary):

Schedule 1
1. Crude oil refinery
2. Thermal power station
3. Storage or disposal of radioactive waste
4. Works for the initial melting of cast iron and steel
5. Installations for asbestos extraction or process
6. Chemical installations for the manufacture of olefins, sulphuric, nitric or hydrofluoric acid; chlorine or fluorine.
7. A special road, a long-distance railway or an aerodrome
8. A port for handling vessels of over 1,350 tonnes
9. Waste disposal installations for the incineration or chemical treatment of special waste
10. Land fill or the deposit of special waste.

Schedule 2
of the Regulations is a long list under eleven subheadings of projects that may require EAs depending on whether they are likely to have significant effects on the environment. They are:

1. Agriculture
   (a) water-management for agriculture, (b) poultry-rearing, (c) pig-rearing, (d) a salmon hatchery, (e) an installation for the rearing of salmon, (f) the reclamation of land from the sea.

2. Extractive industry
   (a) extracting peat, (b) deep drilling, including in particular [(i) geothermal drilling, (ii) drilling for the storage of nuclear waste material, (iii) drilling for water supplies] but excluding drilling to investigate the stability of the soil, (c) extracting minerals (other than metalliferous and energy-producing minerals) such as marble, sand, gravel, shale, salt, phosphates and potash, (d) extracting coal or lignite by underground or open-cast mining, (e) extracting petroleum, (f) extracting natural gas, (g) extracting ores, (h) extracting bituminous shale, (j) extracting minerals (other than metalliferous and energy-producing minerals) by open-cast mining, (k) a surface industrial installation for the extraction of coal, petroleum, natural gas or ores or bituminous shale, (l) a coke oven (dry distillation of coal), (m) an installation for the manufacture of cement.

3. Energy industry
   (a) a non-nuclear thermal power station, not being an installation falling within Schedule 1, or an installation for the production of electricity, steam and hot water, (b) an industrial installation for carrying gas, steam or hot water; or the transmission of electrical energy by overhead cables, (c) the surface storage of natural gas, (d) the underground storage of combustible gases, (e) the surface storage of fossil fuels, (f) the industrial briquetting of coal or lignite, (g) an installation for the production or enrichment of nuclear fuels, (h) an installation for the reprocessing of irradiated nuclear fuels, (j) an installation for the collection or

176

processing of radioactive waste, not being an installation falling within Schedule 1, (k) an installation for hydroelectric energy production.

4. Processing of metals

(a) an ironworks or steelworks including a foundry, forge, drawing plant or rolling mill (not being a works falling within Schedule 1), (b) an installation for the production (including smelting, refining, drawing and rolling) of non-ferrous metals, other than precious metals, (c) the pressing, drawing or stamping of large castings, (d) the surface treatment and coating of metals, (e) boilermaking or manufacturing reservoirs, tanks and other sheet-metal containers, (f) manufacturing or assembling motor vehicles or manufacturing motor-vehicle engines, (g) a shipyard, (h) an installation for the construction or repair of aircraft, (j) the manufacture of railway equipment, (k) swaging by explosives, (l) an installation for the roasting or sintering of metallic ores.

5. Glass making – the manufacture of glass.

6. Chemical industry

(a) the treatment of intermediate products and production of chemicals, other than development falling within Schedule 1, (b) the production of pesticides or pharmaceutical products, paints or varnishes, elastomers or peroxides, (c) the storage of petroleum or petrochemical or chemical products.

7. Food industry

(a) the manufacture of vegetable or animal oils or fats, (b) the packing or canning of animal or vegetable products, (c) the manufacture of dairy products, (d) brewing or malting, (e) confectionery or syrup manufacture, (f) an installation for the slaughter of animals, (g) an industrial starch manufacturing installation, (h) a fish-meal or fish-oil factory, (j) a sugar factory.

8. Textile, leather, wood and paper industries

(a) a wool scouring, degreasing and bleaching factory, (b) the manufacture of fibre board, particle board or plywood, (c) the manufacture of pulp, paper or board, (d) a fibre-dying factory, (e) a cellulose-processing and production installation, (f) a tannery or a leather dressing factory.

9. Rubber industry – the manufacture and treatment of elastomer-based products.

10. Infrastructure projects

(a) an industrial estate development project, (b) an urban development project, (c) a ski-lift or cable car, (d) the construction of a road, or a harbour, including a fishing harbour, or an aerodrome, not being development falling within Schedule 1, (e) canalisation or flood-relief works, (f) a dam or other installation designed to hold water or store it on a long-term basis, (g) a tramway, elevated or underground railway, suspended line or similar line, exclusively or mainly for passenger transport, (h) an oil or gas pipeline installation, (j) a long-distance aqueduct, (k) a yacht marina, (l) a motorway service area; or (m) coast protection work.

11. Other projects

(a) a holiday village or hotel complex, (b) a permanent racing or test track for cars or motor cycles, (c) an installation for the disposal of controlled waste from mines and quarries, not being an installation falling within Schedule 1, (d) a waste water treatment plant, (e) a site for depositing sludge, (f) the storage of scrap iron, (g) a test bench for engines, turbines or reactors, (h) the manufacture of artificial mineral fibres, (j) the manufacture, packing, loading or placing in cartridges of gunpowder or other explosives, (k) a knackers' yard.

12. The modification of a development within Schedule 1.

13. Development within Schedule 1 where it is exclusively or mainly for the development and testing of new products and will not be permitted for more than one year.

Identifying Schedule 2 projects

Not all projects described by the Schedule 2 list need necessarily to have an EA. Equally, some projects in neither Schedule 1 nor Schedule 2 will nevertheless need EAs because of their significant environmental effects. The critical word is 'significant' and it introduces a degree of judgement on the part of those deciding whether or not an EA is necessary.

The view set out in Circ. 15/88 is that only a small proportion of Schedule 2 projects will need EAs. The amount of opposition to a project is not in itself sufficient, nor is the fact that it is in a designated area such as a National Park. Normal planning procedures should deal with the majority of cases. The Circular sets out three types of cases where an EA is needed.

1. Major projects of more than local importance.
2. Some projects on a smaller scale but in sensitive locations.
3. A small number of projects with unusually complex and potentially adverse environmental effects.

Appendix A of the Circular gives indicative thresholds and criteria for projects requiring EA. These criteria include such things as industrial estates larger than 20 ha; urban development projects of more than 5 ha, or more than 10,000 m^2 of shops or offices.

Who decides if an EA is needed?

A developer can take the view that his project requires an EA and can produce an ES with his planning application. Alternatively he can ask the planning authority that would normally deal with the application for its opinion. This is usually a district council, but could be a county council as, for instance, mineral or waste disposal authority. We have used the usual shorthand of LPA.

The LPA can also volunteer its opinion as to whether an EA is needed. The LPA should notify its opinion within three weeks of a request but it can ask for more information on which to form its view (Regulation 5). The developer can accept that opinion or contest it by referring to the Secretary of State; or the Secretary of State can require an EA for a proposal that has been referred to him without one.

Direction under regulation 6

If a developer chooses to contest the view of an LPA, or simply to obtain guidance if the LPA has taken more than three weeks to respond, he does so by applying under Regulation 6 of the Regulations. This is usually to the regional branch of the DETR. The Secretary of State should respond within three weeks (Regulation 6(4)) but there is the usual let-out of 'such longer period as he may

ENVIRONMENTAL ASSESSMENTS

reasonably require'. This response should be a written statement with clear and precise reasons for his decision for an EA; if he thinks an EA is not required he need give no reasons.

Direction under regulation 9

If a planning application has been made to an LPA without an ES, and in the opinion of the LPA it should have had one, the LPA must notify the applicant within three weeks that an ES is required.

The applicant must, within three weeks, write to the LPA saying he accepts their view or saying that he is applying to the Secretary of State for a direction under Regulation 9. The form of the application is essentially the same as under Regulation 6.

Voluntary ES

The completion of an ES for a major project is usually good planning practice whether or not it is required by law. It gives evidence of proper concern by the developer and enables a planning officer to produce a full and accurate report. It is, however, important to make clear that it is a voluntary ES and is not produced for the purposes of the Regulations, otherwise the LPA may assume that the project qualifies for an EA and delays could be incurred.

Contents of an ES

The Regulations are specific about the minimum information required for an ES; they are set out in Schedule 3 of the Regulations and are as follows:

Schedule 3
1. A description of the development proposed, comprising information about the site and the design and size or scale of the development.
2. The data necessary to identify and assess the main effects which development is likely to have on the environment.
3. A description of the likely significant effects, direct and indirect, on the environment of the development, explained by reference to its possible impact on: human beings, flora, fauna, soil, water, air, climate, the landscape, the interaction between any of the foregoing, material assets, the cultural heritage.
4. Where significant adverse effects are identified with respect to any of the foregoing, a description of the measures envisaged in order to avoid, reduce or remedy those effects.
5. A summary in non-technical language of the information specified above.

Schedule 3 also contains a list of further information which could usefully explain and amplify the proposals. It includes:

- physical characteristics, land use and phasing of proposal
- characteristics of the production process
- type and quantity of emissions
- any alternatives considered

- environmental consequences of the use of natural resources or of the emission of pollutants etc.
- forecasting methods
- shortcomings in the data.

Scope of an EA/ES

The relevance of the headings in Schedule 3 and the depth to which they should be covered will vary for each project. The LPA will provide guidance about the critical issues from a planning point of view and the applicant should discuss the contents of the EA/ES with the LPA as early as possible.

Involvement of other public bodies

Once the need for an EA has been established, the LPA informs the relevant public bodies of the fact and of their obligation to supply the developer with any relevant information in their possession. The LPA must tell the developer the names and addresses of these bodies. They include statutory consultees under Article 10 of the GDPO; any principal council other than the LPA; the Nature Conservancy Council and the Countryside Commission and, in certain cases, HM Inspectorate of Pollution.

The developer must provide these bodies with copies of his ES. He may send copies direct to these bodies (free of charge) or he may send them to the LPA for onward transmission. The LPA must also copy the application and ES to a Regional Office of the DETR.

Publicity

The LPA must advertise both on the site and in the local press the fact that an ES has been produced. The Notice is prescribed by Article 8 and Schedule 3 of the GDPO and tells members of the public where they can see or get copies of the ES, how much it will cost, where to send their comments and by what date.

Determining the Application

The period for determining an application with an ES is extended from 8 to 16 weeks during which the LPA can ask for more information and/or extend the period by agreement. Once the application has been determined by the planning committee, an applicant has the normal right of appeal against refusal or conditions. The applicant also has the normal right of appeal against non-determination after 16 weeks if a longer period has not been agreed.

Hazardous Substances

Schedule 1 of the Planning (Hazardous Substances) Regulations 1992 contains a list of 71 substances together with the critical minimum quantity which brings them within the control of the Regulations:

Part A Toxic substances

Hazardous substance	Controlled quantity (in tonnes, unless otherwise stated)
1 Acetone cyanohydrin (2-cyanopropan-2-ol)	200
2 Acrolein (2-propenal)	200
3 Acrylonitrile	20
4 Allyl alcohol (2-propen-1-ol)	200
5 Allylamine	200
6 Ammonia (anhydrous or as a solution containing more than 50% by weight of ammonia)	100
7 Arsenic trioxide arsenious (III) acid and salts	1
8 Arsine (arsenic hydride)	1
9 Bromine	40
10 Carbon disulphide	20
11 Chlorine	10
12 Ethylene dibromide (1, 2-dibromoethane)	50
13 Ethyleneimine	50
14 Formaldehyde (greater than 90%)	50
15 Hydrogen chloride (liquefied gas)	250
16 Hydrogen cyanide	20
17 Hydrogen fluoride	10
18 Hydrogen selenide	1
19 Hydrogen sulphide	50
20 Methyl bromide (bromomethane)	200
21 Methyl isocyanate	150kg
22 Nickel tetracarbonyl	1
23 Nitrogen oxide	50
24 Oxygen difluoride	1
25 Pentaborane	1
26 Phosgene	750kg
27 Phosphine (hydrogen phosphide)	1
28 Propyleneimine	50
29 Selenium hexafluoride	1
30 Stibine (antimony hydride)	1
31 Sulphur dioxide	20
32 Sulphur trioxide (including the sulphur trioxide content in oleum)	15
33 Tellurium hexafluoride	1
34 2, 3, 7, 8-Tetrachlorodibenzo-p-dioxin (TCDD)	1kg
35 Tetraethyl lead	50
36 Tetramethyl lead	50

Part B Highly reactive substances and explosive substances

Hazardous substance	Controlled quantity (in tonnes, unless otherwise stated)
37 Acetylene (ethyne) when a gas subject to a pressure not exceeding 620 millibars above that of the atmosphere and not otherwise deemed to be an explosive by virtue of Order in Council No. 30 as amended by the Compressed Acetylene Order 1947, or when contained in a homogeneous porous substance in cylinders in accordance with Order of Secretary of State No. 9 made under the Explosives Act 1875	50
38 Ammonium nitrate and mixtures containing ammonium nitrate where the nitrogen content derived from the ammonium nitrate exceeds 28% of the mixture by weight other than:	500

(a) mixtures to which the Explosives Act 1875 applies;

(b) ammonium nitrate-based products manufactured chemically for use as fertiliser which comply with Council Directive 80/876/EEC; or

(c) compound fertilisers

39 Aqueous solutions containing more than 90 parts by weight of ammonium nitrate per 100 parts by weight of solution 500

40 Ammonium nitrate-based products manufactured chemically for use as fertiliser which comply with Council Directive 80/876/EEC and compound fertilisers where the nitrogen content derived from the ammonium nitrate exceeds 28% of the mixture by weight 1,000

41 2, 2–Bis(tert-butylperoxy)butane (greater than 70%) 5

42 1, 1–Bis(tert-butylperoxy)cyclohex-ane (greater than 80%) 5

43 tert-Butyl peroxyacetate (greater than 70%) 5

44 tert-Butyl peroxyisobutyrate (greater than 80%) 5

45 tert-Butyl peroxyisopropylcarbonate (greater than 80%) 5

46 tert-Butyl peroxymaleate (greater than 80%) 5

47 tert-Butyl peroxypivalate (greater than 77%) 5

48 Cellulose nitrate other than:

(a) cellulose nitrate to which the Explosives Act 1875 applies; or 50

(b) solutions of cellulose nitrate where the nitrogen content of the cellulose nitrate does not exceed 12.3% by weight and the solution contains not more than 55 parts of cellulose nitrate per 100 parts by weight of solution

49 Dibenzyl peroxydicarbonate (greater than 90%) 5

50 Diethyl peroxydicarbonate (greater than 30%) 5

51 2, 2–Dihydroperoxypropane (greater than 30%) 5

52 Di-isobutyryl peroxide (greater than 50%) 5

53 Di–n–propyl peroxydicarbonate (greater than 80%) 5

54 Di–sec–butyl peroxydicarbonate (greater than 80%) 5

55 Ethylene oxide 5

56 Ethyl nitrate 50

57 3, 3, 6, 6, 9, 9–Hexamethyl–1, 2, 4, 5–tetroxacyclonaonane (greater than 75%) 5

58 Hydrogen 2

59 Liquid oxygen 500

60 Methyl ethyl ketone peroxide (greater than 60%) 5

61 Methyl isobutyl ketone peroxide (greater than 60%) 5

62 Peracetic acid (greater than 60%) 5

63 Propylene oxide 5

64 Sodium chlorate 25

65 Sulphur dichloride 1

Part C Flammable substances (unless specifically named in Parts A and B)

Hazardous substance *Controlled quantity (in tonnes, unless otherwise stated)*

66 Liquefied petroleum gas such as commercial propane and commercial butane, and any mixture thereof, when held at a pressure greater than 1.4 bars absolute 25

67 Liquefied petroleum gas such as commercial propane and commercial butane, and any mixture thereof, when held under refrigeration at a pressure of 1.4 bars absolute or less   50

68 Gas or any mixture of gases which is flammable in air, when held as a gas   15

69 A substance or any mixture of substances which is inflammable in air, when held above its boiling point (measured at 1 bar absolute) as a liquid or as a mixture of liquid and gas at a pressure greater than 1.4 bars absolute   25

70 A liquefied gas or any mixture of liquefied gases which is flammable in air and has a boiling point of less than 0°C (measured at 1 bar absolute), when held under refrigeration at a pressure of 1.4 bars absolute or less   50

71 A liquid or any mixture of liquids not included in entries 68–70 above, which has a flash-point of less than 21°C   10,000

Part D   Interpretation

In this Schedule:

(a) References to percentages are references to parts by weight of the substance per 100 parts by weight of the solution.

(b) 'Compound fertiliser' means a fertiliser containing ammonium nitrate and phosphate or potash.

(c) Part C does not include a substance which is within Part A or Part B.

(d) A substance, or any mixture of substances, shall only be treated as a hazardous substance by virtue of satisfying a description in entry number 37, 66, 67, 68, 69 or 70 when it is in a state in which it satisfies the description.

(e) The controlled quantity of 25 tonnes in entry 69 refers, in the case of a mixture of substances, to the quantity of substances within that mixture which are held above their boiling point (measured at 1 bar absolute).

(f) The controlled quantity of 50 tonnes in entry 70 refers, in the case of a mixture of substances, to the quantity of substances within that mixture which have boiling points below 0°C.

© Crown Copyright

APPENDIX I

Other Agreements and Applications

Planning and infrastructure agreements and applications can be entered into under a range of statutory powers. The main ones are listed below, but there may also be local acts which are relevant.

Section 106 Agreement (1990 Act)

Section 106 and section 278 agreements are probably the most common agreements that are encountered in the course of obtaining planning consent. Updated by section 12(1) of the PCA, 1991, and covered by DETR Circular 1/97, section 106 agreements are typically between the applicant (who must have an interest in the land in question) and the local planning authority as a result of the imposition by the authority of 'planning obligations'. Where agreement cannot be reached, the applicant can make a 'unilateral undertaking'. Such undertakings only come into effect when permission is granted.

The section 106 agreement, which invariably must be completed before the planning consent is issued (despite an approval in principle of the application by the relevant planning committee), restricts or regulates the use or development of land and/or requires the applicant to make a financial contribution (single sum or periodically) to the local authority. This latter provision usually relates to the funding of off-site local facilities such as schools, roads, libraries and public transport, and the cost of maintenance of public open space adopted by the LPA as result of the development. The obligation created, which can be unconditional or subject to conditions, runs with the land and therefore is a local land charge for the purposes of the Local Land Charges Act 1975.

Section 106 agreements are intended to be used where an obligation or restriction cannot properly be the subject of a planning condition because either it would lie outside the application's 'red line', and/ or it involves a financial settlement. Government guidance confirms that planning obligations should only be sought where 'necessary', where 'relevant to planning', 'directly related to the proposed development', 'fairly and reasonably related in scale and kind to the proposed development' and 'reasonable in all other respects'.

Some notable issues relating to section 106 agreements are as follows:

- obligations may include a covenant by the local authority to repay contributions if they are not used for a specified purpose by a specified date;
- local authorities should not use obligations to secure a share in the profits of development (i.e. as a 'betterment levy');

- if a development would exacerbate an existing problem it could, in certain circumstances, be reasonable to seek from a developer the cost of resolving that existing problem;
- planning obligations can be entered into in relation to any Crown or Duchy interest in land under section 299A – see below.

Examples of appropriate planning obligations include arrangements:

- to ensure an acceptable balance of uses in a mixed-use development;
- to secure the inclusion of an element of affordable or special needs housing in a larger residential or mixed-use development;
- to offset, through substitution, replacement or regeneration the loss of, or impact on, a resource on the site;
- to protect or reduce harm to protected sites or species, acknowledged to be of importance.

LPAs should include in their development plans the matters which must be addressed in order for development to proceed, i.e. the development plans should form a framework into which a planning obligation should fit.

Section 278 Agreement (Highway Act 1980)

These are agreements between highway authorities proposing to execute highway works and other persons who would derive a special benefit if those works incorporated particular modifications, additions or features or were implemented in a particular manner or at a particular time. The agreement is that the other party will, on the proposed works satisfying certain criteria, make a contribution to expenses incurred in executing the works. The section 278 agreement can also include a contribution towards maintenance costs. The criteria are:

- a condition that the works by the highway authority will incorporate specified modifications, additions or features;
- a condition that the works will be started or completed before a specified date;
- that the works will be implemented in a specified manner.

The highway authority must be satisfied that the agreement will be to the public benefit. Such an agreement does not permit the authority to use its powers of land acquisition solely for the benefit of the agreement.

There have been instances where the highway authority has refused to enter into, or blocked, a section 278 agreement despite there being a valid planning consent in place. Precedent now indicates that this type of stalling action by a highway authority may be unacceptable to the courts.

APPENDIX I

Section 38 Agreement (Highways Act 1980)

Section 38 agreements relate to the adoption of highways by the relevant highway authorities. The agreement is made with the owner of the land and will specify a date on which the highway becomes maintainable at public expense. The highway to be adopted can be constructed by the developer or by the highway authority on his behalf. The agreement can also cover the maintenance of a bridge or viaduct, and therefore will be made with the relevant railway, canal etc. authority.

Section 94 Agreement (Highways Act 1980)

This form of agreement is between the highway authorities and bridge owners and covers:

- payment by the highway authority of contributions towards the cost of reconstruction, improvement or maintenance of the bridge, or of the highway carried by the bridge, or of the approaches to the bridge;
- transfer to the highway authority of responsibility for the improvement and maintenance of the above;
- for the transfer to the highway authority of the property in the two situations above, and all or any rights and obligations attached to the above.

Section 116 and 117 Applications (Highways Act 1980)

Section 116 applications are ones made to the magistrates' court by the local authority or highway authority to stop up and divert highways. Section 117 applications are ones made to the local authority or highway authority by any person who wishes a highway to be stopped up or diverted. In this instance, if the authority grants the request, it may as a condition require any costs it incurs to be reimbursed.

Section 118 and 119 Applications (Highways Act 1980)

Section 118 applications are ones made to the Secretary of State by the local authority to stop up a footpath or bridleway because it is not needed for public use. An order under this section is referred to in this Act as a 'public path extinguishment order'. Section 119 applications are ones made to the local authority by an owner, lessee or occupier of land crossed by a footpath or bridleway who wishes it to be diverted ('public path diversion order'). In this instance, if the authority grants the request, it may as part of an agreement require a contribution towards any expenses and compensation which may be payable.

Sections 247, 253, 257 and 258 (1990 Act)

All these sections relate to the stopping up or diversion of any highway, footpath or bridleway in accordance with a planning permission. In certain instances there may be a contribution payable in respect of the cost of doing the work or in the compensation paid.

Section 111 Agreement (Local Government Act 1972)

This is a catch-all piece of legislation that allows a local authority to enter into an agreement with whomsoever it wishes. In the cases where it is used as an adjunct to a planning consent, the agreement covers obligations that are not adequately covered by either planning conditions or section 106 agreements. Examples of the types of issue covered by such an agreement include the obligation to carry out planning studies (e.g. a traffic impact study, visual impact study) to be submitted for approval with each of a series of reserve matter applications. These applications could be, for example, for separate buildings forming part of a campus-type phased development such as a business park or a university. Enforcement of section 111 agreements are executed through section 33 of the Local Government (Miscellaneous Provisions) Act 1982.

Section 104 Agreement (Water Industry Act 1991)

These are agreements with statutory sewerage authorities by anyone constructing or proposing to construct a sewer or sewage disposal works, to declare the sewer or works to be adopted by them. The agreement is conditional on the sewer or works being constructed in accordance with the terms of the agreement and may take effect either on completion of the works or at some specified date. The agreement is enforceable against the authority by the owner or occupier of any premises served by the sewer or works.

Section 299A Agreement (1990 Act as amended)

This allows the Crown to enter into planning obligations in the same way as provided for by section 106 Agreements.

APPENDIX J

Local Planning Authorities

Below, in alphabetical order, are addresses of all the local planning authorities in England and Wales. A separate list for Scotland is given on pages 203 and 204. For Northern Ireland, planning applications should be sent to one of six DETR (NI) planning divisions, each of which covers a number of local council districts. Addresses for the planning divisions are given on page 204.

Each LPA has its own version of the title for the officer heading the department that handles planning applications, but until you are aware of that title, we suggest that letters and applications to the LPA should be addressed to the Chief Planning Officer.

LPAs in England & Wales

Adur District Council
Development Services
Civic Centre
Ham Road
Shoreham-by-Sea BN43 6PR
Tel: 01273 455566
Fax: 01273 454847

Allerdale District Council
Planning Department
Allerdale House
Workington, Cumbria CA14 3YJ
Tel: 01900 735524
Fax: 01900 735346

Alnwick District Council
Planning Department
Allerburn House
Alnwick, Northumberland NE66 1YY
Tel: 01665 510505
Fax: 01665 605099

Amber Valley District Council
Planning Department
Borough Services Offices
PO Box 18
Town Hall
Ripley, Derbys. DE5 3SZ
Tel: 01773 570222
Fax: 01773 841523

Arun District Council
Planning and Housing
Arun Civic Centre
Maltravers Road
Littlehampton BN17 5LF
Tel: 01903 716133
Fax: 01903 716019

Ashfield District Council
Planning Department
Council Offices
Urban Road
Kirkby-in-Ashfield, Notts NG17 8DA
Tel: 01623 755755
Fax: 01623 751735

Ashford District Council
Planning Department
Civic Centre
Tannery Lane
Ashford, Kent TN23 1PL
Tel: 01233 637311
Fax: 01233 645654

Aylesbury Vale District Council
Planning Department
Exchange Street
Aylesbury, Bucks HP20 1UB
Tel: 01296 555400
Fax: 01296 398665

Babergh District Council
Planning and Development
Corks Lane
Haleigh
Ipswich IP7 6SJ
Tel: 01473 825858
Fax: 01473 823594

Barking and Dagenham London Borough
Planning Department
Town Hall
Barking IG11 7LU
Tel: 0181 594 3880
Fax: 0181 252 8233

Barnet London Borough
Planning Department
Barnet House
1255 High Road
London N20 0JE
Tel: 0181 359 4481
Fax: 0181 359 4502

Barnsley Metropolitan District Council
Planning Department
Central Offices
Kendray Street
Barnsley, S. Yorks S70 2TN
Tel: 01226 772601
Fax: 01226 772599

Barrow-in-Furness District Council
Planning Department
Town Hall
Barrow-in-Furness, Cumbria LA14 2LD
Tel: 01229 842337
Fax: 01229 842499

Basildon District Council
Planning Department
The Basildon Centre
Pagel Mead
Basildon, Essex SS14 1DL
Tel: 01268 533333
Fax: 01268 294162

Basingstoke and Dean District Council
Planning Department
Civic Offices
London Road
Basingstoke, Hants RG21 4AH
Tel: 01256 845788
Fax: 01256 844708

Bassetlaw District Council
Planning Department
Queens Buildings
Potter Street
Worksop, Notts. S80 2AH
Tel: 01909 475531
Fax: 01909 482622

Bath and North East Somerset Unitary Council
Planning Department
Trimbridge House, Trim Street
Bath BA1 2DP
Tel: 01225 394125
Fax: 01225 394199

Bedford District Council
Planning Department
Town Hall
Bedford MK40 1SJ
Tel: 01234 267422
Fax: 01234 221606

Bedfordshire County Council
Environment & Economic Development
County Hall
Bedford MK42 9AP
Tel: 01234 228004
Fax: 01234 228232

Berkshire County Council
City Environmental Office
Shire Hall
Shinfield Park
Reading RG2 9XA
Tel: 0118 923 4150
Fax: 0118 923 4348

Berwick-upon-Tweed District Council
Planning Department
Council Offices
Wallace Green
Northumberland TD15 1ED
Tel: 01289 330044
Fax: 01289 330540

Bexley London Borough
Planning and Development
Wyncham House
207 Longlands Road
Sidcup, Kent DA15 7JH
Tel: 0181 303 7777
Fax: 0181 308 5010

Birmingham City Council
Planning Department
PO Box 28
Baskerville House
Broad Street
Birmingham B1 2NA
Tel: 0121 235 3163
Fax: 0121 235 7007

Blaby District Council
Planning Department
Council Offices
Narborough
Leicester LE9 5EP
Tel: 0116 275 0555
Fax: 0116 275 3132

Blackburn District Council
Planning Department
Borough Planning Offices
Town Hall
Blackburn, Lancs. BB1 7DY
Tel: 01254 585324
Fax: 01254 680870

Blackpool District Council
Planning Department
PO Box 17
Municipal Buildings
Blackpool FY1 1LZ
Tel: 01253 25212
Fax: 01253 752310

Blaenau Gwent Unitary Council
Planning Department
Municipal Offices
Civic Centre
Ebbw Vale NP3 6XB
Tel: 01495 350555
Fax: 01495 301255

Blyth Valley District Council
Planning Department
Council Offices
Seaton Deleval
Whitley Bay, Tyne and Wear NE25 0DX
Tel: 01670 542000
Fax: 01670 542323

Bolsover District Council
Planning Department
Sherwood Lodge
Bolsover, Derbys. S44 6NF
Tel: 01246 540000
Fax: 01246 2400316

Bolton Metropolitan District Council
Planning Department
Town Hall
Bolton BL1 1RU
Tel: 01204 522311 Ext 6100
Fax: 01204 387153

Boston District Council
Planning Department
Municipal Buildings
Boston, Lincs PE21 8QR
Tel: 01205 357400
Fax: 01205 364604

Bournemouth District Council
Planning Department
Town Hall Annex
St. Stephen's Road
Bournemouth, Dorset BH2 6EA
Tel: 01202 451451
Fax: 01202 451005

Bracknell Forest District Council
Planning Department
Easthampstead House
Town Square
Bracknell, Berks RG12 1AQ
Tel: 01344 424642
Fax: 01344 411875

City of Bradford Metropolitan District Council
Planning and Transportation
Jacobs Well
Bradford BD1 5RW
Tel: 01274 753761/2
Fax: 01274 722840

Braintree District Council
Environmental Services
Causeway House
Bocking End
Braintree, Essex CM7 6HB
Tel: 01376 552525
Fax: 01376 552626

Breckland District Council
Planning Department
The Guildhall
Dereham
Norfolk NR19 1EE
Tel: 01362 695333
Fax: 01362 696771

Brent London Borough
Planning and Streetcare
Brent House
349/357 High Road
Wembley, Middlesex HA9 6BX
Tel: 0181 937 5002
Fax: 0181 937 5010

Brentwood District Council
Planning Department
Council Offices
Ingrave Road
Brentwood, Essex CM15 8AY
Tel: 01277 261111
Fax: 01277 260836

Bridgend Unitary Council
Environmental and Planning Services
Civic Offices
Angel Street
Bridgend CF1 1LX
Tel: 01656 643643
Fax: 01656 668126

Bridgnorth District Council
Environmental Services
Westgate
Bridgnorth, Salop WV16 5AA
Tel: 01746 765131
Fax: 01746 764414

Brighton District Council
Planning Department
Bartholomew House
Bartholomew Square
Brighton, E. Sussex BN1 1JP
Tel: 01273 710000
Fax: 01273 779550

Bristol Unitary Council
Planning Transport and Development
Brunel House
St Georges Road
Bristol BS1 5UY
Tel: 0117 922 2939
Fax: 0117 922 3861

Broadland District Council
Planning Department
Thorpe Lodge
1 Yarmouth Road
Norwich NR7 0DU
Tel: 01603 431133
Fax: 01603 700339

Bromley London Borough
Planning Department
Bromley Civic Centre
Stockwell Close
Bromley
London BR1 3UH
Tel: 0181 313 4441
Fax: 0181 313 0095

Bromsgrove District Council
Planning Department
Council Offices
Burcot Lane
Bromsgrove, W. Midlands B60 1AA
Tel: 01527 873232
Fax: 01527 8756600

Broxbourne District Council
Planning Department
Borough Offices
Bishops College
Churchgate
Cheshunt EN8 9NF
Tel: 01992 631921
Fax: 01992 639391

Broxtowe District Council
Planning Department
Council Offices
Foster Ave
Beeston
Nottingham NG9 1AB
Tel: 0115 925 4891
Fax: 0115 943 1452

Buckinghamshire County Council
Planning and Transport
County Hall
Aylesbury, Bucks HP20 1UA
Tel: 01296 382401
Fax: 01296 382409

Burnley District Council
Planning Department
PO Box 2
Parker Lane
Burnley, Lancs. BB1 2DT
Tel: 01282 425011
Fax: 01282 414799

Bury Metropolitan District Council
Planning Department
Craig House
Bury, Lancs. BL9 0DN
Tel: 0161 253 5319
Fax: 0161 253 5985

Caerphilly Unitary Council
Planning Department
Council Offices
Pontilanfraith
Blackwood NP2 2YW
Tel: 01495 235320
Fax: 01495 235012

Calderdale Metropolitan District Council
Environmental Services
Northgate House
Northgate
Halifax HX1 1UN
Tel: 01422 357257
Fax: 01422 392238

Cambridge City Council
Planning Department
The Guildhall
Cambridge CB2 3QJ
Tel: 01223 457200
Fax: 01223 457109

Cambridgeshire County Council
Planning Department
Shire Hall
Castle Hill
Cambridge CB3 0AP
Tel: 01223 717607
Fax: 01223 717900

Camden London Borough
Environmental Services
Town Hall Extension
Argyle Street
London WC1H 8NL
Tel: 0171 860 5621
Fax: 0171 860 5556

Cannock Chase District Council
Planning and Property Services
Civic Centre
28 Beechcroft Road
Cannock, Staffs. WS11 1BG
Tel: 01543 462621
Fax: 01543 462317

Canterbury City Council
Planning Department
Council Offices
Military Road
Canterbury CT1 1YQ
Tel: 01227 763763
Fax: 01227 763727

Caradon District Council
Planning Department
Luxstowe House
Liskeard, Cornwall PL14 3DZ
Tel: 01579 341000
Fax: 01579 341001

Cardiff Unitary Council
Planning Department
County Hall
Atlantic Wharf
Cardiff CF1 5UW
Tel: 01222 872000
Fax: 01222 872407

Carlisle City Council
Environmental Services
Civic Centre
Carlisle CA3 8QG
Tel: 01228 23411
Fax: 01228 591379

Carmarthenshire Unitary Council
Planning Department
3 Spilman Street
Camarthen, Dyfed SA31 1LE
Tel: 01267 234567
Fax: 01267 221918

Carrick District Council
Planning Department
Carrick House
Pydar Street
Truro TR1 1EB
Tel: 01872 224346
Fax: 01872 42104

Castle Morpeth District Council
Environmental Services
Council Offices
The Kylins Loansdean
Morpeth, Northumberland NE61 2EQ
Tel: 01670 514351
Fax: 01670 510348

Castle Point District Council
Planning Department
Council Offices
Kiln Road
Thundersley
Benfleet, Essex SS7 1TF
Tel: 01268 882200
Fax: 01268 565580

Ceredigion Unitary Council
Environmental Services
Penmorfa
Aberaeron SA46 0PA
Tel: 01545 570881
Fax: 01545 572117

Charnwood District Council
Planning Department
Southfields
Loughborough LE11 2TN
Tel: 01509 634721
Fax: 01509 219723

Chelmsford District Council
Planning Department
Civic Centre
Duke Street
Chelmsford CM1 1JE
Tel: 01245 490490
Fax: 01245 491924

Cheltenham District Council
Planning Department
Municipal Offices
Cheltenham GL50 1PP
Tel: 01242 262626
Fax: 01242 227131

Cherwell District Council
Development & Property Services
Bodicote House
Bodicote
Banbury, Oxon. OX15 4AA
Tel: 01295 252535
Fax: 01295 270028

Cheshire County Council
Planning Department
Commerce House
Hunter Street
Chester CH1 2QP
Tel: 01244 603101
Fax: 01244 603802

Chester City Council
Planning and Building Control
Town Hall
Chester CH1 2HN
Tel: 01244 402213
Fax: 01244 321302

Chester-le-Street District Council
Planning Department
Civic Centre
Newcastle Road
Chester-le-Street, Co. Durham DH3 3UT
Tel: 0191 387 1919
Fax: 0191 387 1583

Chesterfield District Council
Planning Department
Town Hall
Chesterfield, Derbys. S40 1LP
Tel: 01246 277232
Fax: 01246 221085

Chichester District Council
Planning Department
Council Offices
8 North Pallant
Chichester PO19 1TJ
Tel: 01243 785 166
Fax: 01243 776766

Chiltern District Council
Planning Department
Council Offices
King George V Road
Amersham, Bucks HP6 5AW
Tel: 01494 732033
Fax: 01494 729332/729011

Chorley District Council
Technical Services
Council Offices
Gillibrand Street
Chorley, Lancs PR7 2EL
Tel: 01257 244300
Fax: 01257 244390

Christchurch Borough Council
Planning Department
Civic Offices
Bridge Street
Christchurch, Dorset BH23 1AZ
Tel: 01202 486321
Fax: 01202 474457

City of York Unitary Council
Planning Department
9 Saint Leonards Place
York YO1 2ET
Tel: 01904 613161
Fax: 01904 670739

Colchester Borough Council
Environmental Services
PO Box 885
Town Hall
Colchester CO1 1ZE
Tel: 01206 282717
Fax: 01206 282727

Congleton Borough Council
Planning Department
Westfields
Middlewich Road
Sandbach, Cheshire CW11 3HZ
Tel: 01270 763231
Fax: 01270 768460

Conwy Unitary Council
Planning Department
Civic Offices
Colwyn Bay, Clwyd LL32 8DU
Tel: 01492 574000
Fax: 01492 512637

Copeland Borough Council
Planning Department
Council Offices
Catherine Street
Whitehaven, Cumbria CA28 7NY
Tel: 01946 693111
Fax: 01946 693373

Corby Borough Council
Development Services
Civic Centre
George Street
Corby, Northants. NN17 1QB
Tel: 01536 402551
Fax: 01536 402414

Cornwall County Council
Planning Department
County Hall
Truro TR1 3AY
Tel: 01872 322600
Fax: 01872 323808

Cotswold District Council
Development and Heritage
Trinity Road
Cirencester, Gloucs. G17 1PX
Tel: 01285 643643
Fax: 01285 657334

Coventry Metropolitan District Council
City Development
Tower Block
Much Park Street
Coventry CV1 1PY
Tel: 01203 831200
Fax: 01203 831203

Craven District Council
Planning Department
Council Offices
Granville Street
Skipton, N. Yorks BD23 1PS
Tel: 01756 700600
Fax: 01756 700658

Crawley Borough Council
Planning and Environmental Services
Town Hall
The Boulevard
Crawley, W. Sussex RH10 1UZ
Tel: 01293 528744
Fax: 01293 511803

Crewe and Nantwich Borough Council
Planning Department
Municipal Buildings
Earle Street
Crewe CW1 2BJ
Tel: 01270 537600
Fax: 01270 537788

Croydon London Borough
Planning Department
Taberner House
Park Lane
Croydon
Surrey CR9 1JT
Tel: 0181 686 4433
Fax: 0181 760 5406

Cumbria County Council
North Cumbria
Planning Department
Citadel Chambers
Carlisle CA3 8SG
Tel: 01228 606731
Fax: 01228 606755

South Cumbria
Planning Department
County Offices
Kendal, Cumbria LA9 4RQ
Tel: 01539 773407
Fax: 01539 773439

Dacorum Borough Council
Planning Department
Civic Centre
Marlowes
Hemel Hempstead HP1 1HH
Tel: 01442 228583
Fax: 01442 228995

Darlington Borough Council
Development Services
Town Hall
Darlington, Co. Durham DL1 5QT
Tel: 01325 380651
Fax: 01325 382032

Dartford Borough Council
Development and Leisure Services
Civic Centre
Home Gardens
Dartford, Kent DA1 1DR
Tel: 01322 343434
Fax: 01322 343422

Daventry District Council
Planning Department
Lodge Road
Daventry, Northants. NN11 5AF
Tel: 01327 302560
Fax: 01327 76543

Denbighshire Unitary Council
Planning Department
Council Offices
Station Road
Ruthin LL15 1YN
Tel: 01824 706009
Fax: 01824 705026

Derby City Council
Planning Department
Roman House
Friar Gate
Derby DE1 1XB
Tel: 01332 255974
Fax: 01332 255989

Derbyshire Dales District Council
Planning Department
Town Hall
Matlock, Derbys. DE4 3NN
Tel: 01629 580580
Fax: 01629 580482

Derbyshire County Council
Planning and Highways Office
County Offices
Matlock, Derbys. DE4 3AG
Tel: 01629 590000
Fax: 01629 590119

Derwentside District Council
Planning Department
Civic Centre
Medomsley Road
Consett, Co. Durham DH8 5JA
Tel: 01207 218281
Fax: 01207 218280

Devon County Council
Environmental Services
Lucombe House
County Hall
Topsham Rd
Exeter EX2 4QW
Tel: 01392 382149/249
Fax: 01392 382135

Doncaster Metropolitan District Council
Planning and Design Services
2nd Floor Danum House
St. Sepulchre Gate Street
Doncaster, S. Yorks. DN1 1UB
Tel: 01302 734444
Fax: 01302 734949

Dorset County Council
City Planning Offices
County Hall
Dorchester DT1 1XJ
Tel: 01305 251000
Fax: 01305 224482

Dover District Council
Planning and Technical Services
Council Offices
Whitecliffs Business Park
Dover CT16 3PG
Tel: 01304 821199
Fax: 01304 827268

Dudley Metropolitan District Council
Planning and Leisure
3 St. James Rd
Dudley, W. Midlands DY1 1HZ
Tel: 01384 4521500
Fax: 01384 452121

Durham County Council
Environmental Services
County Hall
Durham DH1 5UQ
Tel: 0191 386 4411
Fax: 0191 383 4096

Durham City Council
Planning Department
Ruth First House
Claypath DH1 1XE
Tel: 0191 386 6111
Fax: 0191 384 1529

Ealing London Borough
Planning and Building Services
Percival House
14–16 Uxbridge Road
Ealing
London W5 2HL
Tel: 0181 758 5623
Fax: 0181 758 8171

Easington District Council
Planning Department
Council Offices
Easington
Peterlee, Co. Durham SR8 3TN
Tel: 0191 527 0501
Fax: 0191 527 3797

East Cambridgeshire District Council
Planning Department
The Grange
Nutholt Lane
Ely CB7 4PL
Tel: 01353 665555
Fax: 01353 665240

East Devon District Council
Planning Department
Council Offices
Knowle
Sidmouth, Devon EX10 8HL
Tel: 01395 516551
Fax: 01395 577853

East Dorset District Council
Planning Department
Council Offices
Furzehill
Wimbourne, Dorset BH21 4HN
Tel: 01202 886201
Fax: 01202 849182

East Hampshire District Council
Planning Department
Penns Place
Petersfield, Hants. GU31 4EX
Tel: 01703 266551
Fax: 01703 267366

East Hertfordshire District Council
Planning and Property Department
PO Box 102
Wallfields
Pegs Lane
Hertford SG13 8EQ
Tel: 01279 655261
Fax: 01992 552280

East Lindsey District Council
Planning and Economic Development
Tedder Hall
Manby Park
Louth, Lincs LN11 8UP
Tel: 01507 601111
Fax 01507 600206

East Northamptonshire District Council
Planning Department
East Northamptonshire House
Cedar Drive
Thrapston, Northants NN14 4LS
Tel: 01832 742000
Fax: 01832 734839

East Riding Unitary Council
Planning Department
County Hall
Beverley HU17 9BA
Tel: 01482 887700
Fax: 01482 871137

East Sussex County Council
Planning Department
Southover House
Southover Road
Lewes BN7 1YA
Tel: 01273 481651
Fax: 01273 479040

Eastbourne Borough Council
Planning Department
68 Grove Groad
Eastbourne BN21 1DF
Tel: 01323 415210
Fax: 01323 415995/6

Eastleigh Borough Council
Planning Department
Civic Offices
Leigh Road
Eastleigh, Hants. SO50 9YN
Tel: 01703 614646
Fax: 01703 643952

Eden District Council
Planning Department
Mansion House
Penrith, Cumbria CA11 7YG
Tel: 01768 64671
Fax: 01768 890732

Ellesmere Port and Neston Borough Council
Environmental Services
Council Offices
4 Civic Way
Ellesmere Port, S. Wirral L65 0BE
Tel: 0151 356 6789
Fax: 0151 356 6689

Elmbridge Borough Council
Technical Services
Civic Centre
High Street
Esher, Surrey KT10 9SD
Tel: 01372 474700
Fax: 01372 474910

Enfield London Borough
Planning Department
Borough Planning Offices
PO Box 53
Civic Centre
Enfield
Middlesex EN1 3XE
Tel: 0181 967 9490
Fax: 0181 982 7088

Epping Forest District Council
Planning Department
Civic Offices
High Street
Epping, Essex CM16 4BZ
Tel: 01992 564115
Fax: 01992 578018

Epsom and Ewell Borough Council
Planning and Engineering
Town Hall
The Parade
Epsom, Surrey KT18 5BY
Tel: 01372 732301
Fax: 01372 732337

Erewash Borough Council
Planning Department
Town Hall
Long Eaton, Notts. NG10 1HU
Tel: 0115 946 1321
Fax: 0115 946 1900

Essex County Council
Planning Department
County Hall
Chelmsford CM1 1LF
Tel: 01245 492211
Fax: 01245 258353

Exeter City Council
Planning and Property
Civic Centre
Paris Street
Exeter EX1 1NN
Tel: 01392 277888
Fax: 01392 265265

Fareham Borough Council
Planning Department
PO Box 82
Civic Way
Fareham, Hants. PO16 7TT
Tel: 01329 236100
Fax: 01329 822732

Fenland District Council
Development and Leisure Services
Fenland Hall
March, Cambridgeshire PE15 8NQ
Tel: 01354 54321
Fax: 01354 660219

Flintshire Unitary Council
Planning Department
Shire Hall
Mold CH7 6NB
Tel: 01352 703200
Fax: 01352 703222

Forest Heath District Council
Planning Department
District Offices
College Heath Road
Mildenhall
Bury St Edmunds, Suffolk IP28 7EY
Tel: 01638 719000
Fax: 01638 716493

Forest of Dean District Council
Planning and Leisure Services
Council Offices
Coleford, Gloucs. GL16 8HG
Tel: 01594 810000
Fax: 01594 810134

Fylde Borough Council
Planning and Technical Services
Council Offices
Derby Road
Wesham, Lancs. PR4 3AJ
Tel: 01772 671488
Fax: 01772 671401

Gateshead Metropolitan District Council
Planning Department
Civic Centre
Gateshead, Tyne and Wear NE8 1HH
Tel: 0191 477 1011
Fax: 0191 478 3495

Gedling Borough Council
Planning Department
Civic Centre
Arnot Hill Park
Arnold
Nottingham NG5 6LU
Tel: 0115 967 0067
Fax: 0115 967 0014

Gillingham Borough Council
Planning Department
Municipal Buildings
Gillingham, Kent ME7 5LA
Tel: 01634 282360
Fax: 01634 282309

Gloucester City Council
Planning and Technical Services
Herbert Warehouse
Gloucester Docks
Gloucester GL1 2EQ
Tel: 01452 522232
Fax: 01452 396899

Gosport Borough Council
Planning Department
Town Hall
Gosport, Hants PO12 1EB
Tel: 01705 545401
Fax: 01705 511279

Gravesham Borough Council
Planning Department
Cygnet House
132 Windmill Street
Gravesend, Kent DA12 1BQ
Tel: 01474 564422
Fax: 01474 337546

Great Yarmouth Borough Council
Planning Department
Greyfriars House
Greyfriars Way
Great Yarmouth NR30 2EQ
Tel: 01493 856100
Fax: 01493 846110

Greenwich London Borough
Planning and Regeneration
Peggy Middleton House
50 Woolwich New Road
Woolwich
London SE18 6HQ
Tel: 0181 312 5063
Fax: 0181 317 0806

Guildford Borough Council
Planning Department
Millmead House
Millmead
Guildford GU2 5BB
Tel: 01483 444600
Fax: 01483 444646

Gwynedd Unitary Council
Planning Department
Council Offices
Caernarfon LL55 1SH
Tel: 01286 672255
Fax: 01286 673993

Hackney London Borough
Environmental Services
161 City Road
Hackney
London EC1V 1NR
Tel: 0171 418 8000
Fax: 0171 418 8100

Halton Borough Council
Planning Department
Municipal Buildings
Kingsway
Widnes, Cheshire WA8 7QF
Tel: 0151 424 2061
Fax: 0151 471 7304

Hambleton District Council
Planning and Technical Services
Civic Centre
Stonecross
Northallerton, N. Yorks DL6 2UU
Tel: 01609 779977
Fax: 01609 780017

Hammersmith & Fulham London Borough
Environment Department
Hammersmith Town Hall Extn
King Street
Hammersmith
London W6 9SU
Tel: 0181 748 3020
Fax: 0181 741 5664

Hampshire County Council
Planning Department
The Castle
Winchester SO23 8UE
Tel: 01962 941841
Fax: 01962 846776

Harborough District Council
Planning Department
Council Offices
Adam and Eve Street
Market Harborough, Leics. LE16 7AG
Tel: 01858 410000
Fax: 01858 462766

Haringey London Borough
Planning Department
639 High Road
Tottenham
London N17 8BD
Tel: 0181 885 7538
Fax: 0181 885 7553

Harlow District Council
Planning Department
1 Adams House
Harlow, Essex CM20 1HJ
Tel: 01279 446564
Fax: 01279 446560

Harrogate Borough Council
Planning Department
Knapping Mount
West Grove Road
Harrogate HG1 2AE
Tel: 01423 500600
Fax: 01423 530982

Harrow London Borough
Planning and Transportation Services
Civic Centre
Harrow
Middlesex HA1 2UW
Tel: 0181 424 1442
Fax: 0181 424 1541

Hart District Council
Environmental Services
Civic Offices
Harlington Way
Fleet, Hants. GU13 8AE
Tel: 01252 622122
Fax: 01252 626886

Hartlepool Unitary Council
Planning Department
Bryan Hanson House
Hanson Square
Hartlepool, Cleveland TS24 7BT
Tel: 01429 266522
Fax: 01429 523599

Hastings Borough Council
Planning Department
37 Wellington Square
Hastings, E. Sussex TN34 1PL
Tel: 01424 781066
Fax: 01424 781608

Havant Borough Council
Planning and Development Services
Civic Offices
Civic Centre Road
Havant, Hants. PO9 2AX
Tel: 01705 446500
Fax: 01705 480263

Havering London Borough
Environment and Planning
Mercury House
Mercury Gardens
Romford, Essex RM1 3DU
Tel: 01708 772866
Fax: 01708 772690

Hereford and Worcester County Council
Environmental Services
County Hall
Spetchley Road
Worcester WR5 2NP
Tel: 01905 766780
Fax: 01905 766899

Hereford City Council
Planning Department
Town Hall
Hereford HR1 2PJ
Tel: 01432 364500
Fax: 01432 364504

Hertfordshire County Council
Planning Department
County Hall
Hertford SG13 8DF
Tel: 01992 555200
Fax: 01992 555202

Hertsmere Borough Council
Planning Department
Civic Offices
Elstree Way
Borehamwood, Herts. WD6 1WA
Tel: 0181 207 7458
Fax: 0181 207 7444

High Peak Borough Council
Planning Department
Municipal Buildings
Glossop, Derbyshire SK13 8AF
Tel: 01457 851600
Fax: 01457 860290

Hillingdon London Borough
Planning and Transportation
Civic Centre
Uxbridge, Middlesex UB8 1UW
Tel: 01895 250627
Fax: 01895 250599

Hinckley and Bosworth Borough Council
Technical Services
Council Offices
Argents Mead
Hinckley, Leics. LE10 1BZ
Tel: 01455 238141
Fax: 01455 251172

Horsham District Council
Planning Department
Park House
North Street
Horsham RH12 1RL
Tel: 01403 215100
Fax: 01403 215198

Hove Borough Council
Planning Department
Town Hall
Hove, E. Sussex BN3 4AH
Tel: 01273 775400
Fax: 01273 207277

Huntingdonshire District Council
Planning Department
Pathfinder House
St Mary's Street
Huntingdon PE18 6TN
Tel: 01480 388388
Fax: 01480 388099

Hyndburn Borough Council
Planning Department
Council Offices
Eagle Street
Accrington, Lancs. BB5 1LN
Tel: 01254 388111
Fax: 01254 391625

Ipswich Borough Council
Planning Department
Civic Centre
Civic Drive
Ipswich IP1 2EE
Tel: 01473 262930
Fax: 01473 262936

Isle of Anglesey Unitary Council
Planning and Economic Development
Council Offices
Llangefni LL77 7TW
Tel: 01248 750057
Fax: 01248 750032

Isle of Wight Unitary Council
Planning Department
Sea Close
Fairlea Road
Newport, I.O.W. PO30 1UD
Tel: 01983 823551
Fax: 01983 823563

Islington London Borough
Technical and Environmental Services
New Municipal Offices
222 Upper Street
London N1 2UD
Tel: 0171 447 2350
Fax: 0171 477 2783

Kennet District Council
Planning and Environmental Services
Browfort
Bath Road
Devizes, Wilts. SN10 2AT
Tel: 01380 724911
Fax: 01380 729146

Kensington and Chelsea London Borough
Planning and Conservation
Town Hall
Hornton Street
London W8 7NX
Tel: 0171 361 2075
Fax: 0171 361 3463

Kent County Council
Planning Department
Springfield
Maidstone ME14 2LX
Tel: 01622 696095
Fax: 01622 687620

Kerrier District Council
Planning Department
Council Offices
Dolcoath Avenue
Camborne, Cornwall TR14 8SX
Tel: 01209 712941
Fax: 01209 713369

Kettering Borough Council
Development Services
Bowling Green Road
Kettering, Northants NN15 7QX
Tel: 01536 534252
Fax: 01536 410795

King's Lynn and West Norfolk Borough Council
Planning Department
Kings Court
Chapel Street
King's Lynn, Norfolk PE30 1EX
Tel: 01553 692722
Fax: 01553 691663

Kingston upon Hull Unitary Council
Planning Department
Kingston House
Bond Street
Kingston upon Hull HU1 3ER
Tel: 01482 612003
Fax: 01482 612012

Kingston upon Thames London Borough
Environmental Services
Guildhall 2
Kingston upon Thames, Surrey KT1 1EU
Tel: 0181 547 5320
Fax: 0181 547 5363

Kirklees Metropolitan District Council
Planning Department
PO Box B9
Civic Centre
Huddersfield HD1 2JR
Tel: 01484 442702
Fax: 01484 442768

Knowsley Metropolitan District Council
Planning and Development
PO Box 26
Municipal Buildings
Archway Road
Huyton
Merseyside L36 9FB
Tel: 0151 433 2242

Lambeth London Borough
Planning Department
Courtney House
9–15 New Park Road
London SW2 4DU
Tel: 0171 926 1000
Fax: 0171 926 7155

Lancashire County Council
Planning Department
East Cliff County Offices
Preston PR1 3EX
Tel: 01772 264111
Fax: 01772 264178

Lancaster City Council
Planning Department
Palatine Hall
Dalton Square
Lancaster LA1 1PJ
Tel: 01524 582303
Fax: 01524 582323

Leeds City Council
Planning Department
Headrow Buildings
44 The Headrow
Leeds LS1 8HR
Tel: 0113 247 8176
Fax: 0113 247 8178

Leicester City Council
Planning Department
New Walk Centre
Welford Place
Leicester LE1 6ZG
Tel: 0116 254 9922
Fax: 0116 254 8954

Leicestershire County Council
Planning and Transport
County Hall
Glenfield, Leics. LE3 8RJ
Tel: 0116 265 7000
Fax: 0116 231 4186

Leominster District Council
Planning Department
PO Box 3
Leominster, Hereford HR6 8LU
Tel: 01568 618350
Fax: 01568 616559

Lewes District Council
Planning Services
Lewes House
32 High Street
Lewes, E. Sussex BN7 2LX
Tel: 01273 471600
Fax: 01273 484213

Lewisham London Borough
Urban Regeneration
Laurence House
1 Catford Road
London SE6 4RU
Tel: 0181 695 6000
Fax: 0181 690 4098

Lichfield District Council
Planning Department
District Council House
Frog Lane
Lichfield, Staffs. WS13 6YZ
Tel: 01543 414000
Fax: 01543 250673

Lincoln City Council
Planning Department
City Hall
Beaumont Fee, Lincoln LN1 1DF
Tel: 01522 564471
Fax: 01522 567934

Liverpool City Council
Planning and Development Services
5th Floor Steers House
Canning Place
Liverpool L1 8JA
Tel: 0151 233 5671/2/3
Fax: 0151 233 4290

London, Corporation of London
Planning Department
PO Box 270
Guildhall
London EC2P 2EJ
Tel: 0171 606 3030
Fax: 0171 332 1806

Luton Borough Council
Planning and Development
Town Hall
Luton LU1 2BQ
Tel: 01582 746301
Fax: 01582 746975

Macclesfield Borough Council
Planning Department
Town Hall
Macclesfield, Cheshire SK10 1DX
Tel: 01625 500500
Fax: 01625 504155

Maidstone Borough Council
Planning and Development
13 Tonbridge Road
Maidstone, Kent ME16 8HG
Tel: 01622 602217
Fax: 01622 602444

Maldon Borough Council
Planning Department
District Council Offices
Princes Road
Maldon, Essex CM9 7DL
Tel: 01621 875850
Fax: 01621 852575

Malvern Hills Borough Council
Planning and Technical Services
Brunel House
Portland Road
Malvern, Worcs. WR14 2TB
Tel: 01684 862226
Fax: 01684 862499

Manchester City Metropolitan District Council
Planning and Environmental Health
Town Hall
Manchester M60 2JT
Tel: 0161 234 4501
Fax: 0161 234 4508

Mansfield District Council
Planning Department
Civic Centre
Chesterfield Road South
Mansfield, Notts. NG19 7BH
Tel: 01623 656656
Fax: 01623 420197

Melton Borough Council
Planning Department
Council Offices
Nottingham Road
Melton Mowbray, Leics. LE13 0UL
Tel: 01664 67771
Fax: 01664 410283

Mendip District Council
Planning Department
Council Offices
Cannards Grave Road
Shepton Mallet, Somerset BA4 5BT
Tel: 01749 343399
Fax: 01749 344050

Merthyr Tydfil Unitary Council
Planning Department
Civic Centre
Castle Street
Merthyr Tydfil CF47 8AN
Tel: 01685 723201
Fax: 01685 722146

Merton London Borough
Environmental Services
Merton Civic Centre
London Road
Morden, Surrey SM4 5DX
Tel: 0181 545 3050
Fax: 0181 545 4105

Mid Bedfordshire District Council
Planning Department
23 London Road
Biggleswade, Beds. SG18 8ER
Tel: 01767 313137
Fax: 01767 316717

Mid Devon District Council
Planning Department
Ailsa House
Tidcombe Lane
Tiverton, Devon EX16 4DZ
Tel: 01844 255255
Fax: 01844 255584

Mid Suffolk District Council
Planning and Technical Services
Council Offices
Needham Market, Suffolk IP6 8DL
Tel: 01449 720711
Fax: 01449 721851

Mid Sussex District Council
Environmental Services
Oaklands
Oaklands Road
Haywards Heath RH16 1SS
Tel: 01444 458166
Fax: 01444 497971

Middlesbrough Unitary Council
Planning Department
PO Box 99A
Municipal Buildings
Middlesbrough, Cleveland TS1 2QQ
Tel: 01642 245432
Fax: 01642 263588

Milton Keynes Borough Council
Planning Department
Civic Offices
1 Saxon Gate East
Milton Keynes MK9 3HG
Tel: 01908 692466
Fax: 01908 682456

Mole Valley District Council
Planning Department
Planning Offices
Pippbrook
Dorking, Surrey RH4 1SJ
Tel: 01306 879236
Fax: 01306 876821

Monmouthshire Unitary Council
Planning and Economic Development
County Hall
Cwmbran NP44 2XH
Tel: 01633 838838
Fax: 01633 832990

Neath and Port Talbot Unitary Council
Planning Department
Neath Civic Centre
Neath SA11 3QZ
Tel: 01639 764272
Fax: 01639 764400

New Forest Borough Council
Planning Department
Appletree Court
Lyndhurst, Hants. SO43 7PA
Tel: 01703 285303
Fax: 01703 285223

Newark and Sherwood District Council
Planning Department
Kelham Hall
Newark, Notts NG23 5QX
Tel: 01636 605111
Fax: 01636 708361

Newbury District Council
Development Services
Council Offices
Market Street
Newbury, Berks. RG14 5LD
Tel: 01635 42400
Fax: 01635 519431

Newcastle under Lyme Borough Council
Planning Department
Civic Offices
Merriel Street
Newcastle under Lyme, Staffs. ST5 2AG
Tel: 01782 717717
Fax: 01782 711032

Newcastle upon Tyne City Council
Planning Department
Civic Centre
Newcastle upon Tyne NE1 8PH
Tel: 0191 232 8520
Fax: 0191 211 4998

Newham London Borough
Environment and Planning
Town Hall Annex
Barking Road
London E6 2RP
Tel: 0181 472 1430
Fax: 0181 472 2284

Newport Unitary Council
Planning Department
Civic Centre
Newport, Gwent NP9 4UR
Tel: 01633 244491
Fax: 01633 244721

Norfolk County Council
Director of Planning and Transportation
County Hall
Martineau Lane
Norwich NR1 2SG
Tel: 01603 222222
Fax: 01603 223219

Northampton County Council
Planning and Transportation
PO Box 163
County Hall
Northampton NN1 1AX
Tel: 01604 236650
Fax: 01604 236644

North Cornwall District Council
Planning Department
3-5 Barn Lane
Bodmin, Cornwall PL31 1LZ
Tel: 01208 74121
Fax: 01208 261243

North Devon District Council
Planning Department
Civic Centre
Barnstaple, Devon EX31 1EA
Tel: 01271 388300
Fax: 01271 388451

North Dorset District Council
Planning Department
Norden
Salisbury Road
Blandford Forum, Dorset DT11 7LL
Tel: 01258 454111
Fax: 01258 480179

North East Derbyshire District Council
Planning Department
Council House
Saltergate
Chesterfield, Derbys. S40 1LF
Tel: 01246 231111
Fax: 01246 221086

North East Lincolnshire Unitary Council
Planning and Transportation
Devonshire House
Bull Ring Lane
Grimsby, Lincs. DN31 1ES
Tel: 01472 313131
Fax: 01472 324216

North Hertfordshire District Council
Planning Department
Council Offices
Gernon Road
Letchworth, Herts. SG6 3JF
Tel: 01462 474410
Fax: 01462 474558

North Kesteven District Council
Planning Services
District Council Offices
Kesteven Street
Sleaford, Lincs. NG34 7EA
Tel: 01529 414155
Fax: 01529 413956

North Lincolnshire Unitary Council
Planning Department
Council Offices
Carey Lane
Brigg, Lincs. DN20 8EZ
Tel: 01724 296296
Fax: 01652 658316

North Norfolk District Council
Planning Department
Council Offices
Holt Road
Cromer, Norfolk NR27 9EL
Tel: 01263 513811
Fax: 01263 515042

North Shropshire District Council
Planning Department
Edinburgh House
New Street
Wem, Salop. SY4 5DB
Tel: 01939 22771
Fax: 01939 238422

North Somerset Unitary Council
Planning Department
Town Hall
Weston super Mare, Somerset BS23 1UJ
Tel: 01934 631701
Fax: 01934 634634

North Tyneside Metropolitan District Council
Planning and Development
Graham House
Whitley Road
Benton
Newcastle NE12 9TQ
Tel: 0191 201 0033
Fax: 0191 215 1858

North Warwickshire Borough Council
Planning Department
Council House
South Street
Atherstone, Warks. CV9 1BD
Tel: 01827 719434
Fax: 01827 719363

North West Leicestershire District Council
Planning Department
Council Offices
Coalville, Leics. LE67 3FJ
Tel: 01530 833333
Fax: 01530 510290

North Wiltshire District Council
Planning Department
Monkton Park
Chippenham, Wilts. SN15 1ER
Tel: 01249 443322
Fax: 01249 443152

North Yorkshire County Council
Environmental Services
County Hall
Northallerton, N. Yorks. DL7 8AQ
Tel: 01609 780780
Fax: 01609 777719

Northampton Borough Council
Planning Department
Cliftonville House
Bedford Road
Northampton NN4 0NR
Tel: 01604 233500
Fax: 01604 238795

Northumberland County Council
Planning and Environmental Management
County Hall
Morpeth, Northumberland NE61 2EF
Tel: 01670 533000
Fax: 01670 534160

Norwich City Council
Planning Department
City Hall
Norwich NR2 1NH
Tel: 01603 212500
Fax: 01603 212545

Nottingham City Council
Planning Department
Exchange Buildings North
Smithy Row
Nottingham NG1 2BS
Tel: 0115 948 3500
Fax: 0115 941 0333

Nottinghamshire County Council
Planning and Economic Development
Centenary House
1 Wilford Lane
West Bridgeford
Nottingham NG2 7QZ
Tel: 0115 977 2195
Fax: 0115 945 5391

Nuneaton and Bedworth Borough Council
Planning Department
Town Hall
Nuneaton CV11 5AA
Tel: 01203 376303
Fax: 01203 376340

Oadby and Wigston Borough Council
Planning Department
Council Offices
Station Road
Wigston, Leicester LE8 2DR
Tel: 0116 288 8961
Fax: 0116 288 7828

Oldham Metropolitan District Council
Environmental Services
Civic Centre
West Street
Oldham, Gtr. Manchester OL1 1XN
Tel: 0161 911 3000
Fax: 0161 911 4450

Oswestry Borough Council
Planning services
Council Offices
Castle View
Oswestry, Salop. SY11 1JR
Tel: 01691 677251
Fax: 01691 677348

Oxford City Council
Planning Policy and Economic Development
Clarendon House
52 Cornmarket Street
Oxford OX1 3HD
Tel: 01865 252161
Fax: 01865 252678

Oxfordshire County Council
Environmental Services
County Hall
Oxford OX1 1SD
Tel: 01865 815718
Fax: 01685 246110

Pembrokeshire Unitary Council
Planning Department
Cambria House
Haverfordwest SA61 1TP
Tel: 01437 764551
Fax: 01437 760703

Pendle Borough Council
Planning Services
Town Hall
Market Street
Nelson, Lancs. BB9 7LG
Tel: 01282 617731
Fax: 01282 695180

Penwith District Council
Planning and Environmental Department
Council Offices
St Clare
Penzance TR18 3QW
Tel: 01736 331166
Fax: 01736 331199

Peterborough District Council
Planning Department
Bridge House
Bridge Street
Peterborough PE1 1HS
Tel: 01733 63141
Fax: 01733 890348

Plymouth District Council
Planning Department
Civic Centre
Plymouth PL1 2EW
Tel: 01752 264870
Fax: 01752 264931

Poole Borough Council
Planning Department
Civic Centre
Poole, Dorset BH15 2RU
Tel: 01202 633304
Fax: 01202 633345

Portsmouth City Council
Planning Department
Civic Offices
Guildhall Square
Portsmouth PO1 2AU
Tel: 01705 834334
Fax: 01705 834660

Powys Unitary Council
Planning Department
County Hall
Llandrindod Wells LD1 5LG
Tel: 01597 826000
Fax: 01597 826250

Preston Borough Council
Planning Department
PO Box 10
Lancastria House
Preston PR1 2RL
Tel: 01772 266179
Fax: 01722 266195

Purbeck District Council
Planning Department
Westport House
Worgret Road
Wareham, Dorset BH20 4PP
Tel: 01929 556561
Fax: 01929 552688

Reading Borough Council
Planning Department
Civic Centre
Reading RG1 7TD
Tel: 0118 939 0444
Fax: 0118 958 9770

Redbridge London Borough
Planning Department
Town Hall
High Road
Ilford, Essex IG1 1DD
Tel: 0181 478 3020
Fax: 0181 478 9133

Redcar and Cleveland Unitary Council
Planning Department
Middlesbrough Road
PO Box Southbank 70
Middlesbrough TS6 6EL
Tel: 01642 444000
Fax: 01642 444882

Redditch Borough Council
Planning Department
Town Hall
Alcester Street
Redditch, Worcs. B98 8AH
Tel: 01527 64252
Fax: 01527 65216

Reigate and Banstead District Council
Environmental Services
Town Hall
Castlefield Road
Reigate, Surrey RH2 0SH
Tel: 01737 242477
Fax: 01737 222135

Restormel Borough Council
Planning Department
Borough Offices
Penwinnick Road
St Austell, Cornwall PL25 5DR
Tel: 01726 74466
Fax: 01726 68339

Rhondda Cynon Taff Unitary Council
Planning Department
Llwyn Castan
Libarary Road
Pontypridd CF37 2YA
Tel: 01443 400322
Fax: 01443 405184

Ribble Valley Borough Council
Planning Department
Council Offices
Church Walk
Clitheroe, Lancs. BB7 2RA
Tel: 01200 25111
Fax: 01200 26339

Richmond upon Thames London Borough
Planning and Building Services
Civic Centre
44 York Street
Twickenham TW1 3BZ
Tel: 0181 891 1411
Fax: 0181 891 7702

Richmondshire District Council
Planning and Development
Springwell House
Frenchgate
Richmond, N. Yorks. DL10 4JG
Tel: 01748 850222
Fax: 01748 822535

Rochdale Metropolitan District Council
Planning Department
PO Box 32
Telegraph House
Baillee Street
Rochdale OL6 1JH
Tel: 01706 864307
Fax: 01706 864185

Rochester upon Medway City Council
Planning Department
Civic Centre
Strood
Rochester, Kent ME2 4AW
Tel: 01634 727777
Fax: 01634 732720

Rochford District Council
Planning Department
Council Offices
South Street
Rochford, Essex SS4 1BW
Tel: 01702 546366
Fax: 01702 545737

Rossendale Borough Council
Planning Department
Stubbylee Hall
Stubbylee Lane
Bacup, Lancs. OL13 0DE
Tel: 01706 874333
Fax: 01706 875920

Rother District Council
Planning Department
Town Hall
Bexhill-on-Sea, E. Sussex TN39 3JX
Tel: 01424 216321
Fax: 01424 217869

Rotherham Metropolitan District Council
Planning Department
Bailey House
Rawmarsh Road
Rotherham, S. Yorks. S60 1QT
Tel: 01709 382121
Fax: 01706 823810

Rugby Borough Council
Planning Department
Town Hall
Rugby, Warks. CV21 2LB
Tel: 01788 533750
Fax: 01788 533577

Runnymeade Borough Council
Technical Services
Civic Offices
Addlestone, Surrey KT15 2AH
Tel: 01932 838383
Fax: 01932 855135

Rushcliff Borough Council
Planning Department
Civic Centre
Pavillion Road
Trent Bridge
West Bridgford, Nottingham NG2 5FF
Tel: 0115 981 9911
Fax: 0115 945 5882

Rushmoor Borough Council
Planning Department
Council Offices
Farnborough Road
Farnborough, Hants. GU14 7JU
Tel: 01252 398398
Fax: 01252 524017

Rutland District Council
Planning Department
Catmose,
Oakham, Rutland LE15 6HP
Tel: 01572 722577
Fax: 01572 758307

Ryedale District Council
Planning Department
Ryedale House
Malton, N. Yorks. YO17 0HH
Tel: 01653 600666
Fax: 01653 696801

Salford City Metropolitan District Council
Planning Department
Salford Civic Centre
Chorley Road
Salford, Gtr. Manchester M27 5BW
Tel: 0161 793 3601/793 3621
Fax: 0161 727 8269

Salisbury District Council
Planning Department
Planning Offices
61 Wyndham Road
Salisbury SP1 3AH
Tel: 01722 336272
Fax: 01722 434650

Sandwell Metropolitan District Council
Planning and Development Services
Wigmore
Pennyhill lane
West Bromwich, W. Midlands B71 3RZ
Tel: 0121 569 4052
Fax: 0121 569 4072

Scarborough Borough Council
Planning Services
Town Hall
St. Nicholas Street
Scarborough, N. Yorks. YO11 2HG
Tel: 01723 372351
Fax: 01723 354979

Sedgefield District Council
Planning and Technical Services
Council Offices
Spennymoor, Co. Durham DL16 6JQ
Tel: 01388 816166
Fax: 01388 817251

Sedgemoor District Council
Planning Department
Bridgewater House
King Square
Bridgewater, Somerset TA6 3AR
Tel: 01278 435435
Fax: 01278 444076

Sefton Metropolitan District Council
Planning Environment and Conservation
Balliol House
Bootle, Merseyside L20 3RY
Tel: 0151 934 3543
Fax: 0151 934 3587

Selby District Council
Environmental Services
Civic Centre
Portholme Road
Selby, N. Yorks. YO8 0SB
Tel: 01757 292140
Fax: 01757 292109

Sevenoaks District Council
Planning Department
Council Offices
Argyle Road
Sevenoaks, Kent TN13 1HG
Tel: 01732 741222
Fax: 01732 451332

Sheffield City Council
Planning and Economic Development
Town Hall Extension
Sheffield S1 2HH
Tel: 0114 273 4201
Fax: 0114 273 5002

Shepway District Council
Planning Department
Civic Centre
Folkestone, Kent CT20 2QY
Tel: 01303 850388
Fax: 01303 221720

Shrewsbury and Atcham Borough Council
Planning Department
Oakley Manor
Belle Vue Road
Shrewsbury SY3 7NW
Tel: 01743 231456
Fax: 01743 271593

Shropshire County Council
Environmental Services
The Shirehall
Abbey Foregate
Shrewsbury SY2 6ND
Tel: 01743 252502
Fax: 01743 252505

Slough Borough Council
Planning Department
Town Hall
Bath Road
Slough SL1 3UQ
Tel: 01753 875800
Fax: 01753 692499

Solihull Metropolitan District Council
Environment and Technical Services
PO Box 1
Council House
Solihull, W. Midlands B91 3QT
Tel: 0121 704 6380
Fax: 0121 704 6404

Somerset County Council
Environmental Services
County Hall
Taunton TA1 4DY
Tel: 01823 333451
Fax: 01823 332773/334346

South Bedfordshire District Council
Planning Department
District Offices
79 High Street
North Dunstable, Beds. LU6 1LF
Tel: 01582 472222
Fax: 01582 474009

South Cambridgeshire District Council
Planning Department
South Cambridgeshire Hall
9–11 Hills Road
Cambridge CB2 1PB
Tel: 01223 443151
Fax: 01223 301027

South Bucks District Council
Planning Services
Council Offices
Windsor Road
Slough SL1 2HN
Tel: 01753 533333
Fax: 01753 676269

South Derbyshire District Council
Planning and Economic Development
Civic Offices
Civic Way
Swadlincote, Derbys. DE11 0AH
Tel: 01283 221000
Fax: 01283 550128

South Gloucestershire Unitary Council
Planning Transport and Environmental
Services
The Council Offices
Castle Street
Thornbury, Avon BS13 1HF
Tel: 01454 868686
Fax: 01454 863067

South Hams District Council
Planning Department
Follaton House
Plymouth Road
Totnes, Devon TQ9 5NE
Tel: 01803 861234
Fax: 01803 861166

South Herefordshire District Council
Planning Department
Brockington
35 Hafod Road
Hereford HR1 1SH
Tel: 01432 346300
Fax: 01432 340190

South Holland District Council
Planning Department
Council Offices
Priory Road
Spalding, Lincs. PE11 2XE
Tel: 01775 761161
Fax: 01775 710772

South Kesteven District Council
Planning Department
Council Offices
St Peters Hill
Grantham, Lincs. NG31 6PZ
Tel: 01476 591591
Fax: 01476 591810

South Lakeland District Council
Planning Department
South Lakeland House
Lowther Street
Kendal, Cumbria LA9 4UQ
Tel: 01539 733333
Fax: 01539 740300

South Norfolk District Council
Planning Department
South Norfolk House
Swan Lane
Long Stratton, Norfolk NR15 2XE
Tel: 01508 533633
Fax: 01508 533695

South Northamptonshire District Council
Planning Department
Springfields
Towcester, Northants. NN12 6AE
Tel: 01327 350211
Fax: 01327 359219

South Oxfordshire District Council
Planning Department
PO Box 21
Council Offices
Crowmarsh
Wallingford, Oxon. OX10 8HQ
Tel: 01491 823000
Fax: 01491 826275

South Ribble Borough Council
Planning Department
Civic Centre
West Paddock
Leyland, Lancs. PR5 1DH
Tel: 01772 421491
Fax: 01772 622287

South Shropshire District Council
Environmental Services
Council Offices
Stone House
Corve Street
Ludlow, Salop. SY8 1DG
Tel: 01584 874941
Fax: 01584 872971

South Somerset District Council
Planning Department
Maltravers House
Petters Way
Yeovil, Somerset BA20 2HT
Tel: 01935 462462
Fax: 01935 412955

South Staffordshire District Council
Planning Department
Council Offices
Coldsall, Staffs. WV8 1PX
Tel: 01902 696000
Fax: 01902 696800

South Tyneside Metropolitan District Council
Planning Department
Town Hall and Civic Offices
South Shields, Tyne and Wear NE33 2RL
Tel: 0191 427 1717
Fax: 0191 427 7171

Southampton City Council
Planning Department
Civic Centre
Southampton SO14 7LH
Tel: 01703 832553
Fax: 01703 832607

Southend on Sea District Council
Planning Department
Civic Centre
Southend on Sea SS2 6ER
Tel: 01702 215303
Fax: 01702 251707

Southwark London Borough
Regeneration and Planning
Chiltern House
Portland Street
London SE17
Tel: 0171 525 5358
Fax: 0171 525 5484

Spelthorne Borough Council
Planning Department
Council Offices
Knowle Green
Staines, Middlesex TW8 1XB
Tel: 01784 446352
Fax: 01784 463356

St. Albans City Council
Planning Department
District Council Offices
Civic Centre
St. Albans AL1 3JE
Tel: 01727 866100
Fax: 01727 845658

St. Edmundsbury Borough Council
Planning Department
PO Box 122
St. Edmundsbury House
Western Way
Bury St. Edmunds, Suffolk IP33 3YS
Tel: 01284 763233
Fax: 01284 757378

St. Helens Metropolitan District Council
Planning Department
Town Hall
St. Helens, Merseyside WA10 1HP
Tel: 01744 456000
Fax: 01744 733337

Stafford Borough Council
Planning Department
Civic Offices
Riverside
Stafford ST16 3AQ
Tel: 01785 223181
Fax: 01785 223156

Staffordshire County Council
Development Services
County Buildings
Martin Street
Stafford ST16 2LH
Tel: 01785 277200
Fax: 01785 223316

Staffordshire Moorlands District Council
Planning Department
Moorlands House
Stockwell Street
Leek, Staffs. ST13 6HQ
Tel: 01538 399181
Fax: 01538 387813

Stevenage Borough Council
Planning Department
Daneshill House
Danestrete
Stevenage SG1 1HN
Tel: 01438 766288
Fax: 01438 740296

Stockport Metropolitan District Council
Planning and Development
Hygarth House
103 Wellington Road South
Stockport SK1 3TT
Tel: 0161 474 3506
Fax: 0161 953 0013

Stockton on Tees District Council
Planning Department
PO Box 11
Municipal Buildings
Church Road
Stockton on Tees, Cleveland TS18 1LD
Tel: 01642 393939
Fax: 01642 391282

Stoke on Trent City Council
Planning Department
PO Box 633
Civic Centre
Glebe Street
Stoke on Trent ST4 1RH
Tel: 01782 744241
Fax: 01782 404151

Stratford on Avon District Council
Planning Department
Elizabeth House
Church Street
Stratford upon Avon, Warks. CV37 6HX
Tel: 01789 267575
Fax: 01789 260306

Stroud District Council
Planning Department
Ebley Mill
Westward Road
Stroud, Gloucs. GL5 4UR
Tel: 01453 766321
Fax: 01453 750932

Suffolk County Council
Environment and Transport
St Edmund House
County Hall
Ipswich 1P4 1LZ
Tel: 01473 230000
Fax: 01473 230078

Suffolk Coastal District Council
Planning Department
Council Offices
Melton Hill
Woodbridge, Suffolk IP12 1AU
Tel: 01394 444434
Fax: 01394 385100

Sunderland City Council
Environmental Services
Civic Centre
Sunderland SR2 7DN
Tel: 0191 553 1000
Fax: 0191 553 1460

Surrey County Council
Planning Department
County Hall
Penrhyn Road
Kingston Upon Thames, Surrey KT1 2DT
Tel: 0181 541 9400
Fax: 0181 541 9447

Surrey Heath Borough Council
Planning and Community Services
Surrey Heath House
Knoll Road
Camberley, Surrey GU15 3HD
Tel: 01276 686252
Fax: 01276 222777

Sutton London Borough
Planning and Transportation
24 Denmark Road
Carshalton, Surrey SM5 2JG
Tel: 0181 770 6108
Fax: 0181 770 6112

Swale Borough Council
Planning Department
Swale House
East Street
Sittingbourne, Kent ME10 3HT
Tel: 01795 424341
Fax: 01795 417217

Swansea Unitary Council
Planning Department
County Hall
Swansea SA1 3SN
Tel: 01792 636000
Fax: 01792 636037

Tameside Metropolitan District Council
Planning and Engineering
Council Offices
Wellington Road
Ashton under Lyme
Tameside OL6 6DL
Tel: 0161 342 8355
Fax: 0161 342 3070

Tamworth Borough Council
Planning Department
Marmion House
Lichfield Street
Tamworth, Staffs B79 7BZ
Tel: 01827 311222
Fax: 01827 52769

Tandridge District Council
Planning and Environmental Services
Council Offices
Station Road East
Oxted, Surrey RH8 0BT
Tel: 01883 722000
Fax: 01883 722015

Taunton Deane Borough Council
Environmental Services
The Deane House
Belvedere Road
Taunton TA1 1HE
Tel: 01823 356356
Fax: 01823 356329

Teesdale District Council
Planning Department
43 Galgate
Barnard Castle, Co. Durham DL12 8EL
Tel: 01833 690000
Fax: 01833 637269

Teignbridge District Council
Planning and Environmental Services
Forde House
Newton Abbot, Devon TQ12 4XX
Tel: 01626 61101
Fax: 01626 56803

Tendring District Council
Planning Department
Council Offices
Weeley, Essex CO16 9AJ
Tel: 01255 830455
Fax: 01255 256114

Test Valley Borough Council
Planning Department
Council Offices
Duttons Road
Romsey, Hants. SO51 8XG
Tel: 01794 515117
Fax: 01794 518192

Tewkesbury District Council
Planning Department
Council Offices
Gloucester Road
Tewkesbury GL20 5TT
Tel: 01684 295010
Fax: 01684 290577

Thamesdown Borough Council
Planning Department
Civic Offices
Swindon SN1 2JH
Tel: 01793 526161
Fax: 01793 493276

Thanet District Council
Planning Department
Council Offices
Cecil Street
Margate, Kent CT9 1XZ
Tel: 01843 225511
Fax: 01843 290906

Three Rivers District Council
Planning Department
Three Rivers House
Northway
Rickmansworth, Herts. WD3 1RL
Tel: 01923 776611
Fax: 01923 896119

Thurrock Borough Council
Planning Department
Civic Offices
New Road
Grays, Essex RM17 6SL
Tel: 01375 652267
Fax: 01375 652359

Tonbridge and Malling Borough Council
Planning Department
Park Building
Gibson Drive
Kings Hill
West Malling, Kent ME19 4LZ
Tel: 01732 876256
Fax: 01732 846312

Torbay Borough Council
Planning Department
Borough Planning Office
Town Hall
Torquay TQ1 3DR
Tel: 01803 296244/218600
Fax: 01803 292677/218614

Torfaen Unitary Council
Planning Department
Civic Centre
Pontypool NP4 6YB
Tel: 01495 762200
Fax: 01495 755513

Torridge District Council
Planning Department
Riverbank House
Bideford, Devon EX39 2QG
Tel: 01237 476711
Fax: 01237 478849

Tower Hamlets London Borough
Planning Department
Southern Grove Lodge
Mile End
London E3 4PN
Tel: 0171 364 5314
Fax: 0171 364 5421

Tunbridge Wells Borough Council
Planning Department
Town Hall
Royal Tunbridge Wells TN1 1RS
Tel: 01892 526121
Fax: 01892 534227

Tynedale District Council
Planning Department
Old Grammar School
Hallgates
Hexham, Northumberland NE46 1XA
Tel: 01434 652200
Fax: 01434 652422

Uttlesford District Council
Planning Department
Council Offices
High Street
Dunmow, Essex CM6 1AN
Tel: 01799 510450
Fax: 01799 510499

Vale of Glamorgan Unitary Council
Planning Department
Docks Offices
Subway Road
Barry CF63 4RT
Tel: 01446 700111
Fax: 01446 745566

Vale of White Horse District Council
Planning and Engineering
The Abbey House
Abingdon, Oxon OX14 3JE
Tel: 01235 520202
Fax: 01235 553130

Vale Royal Borough Council
Planning Department
Wyvern House
The Drumber
Winsford, Cheshire CW7 1AH
Tel: 01606 867701
Fax: 01606 862100/862088

Wakefield Metropolitan District Council
Planning and Regeneration
Newton Bar
Wakefield WF1 2TX
Tel: 01924 306090
Fax: 01924 306690

Walsall Metropolitan District Council
Environmental Services
Civic Centre
Walsall WS1 1TP
Tel: 01922 652002
Fax: 01922 720885

APPENDIX J

Waltham Forest London Borough
Planning and Economic Development
Municipal Offices
16 The Ridgeway
London E4 0PS
Tel: 0181 527 5544
Fax: 0181 524 8960

Wandsworth London Borough
Planning Department
Town Hall
Wandsworth High Street
London SW18 2PU
Tel: 0181 871 6626
Fax: 0181 871 7809

Wansbeck District Council
Planning and Environmental Services
Council Offices
Front Street
Bedlington, Northumberland NE22 5TU
Tel: 01670 530033
Fax: 01670 530278

Warrington Borough Council
Planning Department
West Annexe
Town Hall
Warrington WA1 1UH
Tel: 01925 442311
Fax: 01925 244914

Warwick District Council
Planning Department
1 Warwick New Road
Leamington Spa, Warks. CV32 5JD
Tel: 01926 450000
Fax: 01926 226400

Warwickshire County Council
Planning, Transport and Economic
Strategy
PO Box 43
Shire Hall
Warwick CV34 4SX
Tel: 01926 412022
Fax: 01926 414129

Watford Borough Council
Planning and Transportation
Town Hall
Watford WD1 3EX
Tel: 01923 226400
Fax: 01923 226133

Waveney District Council
Planning Department
Rectory Road
Lowestoft, Suffolk NR33 0BX
Tel: 01502 562111
Fax: 01502 564962

Waverley Borough Council
Planning Department
Council Offices
The Burys
Godalming, Surrey GU7 1HR
Tel: 01483 869465
Fax: 01483 869118

Wealdon District Council
Planning Department
Council Offices
Pine Grove
Crowborough, E. Sussex TN6 1DH
Tel: 01892 602405
Fax: 01892 602222

Wear Valley District Council
Planning Department
Civic Centre
Crook, Co. Durham DH7 9PB
Tel: 01388 765555
Fax: 01388 766660

Wellingborough Borough Council
Planning Department
Croyland Abbey
Tithe Barn Road
Wellingborough, Northants NN8 1BJ
Tel: 01933 229777
Fax: 01933 274835

Welwyn Hatfield District Council
Planning Department
Council Offices
Welwyn Garden City, Herts. AL8 6AE
Tel: 01707 331212
Fax: 01707 391537

West Devon Borough Council
Planning Department
Kilworthy Park
Drake Road
Tavistock, Devon PL19 0BZ
Tel: 01822 615911
Fax: 01822 614840

West Dorset District Council
Planning and Environmental Services
Stratton House
58/60 High West Street
Dorchester DT1 1UZ
Tel: 01305 251010
Fax: 01305 251481

West Lancashire District Council
Planning Services
52 Derby Street
Ormskirk, L39 2DF
Tel: 01695 585102
Fax: 01695 585113

West Lindsey District Council
Development Services
26 Spital Terrace
Gainsborough, Lincs. DN21 2HG
Tel: 01427 615411
Fax: 01427 810623

West Oxfordshire District Council
Planning Department
Council Offices
Woodgreen
Witney, Oxon OX8 6NB
Tel: 01993 702941
Fax: 01993 770255

West Somerset District Council
Planning Department
Killick Way
Williton
Taunton TA4 4QA
Tel: 01984 632291
Fax: 01984 633022

West Sussex County Council
Planning Department
County Hall
Tower Street
Chichester, West Sussex PO19 1RL
Tel: 01243 777307
Fax: 01243 777232

West Wiltshire District Council
Planning Department
Bradley Road
Trowbridge, Wilts. BA14 0RD
Tel: 01225 776655
Fax: 01225 770314

Westminster City London Borough
Planning and Environmental Services
Westminster City Hall
Victoria Street
London SW1E 6QP
Tel: 0171 798 2650
Fax: 0171 798 3224

**Weymouth and Portland Borough
Council**
Planning Department
Municipal Offices
Weymouth, Dorset DT4 8TA
Tel: 01305 761222
Fax: 01305 766773

Wigan Metropolitan Borough Council
Planning Department
Borough Planning Offices
Civic Buildings
New Mar
Wigan WN1 1RP
Tel: 01942 404256
Fax: 01942 404222

Wiltshire County Council
Environmental Services
County Hall
Trowbridge, Wilts. BA14 8JD
Tel: 01225 713000
Fax: 01225 713991

Winchester City Council
Planning Department
Avalon House
Chesil Street
Winchester SO23 8HU
Tel: 01962 840222
Fax: 01962 849101

**Windsor and Maidenhead Borough
Council**
Planning Department
Aston House
York Road
Miadenhead, Berks. SL6 1PS
Tel: 01628 798888
Fax: 01628 796438

Wirral Metropolitan District Council
Planning and Economic Development
Municipal Offices
Brighton Street
Wallasey, Merseyside L44 8ED
Tel: 0151 638 7070
Fax: 0151 691 8180

Woking Borough Council
Technical Services
Civic Offices
Gloucester Square
Woking, Surrey GU21 1YL
Tel: 01483 755855
Fax: 01483 768746

Wokingham District Council
Planning Department
Council Offices
Shute End
Wokingham, Berks RG40 1WR
Tel: 0118 978 6833
Fax: 0118 978 9078

Wolverhampton Unitary Council
Planning and Environment
Civic Centre
St. Peters Square
Wolverhampton WV1 1RG
Tel: 01902 315700
Fax: 01902 315650

Worcester City Council
Planning Department
Farrier House
Farrier Street
Worcester WR1 3EW
Tel: 01905 722400
Fax: 01905 722499

Worthing Borough Council
Planning Department
Town Hall
Chapel Road
Worthing, Sussex BN11 1LF
Tel: 01903 239999
Fax: 01903 207365

Wrekin District Council
Planning Department
PO Box 212
Civic Offices
Telford TF3 4LB
Tel: 01952 202537
Fax: 01952 291692

Wrexham Unitary Council
Planning Department
Lambpit Street
Wrexham LL11 1AY
Tel: 01978 292500
Fax: 01978 297502

Wychavon District Council
Planning Department
Civic Centre
Queen Elizabeth Drive
Pershore, Hereford & Worcester WR10 1PT
Tel: 01386 565000
Fax: 01386 561092

Wycombe District Council
Planning Department
District Council Offices
Queen Victoria Road
High Wycombe HP11 1BB
Tel: 01494 461000
Fax: 01494 421108

Wyre Borough Council
Planning Department
Wyre Civic Centre
Breck Road
Poulton le Fylde, Lancs. FY6 7PU
Tel: 01253 891000
Fax: 01253 899000

Wyre Forest District Council
Planning Department
Land Oak House
Chester Road North
Kidderminster
Hereford and Worcester DY10 1TA
Tel: 01562 820505
Fax: 01562 748378

LPAs in Scotland

Aberdeen City Unitary Council
Planning Department
St Nicholas House
Broad Street
Aberdeen AB10 1BW
Tel: 01224 523470
Fax: 01224 636181

Aberdeenshire Unitary Council
Planning Department
Woodhill House
Westburn Road
Aberdeen AB16 5GB
Tel: 01224 665540
Fax: 01224 664888

Angus Unitary Council
Planning Department
7 The Cross
Forfar DD8 1BX
Tel: 01307 461460
Fax: 01307 461968

Argyll and Bute Unitary Council
Planning Department
Council Offices
Kilmory PA31 8RT
Tel: 01546 602127
Fax: 01546 604138

Clackmannan Unitary Council
Planning Department
Clackmannan District Council
Greenfield
Alloa FK10 2AD
Tel: 01259 450000
Fax: 01259 452010

Dumfries and Galloway Unitary Council
Planning Department
Kirkbank
English Street
Dumfries DG1 2DD
Tel: 01387 260150
Fax: 01387 260188

Dundee City Unitary Council
Planning Department
21 City Square
Dundee DD1 3BY
Tel: 01382 434400
Fax: 01382 434666

East Ayrshire Unitary Council
Planning Department
Council Headquarters
London Road
Kilmarnock KA3 7DG
Tel: 01563 576000
Fax: 01563 574062

East Dumbartonshire Unitary Council
Planning Department
The Triangle
Kirkintilloch Road
Bishopbriggs G66 2TR
Tel: 0141 762 9000
Fax: 0141 762 0934

East Lothian Unitary Council
Planning Department
Council Buildings
Court Street
Haddington EH41 3HA
Tel: 01620 827827
Fax: 01620 827888

East Renfrewshire Unitary Council
Planning Department
Council Offices
Eastwood Park
Rouken Glen Road
Glasgow G46 6UG
Tel: 0141 621 3000
Fax: 0141 620 0884

Edinburgh City Unitary Council
Planning Department
1 Cockburn Street
Edinburgh EH1 1BJ
Tel: 0131 469 3844
Fax: 0131 529 7478

Falkirk Unitary Council
Planning Department
Abbotsford House
Davids Loan
Falkirk FK3 4QH
Tel: 01324 504950
Fax: 01324 504850

Fife Unitary Council
Planning Department
Fife House
North Street
Glenrothes KY7 5LT
Tel: 01592 414141
Fax: 01592 414142

Glasgow City Unitary Council
Planning Department
Exchange House
231 George Street
Glasgow G1 1RX
Tel: 0141 287 5701
Fax: 0141 287 5667

APPENDIX J

Highland Unitary Council
Planning Department
Glenurquhart Road
Inverness IV3 5NX
Tel: 01463 702251
Fax: 01463 702298

Inverclyde Unitary Council
Planning Department
6 Cathcart Square
Greenock PA15 1LS
Tel: 01475 882404
Fax: 01475 882468

Midlothian Unitary Council
Planning Department
Midlothian House
Buccleuch Street
Dalkeith EH22 1DJ
Tel: 0131 663 2881
Fax: 0131 660 7565

Moray Unitary Council
Planning Department
Council Offices
Elgin IV30 1BX
Tel: 01343 543451
Fax: 01343 540183

North Ayrshire Unitary Council
Planning Department
Cunningham House
Friar Croft
Irvine KA12 8EE
Tel: 01294 324300
Fax: 01294 324344

North Lanarkshire Unitary Council
Planning and Development
Civic Centre
Motherwell ML1 1TW
Tel: 01698 266166
Fax: 01698 275125

Orkney Island Council
Planning Department
Council Offices
Kirkwall KW15 1NY
Tel: 01856 873535
Fax: 01856 874615

Perth and Kinross Unitary Council
Planning and Development
PO Box 77
2 High Street
Perth PH1 5PH
Tel: 01738 475000
Fax: 01738 475005

Renfrewshire Unitary Council
Planning Department
Municipal Buildings
Cotton Street
Paisley PA1 1BU
Tel: 0141 840 3418
Fax: 0141 887 0361

Scottish Borders Unitary Council
Planning Department
Council Headquarters
Newton Street
Boswells
Melrose TD6 0SA
Tel: 01835 824000
Fax: 01835 823225

Shetland Island Council
Planning Department
Grantfield
Lerwick ZE1 0NT
Tel: 01595 744800
Fax: 01595 695887

South Ayrshire Unitary Council
Planning and Economic Development
County Buildings
Wellington Square
Ayr KA7 1DR
Tel: 01292 612000
Fax: 01292 612143

South Lanarkshire Unitary Council
Planning Department
Council Offices
Almada Street
Hamilton ML3 0AA
Tel: 01698 454444
Fax: 01698 454275

Stirling Unitary Council
Environmental Services
Viewforth
Stirling FK8 2ET
Tel: 01786 443322
Fax: 01786 443394

West Dumbartonshire Unitary Council
Planning and Economic Development
Council Offices
Garshake Road
Dumbarton G82 3PU
Tel: 01389 737599
Fax: 01389 737582

West Lothian Unitary Council
Planning Department
County Buildings
Linlithgow EH49 7EZ
Tel: 01506 775222
Fax: 01506 775255

Western Isles Island Council
Environmental Services
Council Offices
Sandwick Road
Stornoway HS1 2BW
Tel: 01851 703773
Fax: 01851 705349

DETR Planning Divisions in Northern Ireland

Ballymena Divisional Planning Office
County Hall
182 Galgorm Road
Ballymena
Co Antrim BT42 1QF
Tel: 01266 653333

Belfast Divisional Planning Office
Bedford House
Bedford Street
Belfast BT2 7FD
Tel: 01232 252800

Craigavon Divisional Planning Office
Marlborough House
Central Way
Craigavon
Co Armagh BT64 1AD
Tel: 01762 341144

Downpatrick Divisional Planning Office
Rathkeltair House
Market Street
Downpatrick
Co Down BT30 6EJ
Tel: 01396 6112211

Londonderry Divisional Planning Office
Orchard House
Foyle Street
Londonderry BT48 6AT
Tel: 01504 319900

Omagh Divisional Planning Office
Tyrone and Fermanagh Building
Donaghanie Road
Omagh
Co Tyrone BT79 0NR
Tel: 01662 250122

DETR Regional Offices in England

Eastern
Heron House
49–53 Goldington Road
Bedford MK40 3LL
Tel: 01234 276170

East Midlands
Cranbrook House
Cranbrook Street
Nottingham NG1 1EY
Tel: 0115 971 2756

London
River Walk House
157–161 Millbank
London SW1P 4RT
Tel: 0171 217 3146

Merseyside
Graeme House
Derby Square
Liverpool L2 7SU
Tel: 0151 224 6302

North East
Wellbar House
Gallowgate
Newcastle upon Tyne NE1 1TD
Tel: 0191 235 7722

North West
Sunley Tower
Piccadilly Plaza
Manchester M1 4BE
Tel: 0161 952 4000

South East
Bridge House
1 Walnut Tree Close
Guildford
Surrey GU1 4GA
Tel: 01483 882255

South West
The Pithay
Bristol BS1 2PB
Tel: 0117 900 1700

West Midlands
Fiveways Tower
Frederick Road
Birmingham B15 1SJ
Tel: 0121 212 2050

Yorkshire and Humberside
City House
New Station Street
Leeds LS1 4JD
Tel: 0113 280 0600

APPENDIX K

Statutory Consultees for a Planning Application

Before granting planning permission a LPA must, according to Art. 10 of the GDPO, consult with various bodies depending on the type of proposed development and the area in which it is to take place. The essential provisions are as follows:

Consultee	Description of development
Local Planning Authority	Development in Greater London or in a Metropolitan County.
District Planning Authority	Development in a non-Metropolitan County, other than land in a National Park.
County Planning Authority	Development in a National Park.
Health and Safety Executive	Development within a notified area because of the presence in the vicinity of toxic, highly reactive, explosive, or inflammable substances and which involves the provision of: (a) residential accommodation (b) more than $250m^2$ of retail floor space (c) more than $500m^2$ of office floor space (d) more than $750m^2$ of floor space to be used for an industrial process, or which is otherwise likely to result in a material increase in the number of persons working within or visiting the notified area.
Secretary of State for Transport, or Secretary of State for Wales and the operator of the railway network	Development likely to result in a material increase in the volume, or a material change in the character of traffic entering or leaving a trunk road, or using a level crossing over a railway.
Local Highway Authority	Development resulting in a material increase in the volume, or a material change in the character of traffic entering or leaving a classified road or proposed highway. Development likely to prejudice the improvement or construction of a classified road or proposed highway. The formation, laying out or alteration of any means of access to a highway (other than a trunk road).

Development which includes the laying out, or construction of a new street.

The Local Highway Authority concerned, and in the case of a road subject to a concession, the concessionaire	The construction of a highway or private means of access, to premises affording access to a road in relation to which a toll order is in force.
Coal Authority	Development which involves the provision of a building or pipeline in an area of coal working notified by the Coal Authority to the LPA.
Environmental Agency	Development involving:

- Mining operations.
- The carrying out of works or operations in the bed of, or on the banks of a river or stream.
- The refining or storing of mineral oils and their derivatives.
- The deposit of refuse or waste.
- A cemetery.
- Fish farming.

Development relating to the retention, treatment, or disposal of sewage, trade waste, slurry or sludge (where more than ten people will normally reside, work or congregate) and ancillary works.

Secretary of State for Culture, Media and Sport	Development within three kilometres of Windsor Castle, Windsor Great Park or Windsor Home Park or within 800 metres of any other royal palace or park which might affect the amenities (including security) of that palace or park.
Historic Building and Monuments Commission for England	Development in Greater London involving the demolition in whole or part of, or the material alteration of, a listed building.
In Wales, the Secretary of State	Development likely to affect the site of a scheduled monument.

Development likely to affect any registered garden or park of special historic intrest and classified as Grade I or Grade II.

The council which gave, or is to be regarded as having given, the notice	Development in a notified site of special scientific interest, or, within two kilometres of such a site.

APPENDIX K

Theatres Trust

Development involving any land on which there is a theatre.

The Minister of Agriculture, Fisheries and Food, or in Wales, the Secretary of State for Wales

Development which is not for agricultural purposes and is not in accordance or in the provisions of a development plan and involves:

(a) the loss of less than 20 ha which is for the time being used (or was last used) for agricultural purposes; or
(b) the loss of less than 20 ha of 1, 2 or 3a agricultural land which is or was last used for, agricultural purposes, where development is likely to lead to a further loss of agricultural land amounting cumulatively to 20 ha or more.

Waste Disposal Authority

Development within 250 metres of land which: is or has at any time in the 30 years before the relevant application, been used for the deposit of refuse or waste and which has been notified as such to the LPA by the waste regulation authority.

The above are statutory consultees, but LPAs can seek advice on certain aspects of a planning application from the following:

DETR

Demolition of a listed church or a church in a conservation area.

English Heritage

Listed building consent applications, ancient monuments and conservation areas.

Royal Fine Arts Commission

Architectural, town planning and landscape matters. Conservation issues of more than local importance.

In addition, national amenity societies such as the Georgian Society, Ancient Monuments Society, Victorian Society etc., are notified of applications to demolish listed buildings in whole or part.

ST NO	— 24950
ACC NO	064076
CLASS	711
DATE	31/11/05
STAFF	

208

REFERENCES

Acts Relevant to Planning Applications

Town and Country Planning Act 1990 (as amended by PCA 1991):			Town and Country Planning (Scotland) Act 1997:
	Section		**Section**
Part I	1	Local planning authorities: general	1
	54A	Status of development plans	25
Part III	55	Meaning of 'development' and 'new development'	26
	55(1A)	Demolition as development	—
	55(4A)	Fish farming	—
	56	Time when development begun	27
	57	Planning permission required for development	28
	58	Granting of planning permission: general	29
	59	Development orders: general	30
	60	Permission granted by development order	31
	62	Form and content of applications for planning permission	32
	65	Notices etc. for applications for planning permission	34/35
	69	Registers of applications, etc.	36
	70	Determination of applications: general considerations	37
	70A	LPA decline to determine applications	39
	71A	Assessment of environmental effects	40
	72	Conditional grant of planning permission	41
	73	Determination of applications to develop land without compliance with conditions previously attached	42
	74	Directions for dealing with applications	—
	74A	Receipt and determination of applications	—
	82	Simplified planning zones	49
	84	Simplified planning zone schemes: conditions and limitations	51
	88	Planning permission for development in enterprise zones	55
	91	General condition limiting duration of planning permission	58
	92	Outline planning permission	59
	94	Termination of planning permission by reference to time limit	61
	95	Effect of completion notice	62
	97	Power to revoke or modify planning permission	65
	106	Planning obligations	75
	106A	Modification and discharge of planning obligations	75
Part VII	172	Power to issue enforcement notice	139
	191	Certificate of lawfulness of existing use or development	150
	192	Certificate of lawfulness of proposed use or development	151
	193	Certificates under sections 191, 192	152
	194	Offences	153
Part VIII	198	Power to make tree preservation orders	164
	199	Form of and procedure applicable to orders	161
	211	Preservation of trees in conservation areas	172
	220	Regulations controlling display of advertisements	182
	222	Planning permission not needed for advertisements complying with regulations	184
Part XI	263	Meaning of 'operational land'	215
	266	Applications for permission by statutory undertakers	218
	299A	Crown planning obligations	—
Part XV	315	Power to modify Act in relation to minerals	262
	316(1)	Development by LPAs on their own land	—

REFERENCES

Town and Country Planning (Listed Buildings and Conservation Areas) Act 1990:		Planning (Listed Buildings and Conservation Areas) (Scotland) Act 1997:
Section		**Section**
Part I	1	Listing of buildings of special architectural or historic interest	1
	6	Issue of certificate that building not intended to be listed	–
	7	Restriction on works affecting listed buildings	6
	8	Authorisation of works: listed building consent	7
	10	Making of applications for listed building consent	9
	18	Limit of duration of listed building consent	16
	19	Application for variation or discharge of conditions	17
	38	Power to issue listed building enforcement notice	34
	66	General duty as respects listed building in exercise of planning functions	64
Part II	69	Designation of conservation areas	61/62
	72	General duty as respects conservation areas in exercise of planning functions	64
	74	Control of demolition in conservation areas	66

Planning (Hazardous Substances) Act 1990

1	Hazardous substances authorities: general
4	Requirement of hazardous substances consent
6	Hazardous substances consent: general
7	Applications for hazardous substances consent
24	Power to issue hazardous substances contravention notice

Environment Act 1995

	Periodic reviews of mineral permissions	–

The GDPO and the GPDO
The Town and Country Planning (General Development Procedures) Order 1995

Article

3	Applications for outline planning permission
4	Applications for approval of reserved matters
5	General provision relating to applications
6	Notice of applications
7	Certificates in relation to notices
8	Publicity for planning applications
10	Consultation before grant of permission
14	Directions by the Secretary of State
16	Notification of mineral applications
20	Time periods for decision
22	Written notice of decision or determination
24	Certificate of lawful use or development
25	Register of applications
Sch. 1	Letter to applicant on receipt of application
	Notification to applicant on refusal or grant of permission
Sch. 2	Notices under Arts. 6 and 9
	Certificate under Art. 7
Sch. 3	Notices under Art. 8
Sch. 4	Certificate under Art. 24 of lawful use or development

The Town and Country Planning
(General Permitted Development) Order 1995

Article

3	Permitted development
4	Directions restricting permitted development
Sch. 2	Permitted development

PPGs, MPGs and Circulars Relevant to
Planning Applications

DETR ref.		WO ref.
	Development control and general planning issues	
PPG1	General Policy and Principles	
PPG5	Simplified Planning Zones	
PPG12	Development Plans and Regional Planning Guidance	
PPG18	Enforcing Planning Control	
1/97	Planning Obligations	
11/95	The Use of Conditions in Planning Permission	35/95
10/95	Planning Controls over Demolition	31/95
9/95	General Development Order Consolidation	25/95
15/92	Publicity for Planning Applications	35/92
14/91	Planning and Compensation Act 1991	44/91
13/87	T&CP (Use Classes) Order 1987	24/87
18/84	Crown Land Development	37/84
22/80	Development Control – Policy and Practice	40/80
	Fees for planning applications	
31/92	T&CP (Fees for Applications and Deemed Applications) (Amendment) (No. 2) Regulations 1992	73/92
SI 1997 No. 37	T&CP (Fees for Applications and Deemed Applications) (Amendment) Regulations 1997	
	Historic buildings and conservation areas	
PPG15	Planning and the Historic Environment	
PPG16	Archaeology and Planning	
8/87	Historic Buildings and Conservation Areas – Policy and Procedures	
14/97	Planning and the Historic Environment	
	Minerals and hydrocarbons	
MPG1	General Considerations and the Development Plan System	
MPG2	Applications, Permissions and Conditions	
MPG5	Minerals Planning and the General Development Order	
MPG14	Minerals Planning Guidance: Environment Act 1995: Review of Mineral Planning Permissions	
1/88	Planning Policy Guidance and Minerals Policy Guidance	1/88
2/85	Planning Control over Oil and Gas Operations	3/85
115/76	Pipelines Act 1962	89/76

REFERENCES

Retail development

PPG6	Town Centres and Retail Developments	
15/93	T&CP (Shopping Development) (England and Wales) (No. 2) Direction 1993	61/93

Industrial development/small businesses etc.

PPG4	Industrial and Commercial Development and Small Firms

Rural areas, agriculture, forestry and conservation

PPG9	Nature Conservation	
36/78	Trees and Forestry	64/78

Caravans etc.

1/94	Gypsy Sites and Planning	2/94
22/91	Travelling Showpeople	78/91
14/89	Caravan Sites and Control of Development Act 1960 Model Standards	23/89
23/83	Caravan Sites and Control of Development Act 1960	32/83
12/78	Mobile Homes	9/78

Hazardous substances

11/92	Planning Controls for Hazardous Substances: Planning (Hazardous Substances) Act 1990 – Planning (Hazardous Substances) Regulations 1991	20/92
3/92	Environmental Protection (Control of Injurious Substances) Regulations 1992	2/92

Advertisements

PPG19	Outdoor Advertisement Control	
15/94	T&CP (Control of Advertisements) (Amendment) Regulations 1994	70/94
5/92	T&CP (Control of Advertisements) Regulations 1992	14/92

Environmental assessment etc.

PPG14	Development of Unstable Land	
PPG22	Renewable Energy	
PPG23	Planning and Pollution Control	
PPG24	Planning and Noise	
14/96	Environmental Protection Act: Amendment Regulations 1996	39/96
6/96	Environmental Protection Act: Regulations 1996	21/96
13/95	T&CP (Environmental Assessment and Unauthorised Development) Regulations 1995	39/95
3/95	Permitted Development and Environmental Assessment	12/95
7/94	Environmental Assessment: Amendment of Regulations	20/94
17/89	Landfill Sites: Development Control	38/89
24/88	Environmental Assessment of Projects in SPZ	48/88
15/88	T&CP (Assessment of Environmental Effects) Regulations 1988	23/88

Miscellaneous uses

PPG3	Housing	
PPG8	Telecommunications	
PPG13	Transport	
PPG17	Sport and Recreation	
PPG21	Tourism	
13/96	Planning and Affordable Housing	
19/86	Housing and Planning Act 1986: Planning Provisions	57/86

LLYFRGELL COLEG MENAI LIBRARY
SAFLE FFRIDDOEDD SITE
BANGOR   GWYNEDD   LL57 2TP

LLYFRGELL COLEG MENAI LIBRARY
SAFLE FFRIDDOEDD SITE
BANGOR   GWYNEDD   LL57 2TP